MALAYSIA–CHINA RELATIONS
Progress, Partnership, Prospects

MALAYSIA–CHINA RELATIONS
Progress, Partnership, Prospects

Edited by

Chow Bing Ngeow
Universiti Malaya, Malaysia

World Scientific

NEW JERSEY • LONDON • SINGAPORE • BEIJING • SHANGHAI • TAIPEI • CHENNAI

Published by

World Scientific Publishing Co. Pte. Ltd.

5 Toh Tuck Link, Singapore 596224

USA office: 27 Warren Street, Suite 401-402, Hackensack, NJ 07601

UK office: 57 Shelton Street, Covent Garden, London WC2H 9HE

Library of Congress Control Number: 2024056923

British Library Cataloguing-in-Publication Data
A catalogue record for this book is available from the British Library.

MALAYSIA–CHINA RELATIONS
Progress, Partnership, Prospects

Copyright © 2025 by World Scientific Publishing Co. Pte. Ltd.

All rights reserved. This book, or parts thereof, may not be reproduced in any form or by any means, electronic or mechanical, including photocopying, recording or any information storage and retrieval system now known or to be invented, without written permission from the publisher.

For photocopying of material in this volume, please pay a copying fee through the Copyright Clearance Center, Inc., 222 Rosewood Drive, Danvers, MA 01923, USA. In this case permission to photocopy is not required from the publisher.

ISBN 978-981-98-0134-3 (hardcover)
ISBN 978-981-98-0135-0 (ebook for institutions)
ISBN 978-981-98-0136-7 (ebook for individuals)

For any available supplementary material, please visit
https://www.worldscientific.com/worldscibooks/10.1142/14056#t=suppl

Desk Editors: Kannan Krishnan/Lum Pui Yee

Typeset by Stallion Press
Email: enquiries@stallionpress.com

© 2025 World Scientific Publishing Company
https://doi.org/10.1142/9789819801350_fmatter

About the Editor

Ngeow Chow Bing is Associate Professor and Director of the Institute of China Studies at the University of Malaya, and a Nonresident Scholar at Carnegie China. He received his Ph.D. in Public and International Affairs from Northeastern University. He is the editor of the books *Populism, Nationalism and South China Sea Dispute* (Springer, 2022, with Nian Peng), *Researching China in Southeast Asia* (Routledge, 2019), and *Southeast Asia and China: A Contest in Mutual Socialization* (World Scientific, 2017, with Lowell Dittmer). He has published in various academic journals such as *Cold War History, Ocean Development and International Law, China Report, The China Review, Journal of Contemporary China, Asian Politics and Policy, Contemporary Southeast Asia, East Asia: An International Quarterly, Issues and Studies,* and *Problems of Post-Communism*. In addition, he has also published shorter pieces on media and policy-oriented online platforms such as *ThinkChina, East Asia Forum,* and *The Asia Dialogue*.

© 2025 World Scientific Publishing Company
https://doi.org/10.1142/9789819801350_fmatter

List of Contributors

Abdul Majid Ahmad Khan (B.A., Universiti Malaya) is former Ambassador of Malaysia to China and currently President of the Malaysia–China Friendship Association.

Andrew Kam Jia Yi (Ph.D., Australian National University) is Associate Professor at the Institute of Malaysian and International Studies, Universiti Kebangsaan Malaysia.

Choo Kim Fong (Ph.D., Capital Normal University) is Lecturer at Universiti Teknologi MARA.

Fan Pik Shy (Ph.D., Capital Normal University) is Senior Lecturer at the Institute of China Studies, Universiti Malaya.

Fu Congcong (Ph.D., Tsinghua University) is Associate Professor at the School of Asian Studies, Beijing Foreign Studies University.

Guanie Lim (Ph.D., National University of Singapore) is Associate Professor at the National Graduate Institute for Policy Studies, Japan.

Karl Lee Chee Leong (Ph.D., Monash University) is Senior Lecturer at the Institute of China Studies, Universiti Malaya.

viii *List of Contributors*

Kuik Cheng-Chwee (Ph.D., Johns Hopkins University) is Professor at the Institute of Malaysian and International Studies, Universiti Kebangsaan Malaysia.

Lam Choong Wah (Ph.D., Xiamen University) is Senior Lecturer at the Department of International and Strategic Studies, Universiti Malaya.

Lee Pei May (Ph.D., University of Nottingham) is Assistant Professor at the Department of Political Science, International Islamic University of Malaysia.

Li Gengrun (B.A., Beijing Foreign Studies University) is a research assistant at the Center for Southeast Asian Studies, Beijing Foreign Studies University, and is also currently an M.A. student at the University of Michigan-Ann Arbor, USA.

Li Ran (Ph.D., Universiti Malaya) is Senior Lecturer at the Institute of China Studies, Universiti Malaya.

Ling Tek Soon (Ph.D., Tsinghua University) is Senior Lecturer at the Institute of China Studies, Universiti Malaya.

Muhammad Ali Ridha bin Norman (Ph.D., China Foreign Affairs University) is Senior Lecturer at the School of International Studies, Universiti Utara Malaysia.

Nur Shahadah Jamil (Ph.D., Universiti Kebangsaan Malaysia) is Senior Lecturer at the Institute of China Studies, Universiti Malaya.

Ong Sheue-Li (Ph.D., Yokohama National University) is Senior Lecturer at the Department of Economics, Universiti Malaya.

Tee Boon Chuan (Ph.D., National Central University) is Associate Professor at the Institute of Chinese Studies, Universiti Tunku Abdul Rahman.

Tham Siew Yean (Ph.D., University of Rochester) is Emeritus Professor at Universiti Kebangsaan Malaysia and Visiting Senior Fellow at Yusof Ishak Institute of Southeast Asian Studies (ISEAS), Singapore.

Yap Hon Lun (Ph.D., Universiti Tunku Abdul Rahman) is Head of the Institute of Socio-Economic Research, Tunku Abdul Rahman University of Management and Technology.

Yat Ming Ooi (Ph.D., University of Auckland) is Assistant Professor of Innovation Management at the University of Auckland, New Zealand.

Zhang Miao (Ph.D., Universiti Malaya), is Associate Professor at the School of International Relations, Research School for Southeast Asian Studies, Xiamen University.

Zhang Mingliang (Ph.D., Peking University) is Associate Professor at the School of International Studies, Academy of Overseas Chinese Studies, Jinan University.

© 2025 World Scientific Publishing Company
https://doi.org/10.1142/9789819801350_fmatter

Acknowledgment

Some chapters in this edited book were first presented at an international conference titled "Constructing a China-Malaysia Community with a Shared Future: Opportunities, Prospects and Challenges," held in November 2023, and organized jointly by the Institute of China Studies at the Faculty of Arts and Social Sciences, Universiti Malaya; the East Asian International Relations Caucus; and the Institute of Malaysia Studies at the Research School for Southeast Asian Studies, Xiamen University. The Embassy of the People's Republic of China in Kuala Lumpur and the Office of the Deputy Minister of Investment, Trade, and Industry of the Government of Malaysia provided generous support and partial funding for the organization of this conference.

This book serves to commemorate the 10th Anniversary of the Comprehensive Strategic Partnership between Malaysia and China in 2023 and the 50th Anniversary of Diplomatic Relations between Malaysia and China in 2024. It gathers scholars from both countries to comprehensively cover and discuss the diplomatic, security, economic, cultural, and educational aspects of bilateral relations. The editor is confident that this book will be helpful to policymakers, academics and students, private sector communities, journalists, and anyone who is interested in Malaysia–China relations and the implications for regional dynamics in Southeast Asia and beyond.

Finally, the editor would like to thank all the academic and administrative staff of the Institute of China Studies at Universiti Malaya for their contribution to the organization of the above-mentioned conference and the publication of this book.

© 2025 World Scientific Publishing Company
https://doi.org/10.1142/9789819801350_fmatter

Contents

About the Editor	v
List of Contributors	vii
Acknowledgment	xi

Chapter 1   **Malaysia–China Relations: A Journey of Deepening Trust and Bilateral Ties across Five Decades (1974–2024)**   **1**
Dato' Abdul Majid Ahmad Khan

Introduction	1
The Formative Years (1974–1985)	2
Malaysia's Policies toward China under Tun Dr. Mahathir Mohamad (1998–2003) and (2019–2021)	3
Malaysia's China Policy under Dato' Seri Najib Abdul Razak (2009–2018)	6
Malaysia's China Policy under Dato' Seri Anwar Ibrahim (2022-present)	8
Opportunities	9
Future Directions of Malaysia–China Relations	9
Conclusion	11
References	12

xiv *Contents*

Chapter 2	**From Peaceful Rise to Community of Shared Future: How Malaysian Leaders View China's Foreign Policy and Diplomatic Concepts and Initiatives**	**13**

Ngeow Chow Bing and Muhammad Ali Ridha bin Norman

Introduction	13
Peaceful Rise and Good Neighborhood	15
Strategic Partnership and Comprehensive Strategic Partnership	18
Belt and Road Initiative	21
Community of Shared Future and the Three Global Initiatives	24
Conclusion	28
Acknowledgments	29
References	29

Chapter 3	**The Future of Malaysia's China Policy: Factors Determining Small-State Hedging**	**35**

Kuik Cheng-Chwee and Nur Shahadah Jamil

Introduction	35
A Response to the Critics of Malaysian (and Small-State) Hedging	36
Factors Determining the Feasibility and Future of Hedging	41
Concluding Analysis	48
References	50

Chapter 4	**A Chinese Perspective on Managing the South China Sea Issue: The Roles of ASEAN and the United States, and the Lessons of China–Malaysia Interactions in the South China Sea**	**55**

Zhang Mingliang

The Role of ASEAN in the South China Sea Issue: China's Ambiguity	56
Rejecting the Involvement of the United States in the South China Sea Issue	58
China–Malaysia Interactions in the South China Sea Issue	61

Contents xv

| | Conclusion | 63 |
| | References | 64 |

Chapter 5 **Dissecting Malaysia's Low-Profile Posture in the South China Sea Dispute** 67
Lam Choong Wah

Introduction	67
Tracing Malaysia's Claims	68
Conceptualizing the Low-Profile Approach	69
Expansion of Maritime Jurisdiction during Oil Crisis	71
San Francisco Treaty and Terra Nullius	74
The Occupation of Reefs and Rocks	77
Conclusion	78
References	79

Chapter 6 **From Bilateral Trade to Supply Chain Integration: Evolving Patterns of Malaysia–China Economic Relations** 83
Zhang Miao and Li Ran

Introduction	83
Bilateral Trade: Structure, Value-Added, and Free Trade Agreements	85
Bilateral Investment	95
Conclusion	104
References	106

Chapter 7 **Malaysia's Trade and Investment Links with China: An Update** 109
Andrew Kam Jia Yi and Tham Siew Yean

Introduction	109
China's Investments in Malaysia	110
Malaysia–China Trade	118
Conclusion	127
Appendix 1. Product Codes	128
Appendix 2. Bilateral RCA and Intra-Industry Trade Index	128
References	129

xvi *Contents*

Chapter 8 **Analyzing the Middle-Income Trap in Malaysia: Of (Chinese) Investment and Industrial Upgrading** **131**
Guanie Lim and Yat Ming Ooi

Introduction	131
Background Information	132
An On-the-Ground Perspective: Chinese Investment in the Digital Free Trade Zone	136
Conclusion	141
References	142

Chapter 9 **Malaysia's Digital Transformation: Navigating the Digital Silk Road** **145**
Ong Sheue-Li

Introduction: Digital Development Cooperation in the Digital Age	145
Assessing Malaysia's Digital Landscape and Policy Frameworks	146
Exploring China's Digital Silk Road	150
Malaysia's Engagement with the Digital Silk Road Initiative: Opportunities and Challenges	153
Recommendations for Future Implementation	156
Conclusion	157
References	158

Chapter 10 **Prospects of Malaysia–China Climate Cooperation** **161**
Lee Pei May

Introduction	161
China's Role in Global Climate Governance	163
Malaysia–China Collaboration on Climate Action within the ASEAN Framework	164
Malaysia–China Cooperation in Renewable Energy	166
Malaysia–China Collaboration in the Electric Vehicle Industry	167
Other Green Initiatives	169
Malaysia–China Prospective Collaboration on Climate	170
Conclusion	171
References	172

Contents   xvii

Chapter 11   Thirty Years of Islamic–Confucian Dialogue in
Malaysia and China   **179**
Tee Boon Chuan

Introduction: Islamic–Confucian Dialogue as a
Commitment to Avoid the Clash of Civilizations   179
Osman Bakar and Tu Wei-Ming: Engaging Islamic–
Confucian Dialogue in Malaysia and China   181
Thirty Years of Islamic–Confucian Dialogue:
Reflective Observations   186
Conclusion   188
References   189

Chapter 12   The Development of Malay Language Teaching and
Malay Studies in China: A Historical Review from
the Perspective of Knowledge Autonomy   **193**
Fu Congcong and Li Gengrun

Introduction   193
The History of Early Malay Language Education
in China: Before 1949   195
The History of Early Malay Language Education
in China: 1949 to the Present   202
Future Directions: Constructing an Autonomous
Knowledge System   217
Conclusion   221
Acknowledgments   222
References   223

Chapter 13   Xiamen University Malaysia: Origins,
Development, and Future Prospects   **225**
Yap Hon Lun

Introduction   225
The Founding of Xiamen University Malaysia   226
Observations on the Developments of Xiamen
University Malaysia   231
Conclusion   235
References   235

xviii *Contents*

Chapter 14 How Satisfied are China's Students Studying in Malaysia's Higher Education Institutions? An Exploratory Survey **239**
Fan Pik Shy and Choo Kim Fong

Introduction	239
Brief Literature Review and Research Framework	242
Methodology	243
Data and Findings	244
Conclusion	252
References	253

Chapter 15 Malay Public Opinion on China-Related Issues in TikTok: A Case Study of Four TikTokers **257**
Ling Tek Soon and Karl Lee Chee Leong

Introduction	257
Malaysian Perceptions toward China	259
Research Methodology	262
Research Findings	262
Conclusion	267
Appendix 1. Videos of the Four TikTokers	268
References	270

Index 273

© 2025 World Scientific Publishing Company
https://doi.org/10.1142/9789819801350_0001

Chapter 1

Malaysia–China Relations: A Journey of Deepening Trust and Bilateral Ties across Five Decades (1974–2024)

Dato' Abdul Majid Ahmad Khan

Introduction

Malaysia–China relations have been characterized by complexity, evolution, and transformation over the years, shaped by the leadership and policies of both nations. The signing of the Joint Malaysia–China Communique between Prime Minister Tun Abdul Razak and Premier Zhou Enlai on the 31st of May, 1974, which formalized diplomatic relations between the two countries, was a game changer. It ushered into a new and promising era in Malaysia–China relations.

This essay is a narration of the evolution and transformation of Malaysia–China ties over the last fifty years since 1974. The assessment of the upward trajectory of the two countries' relations is mainly based on the observation and engagement of this author during his diplomatic posting in China in the 1980s and late 1990s, as well as his continuing involvement in promoting Malaysia–China understanding and cooperation after retirement from active diplomatic service, in his capacity of the President of the Malaysia–China Friendship Association since 2005.

It can be surmised that Malaysia–China relations have been carefully nurtured and managed over the years toward what it is today a healthy and robust relationship. The initial atmosphere of fear and suspicion in the bilateral relationship in the formative years has been transformed into one that is based on trust, respect, and partnership. The Malaysia–China relationship is one of the most successful stories of Malaysia's foreign policy. All nine Prime Ministers of Malaysia after Tun Abdul Razak shared his strategic vision and his conviction in the importance of having good relations with China. Each of these leaders during their respective administrations made a positive contribution to further consolidating Tun Abdul Razak's legacy. For this chapter, the author will focus more on the administrations of Tun Dr. Mahathir Mohamad, Dato' Seri Najib Abdul Razak, and Dato' Seri Anwar Ibrahim. This author believes that during these three administrations, Malaysia–China relations underwent a significant and impactful transition, through the deepening of mutual trust and a successful economic partnership. It has brought mutual benefit to Malaysia and China as well as the region.

The Formative Years (1974–1985)

While Tun Abdul Razak laid the foundation for Malaysia to chart a new direction in Malaysia–China relations following his visit to Beijing in 1974, the actualizing of his objective progressed slowly. Two principal factors contributing to this state of affairs can be identified. Firstly, the domestic situation in China was still unsettled and fluid in the late 1970s. A power struggle ensued between the reformists and the conservatives in the Communist Party of China following the demise of Chairman Mao Zedong. When Deng Xiaoping returned back to the corridors of power after the end of the Cultural Revolution, the consolidation of his power was only gradually established. At one stage, China's domestic as well as foreign policy direction was a serious concern to Malaysia's policymakers. As a young diplomat in Beijing, this author recalls well that the prevailing conversations among the foreign diplomats in Beijing then were whether Deng Xiaoping's practical policy of opening up China to the world would prevail and endure. As it turned out, Deng Xiaoping eventually emerged victorious, implementing his reform and opening-up rigorously and paving the way for China to focus on improving its relations with the outside world, including Malaysia. Deng Xiaoping made an official visit to Malaysia in 1978, and the then Prime Minister of Malaysia, Tun Hussein Onn, reciprocated with his visit to China in 1980.

The second issue which was more fundamental to Malaysia's interests was China's continued (moral) support to the Communist Party of Malaya after the establishment of diplomatic relations. Malaysia had been insistent since the commencement of bilateral negotiations for establishing diplomatic relations that one of the conditions to do so was the cessation of China's support to the Communist Party of Malaya. As commented by a researcher, "China's moral support and fraternal ties with the local communist movement of Malaya had a direct impact on how Kuala Lumpur views the PRC" (Abdul Razak Baginda, 2002: 228). This lingering concern and preoccupation of Malaysia's had an impact on the progress of bilateral exchanges. In the 1980s, the Embassy of Malaysia in Beijing (when this author was posted there) was constantly urged by the Chinese Foreign Ministry officials to step up bilateral exchanges between the two countries, especially at the level of people-to-people exchanges. Malaysia stood firm on its position, insisting that China's cessation of support to the Communist Party of Malaya was a prerequisite for the activation of bilateral interaction. The Chinese persistently argued that the linkage between the Communist Party of China and the Communist Party of Malaya was only a form of party-to-party relations and had nothing to do with government-to-government affairs and that China's moral support to the Communist Party of Malaya was an international obligation on its part, reasons which were not acceptable to Malaysia.

The Chinese position gradually changed following Deng Xiaoping's visit to Malaysia and Singapore in 1979. In 1982, the first Prime Minister of Malaysia, Tunku Abdul Rahman, visited China in his capacity as the President of RISEAP (Regional Islamic Dahwah Council of Southeast Asia and the Pacific) at the invitation of the Chinese Islamic Association, and this was a significant symbolic visit reflecting the change in Malaysia's perception of China as the Tunku had been a staunch anti-Communist personality.

Malaysia's Policies toward China under Tun Dr. Mahathir Mohamad (1998–2003) and (2019–2021)

Tun Mahathir Mohamad became the fourth Prime Minister of Malaysia in 1981 and took an active role in directing Malaysian foreign policy priorities, including the policy toward China. His foreign policy thrust was "economic diplomacy" to secure trade opportunities and investments for

Malaysia's development. Tun Mahathir Mohamad viewed China from two perspectives: from the bilateral dimension and from the regional and international dimension. From the Malaysia–China bilateral perspective, Mahathir viewed China from an economic lens and was less concerned with the ideological issue. He was convinced that the reform and opening-up policy initiated by Deng Xiaoping was genuine and that China was ready for international cooperation and business. Prime Minister Mahathir saw China's emerging market potential and the related opportunities following its program of modernization. He strongly felt that Malaysian businesses should not miss such an opportunity. With such conviction, Mahathir jump-started Malaysia–China relations. He organized a huge delegation of 200 people, consisting of cabinet ministers, senior officials, and private sector representatives, that visited China in 1985. This visit broke the impasse and paved the way for the actualization of Malaysia's economic cooperation with China. He created a conducive environment through bilateral agreements with China on facilitating trade, investment, and taxation arrangements. He wanted Malaysians to dim their perception of fear toward China. The 1985 Malaysian delegation's visit was indeed an eye-opener for business delegates on China's potential economic opportunities. Some of the private sector groups that had joined the delegation later became successful investors in China. Prime Minister Mahathir did not stop at this first visit but followed up with several other visits to China during his 22-year rule. He wanted to secure Malaysia's economic advantage in the Chinese modernization program. Under his administration, he also encouraged a special visit program for the civil service to update themselves on the ongoing process of changes in China and realize that Malaysia too should open up to China. He directed relevant agencies to review regulations that had placed unnecessary travel restrictions that had impeded business and tourist flow between the two countries. Tun Mahathir felt that Malaysia should not be too clouded by the ideological perception of China, which was eventually resolved with the end of the Cold War in 1989 and the signing of a peace agreement between the Malaysian Government and the Communist Party of Malaya.

On the international front, Prime Minister Mahathir, in the 1990s, became a strong advocate of China's rise. He dismissed the "Chinese Threat Theory." Like his predecessor Tun Abdul Razak, Mahathir also believed that China has a legitimate role and responsibility in global affairs and that its legitimate rise should not be contained or denied.

In many of his conversations with Chinese leaders, Mahathir encouraged China to be more active in contributing to stability and development regionally and internationally. Malaysia under the Mahathir administration played a leading role in inviting China to be an active member of the ASEAN Dialogue Process, ASEAN Plus Three, and East Asia Summit. In the year 2000, this author, as the Ambassador to China, accompanied Mahathir to Dalian for a meeting with President Jiang Zemin to secure China's support for Malaysia's proposal to establish the East Asia Economic Group (EAEG). This author recalls a beaming Mahathir as he left the room of President Jiang Zemin, as China had expressed support for Malaysia's EAEG proposal. Many analysts were of the view that Mahathir's positive support for China's active regional and international involvement was a strategy to have China act as a counterweight to the United States and the West in global politics.

The Mahathir administration's contribution to Malaysia–China cooperation and understanding as well as Mahathir's positive statements on China's good intentions and global responsibility earned Malaysia China's goodwill and appreciation. Mahathir provided the catalyst for the transformation of Malaysia's skeptical perception of China to a more positive outlook. His approach of being friendly toward China was motivated by what he saw as opportunities Malaysia could gain from China's development. Following his retirement in 2003, Mahathir was specifically invited by Jiang Zemin to a special lunch hosted at the Zhongnanhai leadership compound, reflecting China's appreciation for Mahathir's contribution to the deepening and consolidation of Malaysia–China ties and friendship. In 2018, Mahathir was once again appointed as the Prime Minister of Malaysia. The then Chinese Premier Li Keqiang, on welcoming the appointment, described Mahathir as a senior politician who has contributed much to Malaysia–China relations as well as to China's relations with ASEAN and East Asia.

There was some anxiety over Malaysia–China relations following Mahathir's return to power as the sixth Prime Minister, following his critical comments on China's infrastructure projects in Malaysia during and before the elections in 2018. Those projects were initiated under Dato' Seri Najib Abdul Razak's administration. Mahathir's comments, however, should not be viewed as a direct criticism of China but rather more reflective of his dissatisfaction with Najib's management and negotiation related to these projects in Malaysia. This uncertainty was cleared with

Mahathir's attendance at the second Belt and Road Summit in Beijing, where he reiterated Malaysia's commitment to further strengthening bilateral cooperation and endorsed China's Belt and Road Initiative (BRI).

Tun Abdullah Badawi, who succeeded Mahathir as the fifth Prime Minister in 2003, continued to expand and deepen the scope of bilateral cooperation with China. Tun Abdullah Badawi was a familiar face in China as he was the Foreign Minister under the Mahathir administration. He had implemented many China-related policies of the government and had helped in forging closer relations with China. Tun Abdullah Badawi also sought to bring China closer to ASEAN and the regional development agenda. He was a likable personality in China and was treated with much respect as the Prime Minister.

Malaysia's China Policy under Dato' Seri Najib Abdul Razak (2009–2018)

During Dato' Seri Najib Razak's nine-year administration, Malaysia–China relations ascended to their highest and best level. He anchored his dedication to Malaysia–China ties on deepening the legacy of his late father Tun Abdul Razak. The Chinese have always held Tun Abdul Razak in high esteem for his courageous and bold move to normalize the relationship with China during the turbulent period in the 1970s. In 2014, at an event celebrating the 40th Anniversary of Malaysia–China Diplomatic Relations, Najib visited the exact location in Beijing — the Great Hall of the People — where, 40 years earlier, Tun Razak signed the Malaysia–China Joint Communique. Najib stated, "It is here today, that I feel not just the responsibility of the government, but the responsibility to my father — to continue his legacy and ensure deepening of the Malaysia–China ties" (Najib Abdul Razak, 2014).

Najib subsequently delivered what he promised. He elevated Malaysia-China relations to a Comprehensive Strategic Partnership and expanded Malaysia's collaboration with China into new areas, such as defense cooperation (including joint exercises and purchase of defense assets from China). He also strongly supported the BRI. That period also witnessed expanded cooperation in education, demonstrated by the establishment of the Xiamen University branch campus in Malaysia, the setting up of two additional Chinese commercial banks, and increased people-to-people exchanges. It was also during this period that investment from China to Malaysia soared to its highest level. Industrial and infrastructure projects such as the Malaysia–China Kuantan Twin Industrial Park, the expansion of the Kuantan Port, and the East Coast Railway Line, as well as new Chinese investments in telecommunication, e-commerce, construction, and manufacturing, became the hallmarks of Malaysia–China economic cooperation. During the Najib administration, two Chinese pandas were loaned to the National Zoo of Malaysia, a symbolic gesture demonstrating the close affinity and friendship between the two nations. At a personal level, Najib also established a good rapport with the Chinese leadership, particularly with President Xi Jinping.

The scale of Chinese investment and bilateral projects during Najib's administration was very much welcomed and appreciated. However, it did raise concerns in some quarters in Malaysia about whether Malaysia had abandoned its balanced approach to foreign investment or whether ordinary Malaysians could benefit from such large-scale investment. These concerns were gradually addressed and the projects were continued, and in some cases competed in the post-Najib era. On balance, despite some controversies during Najib's administration, Malaysia–China relations continued to move forward, further enhancing the foundation that was laid in the early years. Malaysia continues to welcome China's economic participation in its development and growth.

During the short administrations of both Tan Sri Muhyiddin Yassin and Dato' Seri Ismail Sabri Yaakob, the significance of China to Malaysia continued to be emphasized. There were no changes in policies, but given the restrictions imposed by the global pandemic, there were minimal bilateral exchanges. It should however be noted that during the Tan Sri Muhyiddin and Dato' Seri Ismail Sabri administrations, Malaysia and China demonstrated the true spirit of Malaysia–China friendship, as both countries supported each other in meeting the challenges posed by the pandemic. China shared its experiences and supplied medical equipment and vaccines to Malaysia during this critical time, while Malaysia also provided critical support when the early outbreak of the pandemic hit China. The mutual support demonstrated by Malaysia and China during the pandemic is a testament to the lasting legacy of the enduring friendship between the two nations.

Malaysia's China Policy under Dato' Seri Anwar Ibrahim (2022-present)

After coming to power in November 2022, Prime Minister Dato' Seri Anwar Ibrahim made an impact on the policies toward China. During his two visits to China in 2023, Anwar reaffirmed Malaysia's commitment to furthering existing bilateral ties and emphasized the importance of the economic linkages between the two countries in terms of trade, investment, tourism, and connectivity. Reflecting China's confidence in his administration, Prime Minister Anwar Ibrahim secured Chinese commitment of investment to the value of RM 170 billion during his first visit to China in March–April 2023. His administration also further eased and facilitated people-to-people exchanges through a new visa-free policy for Chinese visitors to Malaysia and China reciprocated the Malaysian initiative, which was implemented since late 2023. It was indeed a strategic step taken by both countries to relax travel requirements for each other's citizens, reflecting the trust and confidence between the two countries built over the last 50 years.

Like all his predecessors, Prime Minister Anwar Ibrahim also reiterated Malaysia's position of supporting China's legitimate international role. He expressed that Malaysia will continue to pursue its independent foreign policy of not choosing sides in the ongoing Sino-US strategic competition. Some observers have pointed out that Prime Minister Anwar Ibrahim has added another layer to Malaysia's approach toward China, which is referred to as the "Civilizational Lens" (Ngeow, 2023). Both Prime Minister Anwar Ibrahim and President Xi Jinping share similar views on the advocacy of dialogue among civilizations for better mutual understanding, while they also share a similar view on the promotion of Asian values and the emphasis on humanity and ethical values as equally important in the process of development. In this context, Anwar has expressed support for President Xi's Global Civilization Initiative and the pursuit of a community of shared future. This spiritual, "civilizational" approach to development and peace is akin to the "Madani Malaysia" initiative advocated by the Anwar administration and is expected to be an additional bonding platform between the two leaders. Going forward, both Malaysia and China can be expected to emphasize the importance of value-driven development.

Opportunities

As the Malaysia–China relationship embarks upon the next phase, there is immense potential for deeper collaboration, enhanced connectivity, and shared prosperity. Several developments, including the following, are likely to shape the future trajectory of the bilateral ties:

1. Economic integration through platforms such as the BRI, ASEAN–China Free Trade Agreement, and RCEP which will enhance connectivity, infrastructure development, trade facilitation, supply chain linkage, industrial diversification, and economic growth.
2. In terms of cooperation in innovation and technology, China can offer Malaysia opportunities related to digitalization, artificial intelligence, renewable energy, and emerging technologies such as electrical vehicles and batteries.
3. Malaysia can learn from China's experiences in its successful modernization programs in the areas of poverty eradication, project delivery and implementation, talent and technical skills training, upgrading of the skills of small and medium enterprises, trade promotion, modernization of agriculture, food security, and public health.
4. There are numerous opportunities for cooperation in research and development, education, tourism, student exchanges, and other fields that can further intensify people-to-people exchanges for mutual understanding and friendship.

Future Directions of Malaysia–China Relations

Tun Abdul Razak in his concluding remarks following the signing of the Malaysia–China joint communique on 31st May 1974 had expressed the hope that "This goodwill that exists between us must be carefully nurtured" (Abdul Razak, 1974). Looking back at the last five decades, on the journey of Malaysia–China relations, it can be said that Tun Abdul Razak's expectations have been fulfilled. Malaysia–China relations today are in full bloom, based on a solid foundation anchored on mutual trust, respect, and benefit. The content of the bilateral exchanges has been enriched with multifaceted and strategic cooperation involving almost all sectors.

10 *Abdul Majid Ahmad Khan*

What would then be the appropriate strategy going forward in navigating Malaysia–China relations? As we embrace the next phase of our bilateral cooperation, there are both opportunities and challenges. It is to be noted that we are now living in a new regional and global environment characterized by evolving geopolitical shifts and uncertainties, growing nationalism and protection, and rapid technological advancement as well as the disruptions that have been caused by such advancement.

For Malaysia, this author considers the following measures to be appropriate:

1. Malaysia should continue to invest in bilateral cooperation and friendship with China. Malaysia should take advantage of the geographical proximity to China as well as China's growing prosperity and global influence to benefit its own development and prosperity. China will be the fulcrum of the new Asian growth story and prosperity.
2. Malaysia should continue its policy of active neutrality in the Sino-US strategic rivalry, as Malaysia draws benefits from the respective strengths of the two powers as well as other external powers and partners.
3. Malaysia should continue to be alert on sensitive issues or the "red line" that could undermine the cordial relationship between Malaysia and China.
4. Malaysia should consolidate its consultation process with China. Malaysia needs to revise and upgrade the existing bilateral mechanism/platform to secure a more beneficial outcome, such as market access to China, investment and technology flow, tourism, human resource development, and connectivity. Malaysia's approach must be more proactive and strategic.
5. Malaysia should continue to have a comprehensive understanding of various regional and international platforms and architecture, especially those pertaining to the evolving world order, as initiated by China. China's three initiatives, namely, the Global Development Initiative, Global Civilization Initiative, and Global Security Initiative, anchored on the BRI platform, will be China's foreign policy priorities going forward. Thus, Malaysia needs to pay more attention to these.
6. Malaysia needs to continuously encourage China to produce more public goods and enhance support for the economic growth of the developing world.

7. Malaysia should strategically take advantage of China's "Good Neighborly Policy." As China prospers, Malaysia should also gain from the spillover effect.
8. The South China Sea issue could potentially affect the bilateral sentiment negatively if it is not prudently managed. Hence, for Malaysia, there is a need to have effective communication channels with China, as well as strong internal interagency monitoring and coordination mechanisms.

Conclusion

Malaysia–China relations have traversed a remarkable journey since 1974, evolving from historical connections to strategic partnership and comprehensive cooperation. The resilience and dynamism of the bilateral relations have reflected the common aspiration, mutual respect, and mutual interests of both countries and their peoples. Malaysia's rapprochement with China, despite the differences in ideology and social system, has benefited Malaysia enormously, contributing to both its prosperity and security. The strategic engagement has also brought about regional peace and development.

Despite the changes in the leadership in both Malaysia and China over the past five decades, not only has the policy remained constant but bilateral content has also been enriched and deepened. Malaysia has also benefited from the leadership of all its Prime Ministers since Tun Abdul Razak's journey of friendship to Beijing in 1974. All the Malaysian Prime Ministers have continued their policies toward a stronger and enduring relationship and cooperation with China. In this essay, the author has highlighted the role of the administrations of Tun Dr. Mahathir Mohamad, Dato' Seri Najib Abdul Razak, and Dato' Seri Anwar Ibrahim, which have made strategic advancements in consolidating trust and bilateral relations. It is also to be noted that in building up collaboration and friendship with China, there have been many other players, such as NGOs, associations, chambers of commerce, and certain personalities, that have helped and contributed a lot to the relationship between Malaysia and China. Hence, the celebration and welcoming of the 50th Anniversary of Malaysia–China diplomatic relations in 2024 is a successful embodiment of the past achievements in nurturing and managing the Malaysia–China relationship to what it is today. There are many expectations among people for even better opportunities and stronger relations ahead as the beginning of the new stage of Malaysia–China relations dawns.

It should be noted, however, that as we embrace a positive mood of the 50th Anniversary celebration, we should recognize that there are still pockets of concern about China's rise and its global status, especially its impacts on the smaller states in the neighborhood. These are legitimate expressions of concern that should be noted.

In conclusion, this author believes that based on the trust and goodwill that Malaysia and China have enjoyed over the past 50 years, there is no doubt that our relations will remain robust in the years ahead. Both Malaysia and China must seize opportunities, address challenges, and further build upon the foundation of trust and friendship established by our leaders. By fostering dialogue, innovation, and connectivity, both countries can unlock new avenues for collaboration and realize their shared vision of prosperity and an interconnected future.

References

Abdul Razak (1974). "Speech at the Signing of the Malaysia–China Joint Communique Establishing Diplomatic Relations on 31st May 1974, at the Great Hall of the People, Beijing, China."

Abdul Razak Baginda (2002). "Malaysian Perceptions of China: From Hostility to Cordiality." In Herbert Yee and Ian Storey (eds.), *The China Threat: Perceptions, Myths and Reality*, pp. 227–247. London: Routledge.

Najib Abdul Razak (2014). "Speech at the 40th Anniversary of Malaysia–China Establishment of Diplomatic Relations Ceremony at the Great Hall of People in Beijing, 31 May 2014." https://www.idfr.gov.my/images/stories/DiplomaticVoice/diplomatic%20voice%20vol%202%202014.pdf.

Ngeow, Chow Bing (2023). "PM Anwar's Civilizational Approach to the Malaysia-China Relationship." *ThinkChina*, 8 May. https://www.thinkchina.sg/pm-anwars-civilisational-approach-malaysia-china-relationship.

© 2025 World Scientific Publishing Company
https://doi.org/10.1142/9789819801350_0002

Chapter 2

From Peaceful Rise to Community of Shared Future: How Malaysian Leaders View China's Foreign Policy and Diplomatic Concepts and Initiatives

Ngeow Chow Bing and Muhammad Ali Ridha bin Norman

Introduction

Following the implementation of economic reforms under Deng Xiaoping, China embarked on a path of market-based economic reforms, rapid modernization, and technological development. China's foreign policy priorities shifted to place more emphasis on securing economic opportunities in what Deng Xiaoping deemed as the era of "peace and development." Engagement with and opening up to global capitalism became the means for China to attain prosperity. Forty-five years after the reform and opening-up, China has now become a global power with a stature similar to that of the United States.

Malaysia established diplomatic relations with China in 1974, but from 1974 to the mid-1980s, there were not many economic exchanges between the two countries. In fact, travel between the people of the two countries was heavily regulated and restricted. But with China's reform and opening-up, Malaysia came to recognize the economic dynamism and growing opportunities of its giant neighbor and decided to engage with China in a more concerted manner. In 1985, an important visit to China, with a large business delegation, was undertaken by the then prime minister Mahathir Mohammad. The visit emphasized exploring opportunities for expanding economic ties. Malaysia's major security concerns about China, including its support for the Communist Party of Malaya and its policy toward overseas ethnic Chinese, were largely fading, while the South China Sea issue remained largely latent at that time (Leong, 1987; Ngeow 2021a). The end of the Cold War in the late 1980s and early 1990s further removed any remaining impediment to Malaysia's policy of economic engagement with China. Since the 1990s, Malaysia and China experienced rapid growth of bilateral economic and people-to-people ties. As China's economic and geopolitical influences have continued to expand since the dawn of the 21st century, Malaysia has also been firmly committed to pursuing various avenues of collaboration and partnership, viewing China's ascent as an opportunity rather than a threat.

As China's role in the world became more important, the country's leadership also articulated a series of concepts relating to foreign policy, diplomacy, and international relations, especially since entering the 21st century. These concepts form the core of the repertoire of the Chinese diplomatic lexicon. Put together, these concepts offer a coherent narrative regarding the overarching ideals and vision about China's position in the world and how the country's elites assess and judge the nature of international relations, world order, and global trends and developments. They form the ideational foundation to guide the more concrete actions and policies of the country's officials. These concepts are certainly scrutinized and contested outside of China, especially in the West (and also in some developing countries such as India), and questions remain about how sincere China is in implementing these concepts and whether China's actions deviate from the supposed loftiness contained in these concepts. Nonetheless, China takes these concepts seriously and has consistently sought to explicate them to the international community. For the most part, to what extent other countries echo these concepts is an indication, at a normative level, of the degree of convergence or alignment with China on certain beliefs regarding China's role in the world and the nature of international relations.

Based on this premise, this chapter explores how Malaysia's leaders view and understand China's foreign policy and diplomatic concepts and initiatives in the 21st century, from the notion of the "Peaceful Rise" to the vision of a "Community of Shared Future." The chapter points out that, by and large, Malaysia finds these concepts largely agreeable and that many of these concepts also resonate with Malaysia's own conception of the nature of international relations and world order. These conceptual convergences have served as an important foundation for the development of bilateral relations in the 21st century.

Peaceful Rise and Good Neighborhood

China enjoyed spectacular growth in the 1990s and entered the 21st century with the newly acquired membership to the World Trade Organization (WTO), which further propelled China to become the world's premier manufacturing and export powerhouse. However, the rapid rise of China also led to growing discussions of the "China Threat" theory, especially in the United States (Yee and Storey, 2002). There were various strands of the "China Threat" thesis. Some postulated along the conventional power transition dynamic between established and emerging powers, while others argued that China's economic growth without liberalization would create an enhanced authoritarian power whose interests remained fundamentally at odds with those of the US and the broader Western world. To the Chinese scholars and officials, the idea of the "China Threat" was inimical and completely contrary to the way China had perceived the world, which was fundamentally about "peace and development" after the Cold War ended. The "Peaceful Rise" concept was articulated and put forward by Zheng Bijian, a senior scholar at the Central Party School, as China's most definitive answer to the "China Threat" thesis. The "Peaceful Rise" concept would play a key role in China's diplomatic strategy under the Hu Jintao leadership (2002–2012) and beyond.

Writing in the mid-2000s, Zheng Bijian argued that despite China having made significant progress, the country continued to face significant domestic challenges in terms of resource scarcity, technological backwardness, economic gaps between the rich and the poor, a low level of urbanization, and growing environmental pollution. Coping with and resolving all these challenges, according to Zheng, would require China to transcend the old model of modernization or industrialization and instead embrace a new form of modernization based on technology, economic efficiency, sustainable use of resources, curtailed pollution, and optimal allocation of human resource. China henceforth would not employ the old ways of the hegemonic rise of great powers by plundering resources of other countries. Instead, China's ambition to become a great power would be achieved by embracing globalization, striving for peace and development, and cooperating with other countries (Zheng, 2005). Hence, at its core, the peaceful rise concept aimed to emphasize that China's rise would not proceed through coercion but through peaceful means born out of win-win cooperation because "a developing China needs peaceful external environment and a favorable climate in its periphery" (Gill, 2010: 10).

The terminology peaceful rise was later changed to peaceful development in China's official discourse, displaying the cautiousness still prevalent in China during the Hu Jintao era ("development" sounds less ominous compared to "rise"). Regardless, this concept of peaceful rise/peaceful development has remained in use, as China seeks to reassure major powers such as the US and its neighboring countries that China's rise will not pose any threat. Instead, China often argues that foreign countries, especially China's neighbors, can benefit from China's increasing power and influence, as the peaceful rise prioritizes the path of economic development and cooperation (Guo, 2006). David Shambaugh, a well-known American China-watcher, also observed that China's new regional posture in the 2000s rested on four pillars to facilitate its peaceful rise, namely, its participation in regional organizations, the establishment of strategic partnerships and the deepening bilateral ties, the expansion of regional economic ties, and the reduction of distrust in its strategic sphere (Shambaugh, 2004).

Concomitant with the emergence and popularization of the peaceful rise concept in the early 2000s was the introduction of the good neighborhood policy (Cai, 2005), in particular in the Sixteenth Party Congress Report in 2002. Fostering friendly and cooperative relationships with neighboring countries was not new, but it was in the Sixteenth Party Congress Report that the idea was more formally articulated. The good neighborhood policy proclaimed that China intended to build "friendship and partnership with neighboring countries" and pursue "the policy of bringing harmony, security and prosperity to neighbors." Hence, peaceful rise and good neighborhood formed the context of China's active engagement with countries of the Association of Southeast Asian Nations (ASEAN) from the 2000s onward.

ASEAN countries overall were receptive to the emerging influence of China, but there were also concerns and anxieties over the nature and implications of China's rising power, especially in the context of the unresolved disputes in the South China Sea. China sought to send a positive message of reassurance, that China's growing power should not be perceived as a threat to the region but rather as a source of economic and trade-related opportunities. China's reassurance under the peaceful rise and good neighborhood concepts was manifested through the China–ASEAN Free Trade Agreement (signed in 2002) to address ASEAN's anxiety over its economic rise and the "Declaration on the Conduct of Parties in the South China Sea" (DOC, also signed in 2002) that showcased China's commitment to decreasing tensions and facilitating peaceful management of the disputes. In 2003, China took a significant step by becoming the first major power to accede to the ASEAN Treaty of Amity and Cooperation (TAC), which theoretically binds China to ASEAN regional norms, values, and rules (Shambaugh, 2004). Furthermore, in 2003, China's status vis-à-vis ASEAN was upgraded to that of "Strategic Partner," effectively marking the transition from China's passive attitude toward ASEAN to a more active position in ASEAN-led regional institutions (Suehiro, 2017) (ASEAN and China further upgraded their relationship to "Comprehensive Strategic Partnership" in 2022). The Hu Jintao era also witnessed China's proactive engagement in ASEAN-led forums such as the ASEAN Regional Forum (ARF), ASEAN Plus Three (China, Japan, and South Korea), and the East Asian Summit (EAS). These developments were often cited by China to confirm its commitment to dialogue and cooperation, and also to attest to Beijing's support for ASEAN's centrality in developing inclusive regional architecture.

The articulation of the peaceful rise concept and the pursuit of a good neighborhood policy found receptive responses in Malaysia. Although China's claim in the South China Sea remained a security concern to Malaysia, especially among the defense establishment, the political leadership generally rejected the notion of the "China Threat." Tun Mahathir Mohammad, Malaysia's longest-serving Prime Minister (1981–2003; 2018–2020), in a 1995 speech, articulated a very similar line of argument on why China should not be seen as a threat. In this speech, Mahathir contended that "[to] perceive China as a threat and to fashion our security order around this premise would not only be wrong policy, but it would also be a bad and dangerous one." Instead, Mahathir believed "that China is deeply committed to the perpetuation of a peaceful, regional security environment. It wants this for its own national political and economic interests. China believes, as we do, that peace is a pre-requisite for its own internal development.

This conviction is unlikely to change in the foreseeable future" (Mahathir Mohammad, 1995). In his memoir, published after his first retirement from politics, Mahathir reiterated that Malaysia "must not fall into the American trap of regarding China as a potential enemy. When you regard a country as a potential enemy, you can be sure that that country will regard you as is current enemy" (Mahathir Mohammad, 2011: 432).

Mahathir's successor, Prime Minister Tun Abdullah Badawi (2003–2009), in his speech at the 2005 Asia-Pacific Roundtable, argued that "the China or tomorrow, no less than the China of today, will be a force for peace and stability unless its integrity and vital interests are threatened." In the same speech, Abdullah also expressed his optimism and confidence that China would not turn "hegemonic" as both Malaysia and China were committed to non-hegemony in the regional order (Abdullah Badawi, 2005). Similarly, Abdullah's deputy and later his successor, Prime Minister Dato' Seri Najib Abdul Razak (2009–2018), expressed in numerous speeches his belief in the peaceful rise of China. In a 2005 speech, he said, "I beg to defer from the many that have cited China as a threat to global stability. I firmly believe that it is in China's interests to work with the nations of the world, not against them" (Najib Abdul Razak, 2005). In 2014, as Prime Minister, he reiterated in a speech delivered in the United States that "we have seen that a China which pursues peace, stability and mutual development is an invaluable partner for developed and developing countries alike. We welcome the peaceful rise of China" (Najib Abdul Razak, 2014).

The consistency of the message in all these speeches can be seen as evidence of Malaysia's reading of China as a benign power. Of course, one could argue that in private Malaysian leaders could hold a more reserved view toward China, but public speeches, articulated by these leaders in their official capacity, have to be understood as expressions of authoritative or official positions of the government. It is clear that the above-cited Malaysian leaders intended to express their views agreeing with the concept of the peaceful rise of China.

Strategic Partnership and Comprehensive Strategic Partnership

In contrast to the defense alliance relationships that the US upholds and is often proud of, China's officials and scholars often argue that pursuing "Strategic Partnerships" is more efficacious than pursuing alliances, as partnerships are built on mutual benefits and equality, not targeting any third party, and are not bound by a form of protector–protected unequal relationship (Feng and Huang, 2014). Guided by this logic, strategic partnership (with a variety of themes and labels for different countries, and with varying degrees of depth) rather than alliance has been China's preferred mode of engagement with other countries in the world to achieve its peaceful rise. Malaysia has welcomed this strategic partnership diplomacy, as it has also eschewed formal defense alliances with other powers and has committed to a neutrality-based foreign policy (Savaranamutu, 2010).

Building on the confidence in a China committed to a peaceful rise, Malaysia expanded its engagement and collaboration with China. Prime Minister Abdullah Badawi signed Joint Communiques with China in 2004 and 2005 and agreed to define the bilateral relationship as one of Strategic Partnership in 2004. As explained by Tan Sri Syed Hamid Albar, Malaysia's Foreign Minister from 1999 to 2008, the strategic partnership would "pave the way for the further enhancement of relations at all levels and all sectors of society." He further said that "Malaysians and Chinese alike are now well aware that we are both compatible and capable of forging a partnership and camaraderie for our mutual benefit and also for the good of our people, the region, and the international community" (Syed Hamid Albar, 2004/2005: 512). Najib Abdul Razak, in his capacity as Deputy Prime Minister during the tenure of Abdullah Badawi, affirmed in a speech that the strategic partnership "goes beyond bilateral ties" as both Malaysia and China "share common global perceptions and... stand together on international issues which have helped to form consensus among developing and even developed states" (Najib Abdul Razak, 2004/2009: 147–148).

Malaysia's endorsement of forming a strategic partnership with China in 2004 created a strong positive upward trend during Abdullah's tenure, and this could be seen in the substantial increase in the volume of trade, investment, and mutual visits between Malaysia and China. In 2008, China became Malaysia's fourth largest trading partner, while Malaysia emerged as the largest trading partner of China within the ASEAN region. China also became the fourth largest source of tourism to Malaysia. With China assessed positively, Malaysia also began to cooperate with China in the defense and security sector. Traditionally, Malaysia's defense partnerships were mostly Western powers such as the US, Great Britain, and Australia, but in 2005, Malaysia and China signed a Memorandum of Understanding on Defense Cooperation, which paved the way for more regular exchanges and mutual visits by defense officials, exploration into arms procurement, and almost a decade later, bilateral exercises.

Najib succeeded Abdullah in 2009 with a continuous commitment to this strategic partnership. He visited China two months after assuming the Prime Minister's office and witnessed the signing of a "Joint Action Plan on Strategic Cooperation" outlining 13 key areas for future collaboration across a broad spectrum of domains (Wong and Chow, 2009). In around 2012, together with the then Chinese Premier Wen Jiabao, Najib launched the China–Malaysia Qinzhou Industrial Park and Malaysia–China Kuantan Industrial Park, in what would later come to be known as the "two countries, twin parks" cooperation. This industrial park cooperation provided the impetus for significantly greater investment, in particular from China into Malaysia, and would later also be enveloped into the Belt and Road Initiative (BRI) as a flagship project.

In 2012, Xi Jinping was appointed the General Secretary of the Communist Party of China, and in 2013 Xi assumed the position of China's President. Xi's leadership of China proved to be transformational, whether in terms of domestic or foreign policies (Economy, 2018; Wang, 2018; Zhao, 2022). Successful domestic policies such as anti-corruption, poverty alleviation, protection of the environment, and technological and industrial upgrading, together with a stronger emphasis on party leadership, political discipline, and ideological and cultural self-confidence, have transformed Chinese society significantly. In terms of foreign policy, Xi's leadership has ushered in a more proactive phase of Chinese diplomacy, with signature new ideas and initiatives such as the BRI and the Community of Shared Future now becoming standard references in China's diplomatic outreach.

Xi visited Malaysia in late 2013. During the visit, Xi and Najib agreed that the bilateral relationship should be upgraded from a strategic partnership to a comprehensive strategic partnership. Najib returned with this second official visit to China in May–June 2014 and signed a Joint Communique with China that formalized the upgrading of the bilateral relationship into a comprehensive strategic partnership. These mutual visits between 2013 and 2014 marked a significant diplomatic milestone in deepening and widening the bilateral ties between the two nations (Ngeow, 2019a: 104–106).

With the comprehensive strategic partnership and throughout the tenure of the Najid administration, Malaysia–China relations were characterized by close collaboration across numerous sectors. On the economic front, China emerged as Malaysia's largest trading partner since 2009, while Malaysia for many years retained its position as China's largest trading partner within ASEAN and the third largest in Asia after Japan and South Korea. China came to be the leading foreign investor in Malaysia under Najib's tenure. In 2017, Malaysia rose to become the fourth largest recipient of China's overseas foreign direct investment (FDI) worldwide. Malaysia formulated a five-year economic and trade program with China to identify key sectors of economic cooperation with China while also endorsing China's BRI strongly. Both countries also held common views regarding regional trade integration such as the ASEAN–China Free Trade Area (ACFTA) and the Regional Comprehensive Economic Partnership (RCEP). Sociocultural exchanges also flourished, especially with the inauguration of Xiamen University Malaysia and the steady increase of enrollment of both Chinese students in Malaysia's higher education institutions and Malaysian students in China's universities (Ngeow and Fan, 2024). Defense cooperation also increased significantly during the time of Najib's administration, as can be seen in a major arms procurement agreement, increased exchanges of military academies, increased port visits by China's navy vessels, and the launch of several bilateral military exercises (Ngeow, 2021b).

Belt and Road Initiative

The BRI is perhaps the most discussed and promoted concept emerging from China. Xi first proclaimed the idea of a Silk Road Economic Belt during his visit to Kazakhstan in September 2013, followed by the announcement of the 21st Century Maritime Silk Road during his visit to Indonesia in October 2013. Together, the "BRI" envisioned a stronger interconnected world that would enable a greater flow of people, goods, capital, and ideas, enriching participating countries from all corners. In his speech at the First Belt and Road Forum held in Beijing in 2017, Xi argued that the BRI was consistent with the ideals of peace and development, openness and inclusiveness, mutual learning, and mutual benefit. In pursuing BRI cooperation, China accordingly will not "resort to outdated geopolitical maneuvering." What China aims to achieve is "a new model of mutually beneficial cooperation" and China has no intention of creating "a small group [of countries] detrimental to stability." Instead, China hopes to create "a big family of harmonious coexistence" (Xi, 2017b: 563).

When the BRI was presented to Malaysia, Najib strongly welcomed and supported the initiative. Within a few years, a few major infrastructure projects were announced and launched under the auspices of the BRI, the most important of which is the East Coast Rail Link (ECRL), a project that will connect the east coast and west coast of Peninsular Malaysia via railway. The project, however, when announced in late 2016, elicited controversy and criticism over its lack of transparency and terms of financing. Internationally, the criticism that emerged mostly within Western media and think tank circles was that the BRI was China's tool to impose financial burden and debt. The Najib administration nonetheless remained steadfast in maintaining BRI cooperation with China. Najib echoed Xi's conceptualization of the BRI when he argued that the it is "truly an example of win-win cooperation" and on such basis, countries "should all welcome it...contribute to and participate in it" (Najib Abdul Razak, 2017). He praised the BRI as having "the potential to create the world's largest platform for economic cooperation" and insisted that it would not be in Malaysia's national interests to turn its back on the BRI (Syed Umar Ariff and Luqman Karim, 2018).

Malaysia experienced the first change of ruling government after the general elections held in May 2018, with Tun Mahathir Mohammad, the former Prime Minister, leading a reform-oriented coalition of parties (called Pakatan Harapan or the Hope Alliance) and securing a parliamentary majority, resulting in Mahathir being sworn in as the seventh Prime Minister of Malaysia. Malaysia's bilateral relationship with China came under scrutiny as the incoming government was either skeptical or critical of several major infrastructure projects (including the ECRL and two gas pipeline projects) with financing from China that were agreed upon under the Najib administration. The new government postponed or canceled these projects, leading to questions about whether the new government was adopting a less friendly policy toward China. However, Mahathir, key cabinet officials, and senior leaders of the Pakatan Harapan coalition all at one point dismissed the perception that they were somehow "anti-China" and, in fact, all reaffirmed the importance of the ties between Malaysia and China and cooperation on the BRI (Ngeow, 2019b). In fact, as noted by political scientist Khoo Boo Teik, Mahathir shared and empathized with the BRI vision of resurrecting the ancient land and maritime trade routes in the modern context. The BRI's emphasis on connectivity and infrastructure could well be harnessed for addressing the developmental imperatives of developing countries in the age of globalization (Khoo, 2021).

The ECRL project was also eventually revived after being successfully renegotiated in April 2019, and thus an uncertain factor that overshadowed bilateral relations was successfully removed. Mahathir attended the Second Belt and Road Forum in Beijing in 2019 and lauded the BRI idea as "great" since "it can bring the land-locked countries of Central Asia closer to the sea. They can grow in wealth and their poverty reduced. Everyone will benefit from the ease of travel and communication that the development of the Belt and Road project will bring" (cited in Ngeow and Nur Shahadah Jamil, 2022: 12).

Essentially, Malaysia's approach toward China remained unchanged, especially after the April 2019 renegotiation of the ECRL project; however, the relationship was also disrupted by two factors subsequently, namely, the frequent political changes within Malaysia between 2020 and 2022 and the COVID-19 pandemic that seriously restricted international travel and interactions. Both Tan Sri Dato' Muhyiddin Yassin (2020–2021) and Dato' Sri Ismail Sabri Yaakob (2021–2022), the two short-stint Prime Ministers after Mahathir Mohammad stepped down from power in 2020, had to focus on fighting the pandemic while reviving the economy amid fluid domestic political dynamics. Although more focused on the domestic front, both leaders acknowledged China to be a crucial partner in fighting the pandemic and also for Malaysia's post-pandemic economic revival, and both affirmed the BRI as a major platform for cooperation. In November 2022, Malaysia's Fifteenth General Elections concluded with the emergence of a Unity Government composed of several coalitions and led by Prime Minister Dato' Seri Anwar Ibrahim (2022 to the present). Since entering office, Anwar has been consistently positive on the BRI vision, urging the BRI to regain its momentum after the pandemic and hailing it as the exemplification of "translating lofty ideals into practical reality, solidarity and cooperation" (Zunaira, 2023).

From 2013 to 2023, despite Malaysia having witnessed five different prime ministers, Malaysia's supportive stand on the BRI has not fundamentally changed (Nur Shahadah Jamil, 2023). While due to the ECRL episode, there is a greater recognition that the implementation of the BRI can and has to be done in a more diligent way, the general consensus across the political spectrum in Malaysia is that the BRI can be a good platform to promote economic and functional cooperation for common and mutual benefit.

Community of Shared Future and the Three Global Initiatives

Another major concept fashioned by Xi Jinping is the community of shared future, first systematically articulated in his speech at the United Nations General Assembly in September 2015. In this long speech, Xi urged countries in the world to renew "commitment to the purposes and principles of the Charter of the United Nations, build a new model of international relations featuring mutually beneficial cooperation, and create a community of shared future of mankind." He also stated that efforts should be made to "build partnerships in which countries treat each other as equals, engage in extensive consultation, and enhance mutual understanding," "commit to... multilateralism and reject unilateralism," "create a security environment featuring fairness, justice, joint efforts, and shared interests," "promote open, innovative and inclusive development that benefits all," "increase inter-civilization exchanges to promote harmony, inclusiveness, and respect for differences," and "build an ecosystem that puts Mother Nature and green development first." Xi also called on countries to reject "outdated mindset of zero-sum game" and "abandon the Cold War mentality in all its manifestations" (Xi, 2015/2017). In another speech addressed to the United Nations in 2017, Xi elaborated that the building of a community of shared future is guided by principles established in the United Nations Charter, the five principles of peaceful coexistence, and other principles that have "emerged in the evolution of international relations" that "have been widely accepted." While the principle of sovereign equality was specially held as the supreme principle in this speech, Xi also extolled that all states should "uphold the authority of the international rule of law, exercise their rights in accordance with the law, and fulfill their obligations in good faith." Xi reiterated that countries should "foster partnerships based on dialogue, non-confrontation and non-alliance," "build a world of common security for all through joint efforts," "build a world of common prosperity for all through win-win cooperation," "build an open and inclusive world through exchanges and mutual learning," and "make the world clean and beautiful by pursuing green and low-carbon development" (Xi, 2017a).

The ideas contained in these speeches eventually crystallized into three initiatives that were launched in the years between 2021 and 2023, namely, the Global Development Initiative (2021), the Global Security Initiative (2022), and the Global Civilization Initiative (2023). The Global Development Initiative (GDI) was first proposed by China at the General

Debate of the 76th Session of the United Nations General Assembly, whereby China called for "international commitment to development as a priority, a people-centered approach, benefits for all, innovation-driven development, harmony between man and nature, and results-oriented actions." The GDI is aligned with the United Nations Sustainable Development Goals (SDGs), and prioritizes cooperation in eight areas, namely, "poverty alleviation, food security, pandemic response and vaccines, financing for development, climate change and green development, industrialization, digital economy, and connectivity in the digital era" (Center for International Knowledge on Development, 2023: 1–2).

The Global Security Initiative (GSI) was first mentioned by Xi Jinping at the annual Bo'ao Forum for Asia meeting in April 2022, and the official concept paper of the GSI was published in 2023. In the concept paper, the "vision of common, comprehensive, cooperative and sustainable security" is especially highlighted. It argues that this "new vision of security" is to "advocate a concept of common security, respecting and safeguarding the security of every country; a holistic approach, maintaining security in both traditional and non-traditional domains and enhancing security governance in a coordinated way; a commitment to cooperation, bringing about security through political dialogue and peaceful negotiation; and pursuit of sustainable security, resolving conflicts through development and eliminating the breeding ground for insecurity." It also advances the notion that "humanity is an indivisible security community" and that the "legitimate security concerns of all countries" should be "taken seriously and addressed properly, not persistently ignored or systematically challenged." "Security of one country should not come at the expense of that of others." The concept paper also reinforces the supreme importance of respecting the sovereignty and territorial integrity of all countries, abiding by the principles of the United Nations Charter, commitment to peaceful resolution of conflicts, and the maintenance of both traditional and non-traditional security (Ministry of Foreign Affairs of the People's Republic of China, 2023).

Finally, the Global Civilization Initiative (GCI) was unveiled by Xi in March 2023, during a high-level meeting between the Communist Party of China and other political parties in Beijing. The GCI calls for "respecting the diversity of civilizations, advocating the common values of humanity, valuing the inheritance and innovation of civilizations, and strengthening international people-to-people exchanges and cooperation" It aims to underscore that "differences in histories, cultures, political systems and development phases" are not obstacles to sharing "common aspiration for peace, development, equity, justice, democracy and freedom" but that "people need to keep an open mind in appreciating how different civilizations perceive values, and refrain from imposing their own values or models on others, and from stoking ideological confrontation" (State Council Information Office, 2023a).

The ideas informing these initiatives are not necessarily new *per se* and have been expressed by the Chinese government in the 1990s or 2000s. The core ideas of the GSI, for example, can find precedents in the new security concept that emerged in China in the 1990s. Nevertheless, the more systemic postulation of these three initiatives, integrated with the conception of the community of shared future (encapsulated in the official White Paper *A Global Community of Shared Future: China's Proposals and Actions,* issued in September 2023), represents the most systematic articulation of a "blueprint for the future" by China and has been presented as China's answer to the myriad challenges facing the international community (State Council Information Office, 2023b). China is seemingly advancing a world vision that aims to transcend the conventional understanding of development, security, and political values that have long been dominated by norms and institutions that originated and developed in the West and have been preserved by Western powers. The GDI puts more focus on South–South cooperation in bringing sustainable development to the Global South. The GSI implicitly criticizes the security architecture based on military alliances of the Western powers as being exclusivist and zero sum in nature, becoming the source of insecurity for others whose security interests are ignored. The GCI's vision of a pluralistic world consists of different civilizations underpinned and shaped by different ideologies, political systems and values, histories and cultures. This vision is in contrast with the West and the Western strong emphasis on universal values of democracy and human rights, and the general tendency in the West to categorize countries based on the binary categories of democracy versus autocracy.

These concepts and initiatives have generated mostly skeptical, if not hostile, reactions in the West. A characteristic Western exposition of these concepts and initiatives views them as a "manifesto for an alternative system of international affairs to the current rules-based order led by the United States and its partners in Europe and the Indo-Pacific," meant "to usurp the international dialogue on the global development agenda, place it under Chinese tutelage, and infuse it with (supposed) Chinese principles," and to promote "a state-focused and state-defined values system and marks another effort by Beijing to eliminate universal values" (Schuman, Fulton and Tering, 2023).

Malaysia evaluates the whole corpus of these Chinese narratives from a different premise, one that is more focused on seeking common ground rather than highlighting differences. In fact, many ideas informing the community of shared future and the three initiatives are not incongruent with Malaysia's own foreign policy tradition, norms, and historical experiences. Tun Ghazalie Shafie, Malaysia's Foreign Minister from 1981 to 1984 and one of the key architects and enduring figures in Malaysian foreign policy, in a 1991 speech highlighted the faith in the concept of "togetherness" and alluded to an Asia "where fate and destiny are commonly and equally shared" (Ghazalie Shafie, 1991/2000: 119). Syed Hamid Albar also spoke of an East Asian community that "is open and inclusive rather than closed and antagonistic" and "where large or small states can live in peace and harmony," believing in "egalitarianism and non-hegemony" (Syed Hamid Albar, 2005: 73). The developmental agenda driven by the BRI and the GDI generally converge with the long-standing Malaysian commitment to greater South–South cooperation, sustainable development, and SDGs. Malaysia, being a multicultural country, has also been a firm believer in civilizational dialogues and mutual exchange, and the current Prime Minister Anwar has been a strong advocate of such endeavors for decades (Anwar Ibrahim, 1997).

The vision of "common, comprehensive, cooperative and sustainable security" is not alien to Malaysia either. In a keynote address delivered to the ASEAN–Australia Dialogue in 2018, His Royal Highness Sultan Nazrin Muizzuddin Shah, the Sultan of Perak in Malaysia, remarked that "prospects may become brighter if adversarial military alliances could morph into more inclusive and cooperative security arrangements that bind friends and foes alike, in pursuit of mutual peace. Such a collaborative structure would be more in consonance with a globalized world, where security is indivisible and not zero sum. Ideology need not be an obstacle" (Sultan Nazrin Shah, 2018). This statement was remarkably similar to the basic notion underpinning China's GSI.

During Anwar's official visit to China in 2023, he "expressed support for the principles and values of President Xi Jinping's global initiatives and his vision of a Community for a Shared Future for Mankind, including the proposal for a Malaysia–China Community for a Shared Future" (Ministry of Foreign Affairs of Malaysia, 2023). With this endorsement,

Anwar evidently views China's narrative of the community of shared future as compatible with Malaysia's own values, interests, and norms, as well as his own "Madani" concept in governing Malaysia. The bilateral Joint Statement issued in June 2024, in the wake of Chinese Premier Li Qiang's visit to Malaysia, also affirmed this commitment (Ministry of Foreign Affairs of Malaysia, 2024). Malaysia appears to see that, by agreeing with China on this core concept, there are a lot of opportunities to shape a better regional environment that is beneficial to its own interests and that of others.

Raja Nushirwan Zainal Abidin, Malaysia's current Director General of the National Security Council and former Ambassador to China (2019–2023), explicated Malaysia's philosophy of "strategic embedment" in a 2024 speech, in which he contended that Malaysia's approach is "to integrate as deeply as possible with as many regional initiatives as possible in order to not only to develop close links with partner countries within the region, but to achieve maximum strategic space by working with others to influence the regional strategic environment. This philosophy animates Malaysia's desire to always be at the heart of ASEAN, including to be involved in sub-regional organizations, strategic partnerships or even initiatives such as the Malaysia–China Community for a Shared Future" (Raja Nushirwan Zainal Abidin, 2024).

Malaysia's agreement with China's community of a shared future, however, should not be misconstrued as Malaysia "taking a side" or rejecting the existing international order in favor of a new Chinese hegemonic order. Malaysia does not share the view, often more prevalent in the West, that the current international rules-based order is necessarily a fixed construct defined and monopolized solely by the West (Kuik, 2023), whereby emerging China's concepts and ideas represent a fundamental assault on the order (Ngeow, 2023). An "either–or" conception also undermines the creation of accommodative space that would allow for pragmatic mutual adjustments.

Conclusion

In the 21st century, as China's material power has increased substantially, it has also sought to increase its ideational influence and soft power. A series of foreign policy and diplomatic concepts and initiatives have been articulated and offered by China, ranging from "Peaceful Rise" to the "Community of Shared Future." This chapter has documented how Malaysian leaders have publicly expressed their views about these concepts and initiatives, or how their own views also tend to converge with those concepts and initiatives.

Of course, the public statements of leaders should not be taken entirely at face value, while difficult issues, disagreements, and challenges also exist between Malaysia and China. While Malaysia does not see China as an adversary, it has to be firm in protecting its own rights and interests (in the South China Sea dispute, for example). Whether China can consistently uphold the principles as elucidated in its own concepts and initiatives will be of great consequence as well. Overall, however, Malaysia and China do share similar views on a range of issues, and this ideational or normative convergence between Malaysia and China provides a sound foundation for bilateral relations to develop.

Acknowledgments

Ngeow Chow Bing would like to acknowledge support from the Korea Foundation's Policy-Oriented Research Grant (Project Code: 2221100-1463) for the research included in this chapter.

References

Abdullah Badawi (2005). "Keynote Speech at the Asia Pacific Roundtable." 1 June. https://www.pmo.gov.my/ucapan/index.php?m=p&p=paklah&id=2957.

Anwar Ibrahim (1997). "Islam-Confucianism Dialogue and the Quest for a New Asia." In Osman Bakar and Cheng Gek Nai (eds.), *Islam and Confucianism: A Civilizational Dialogue*, pp. 11–18. Kuala Lumpur: Centre for Civilizational Dialogue, University of Malaya.

Cai, Bingkui (2005). "China's Peaceful Development and Relations with its East Asian Neighbors." In Saw Swee-Hock, Sheng Lijun, and Chin Jin Wah (eds.), *ASEAN-China Relations: Realities and Prospects*, pp. 27–30. Singapore: ISEAS.

Center for International Knowledge on Development (2023). *Progress Report on the Global Development Initiative 2023*. Beijing: Center for International Knowledge on Development. https://www.mfa.gov.cn/mfa_eng/topics_665678/GDI/wj/202306/P020230620670430885509.pdf.

Economy, Elizabeth (2018). *The Third Revolution: Xi Jinping and the New Chinese State*. Oxford: Oxford University Press.

Feng, Zhongping and Huang Jing (2014). *China's Strategic Partnership Diplomacy: Engaging with a Changing World*. European Strategic Partnership Observatory Working Paper No. 8. https://www.files.ethz.ch/isn/181324/China%E2%80%99s%20strategic%20partnership%20diplomacy_%20engaging%20with%20a%20changing%20world%20.pdf.

Ghazalie Shafie (ed.) (1991/2000). "The Making of a New Southeast Asia: Our Regional Vision." In *Malaysia, ASEAN and the New World Order*, pp. 107–120. Bangi: Penerbit Universiti Kebangsaan Malaysia.

Gill, Bates (2010). *Rising Star: China's New Security Diplomacy*. Washington: Brookings Institution Press.

Guo, Sujian (ed.) (2006). "Introduction: Challenges and Opportunities for China's 'Peaceful Rise'." In *China's 'Peaceful Rise' in the 21st Century*, pp. 1–14. Aldershot: Ashgate Publishing.

Khoo, Boo Teik (2021). "China's Belt and Road Initiative: A View from a Mahathirist Imaginary." *Singapore Economic Review*, Vol. 66, No. 1, pp. 293–312.

Kuik, Cheng-Chwee (2023). "Malaysian Conceptions of International Order: Paradoxes of Small-State Pragmatism." *International Affairs*, Vol. 99, No. 4, pp. 1477–1497.

Leong, Stephen (1987). "Malaysia and the People's Republic of China in the 1980s: Political Vigilance and Economic Pragmatism." *Asian Survey*, Vol. 27, No. 10, pp. 1109–1126.

Mahathir Mohammad (1995). Speech at the *International Trade and Investment Conference Malaysia and China in the 21st Century: Prosperity and Cooperation*, 23 January. https://www.pmo.gov.my/ucapan/index.php?m=p&p=mahathir&id=1189.

Mahathir Mohammad (2011). *A Doctor in the House: The Memoirs of Tun Dr Mahathir Mohamad*. Petaling Jaya: MPH.

Ministry of Foreign Affairs of the People's Republic of China (2023). "The Global Security Concept Paper." https://www.mfa.gov.cn/eng/wjbxw/202302/t20230221_11028348.html.

Ministry of Foreign Affairs of Malaysia (2023). "Historic Meeting between YAB Prime Minister Dato' Seri Anwar Ibrahim and His Excellency President Xi Jinping, 31 March 2023." Press Release of the Ministry of Foreign Affairs, 1 April. https://www.kln.gov.my/web/guest/-/historic-meeting-between-yab-prime-minister-dato-seri-anwar-bin-ibrahim-and-his-excellency-president-xi-jinping-31-march-2023.

Ministry of Foreign Affairs of Malaysia (2024). "Joint Statement between the People's Republic of China and Malaysia on Deepening the Comprehensive Strategic Partnership towards China-Malaysia Community with a Shared Future." 20 June. https://www.kln.gov.my/web/guest/-/joint-statement-between-the-people-s-republic-of-china-and-malaysia-on-deepening-the-comprehensive-strategic-part-nership-towards-china-malaysia-commun.

Najib Abdul Razak (ed.) (2004/2009). "Malaysia-China Relations: Strategic Partnership." In *Moving Ahead: Malaysia-China Relations*, pp. 147–154. Petaling Jaya: MPH Group Publishing.

Najib Abdul Razak (2005). "Speech at Malaysia-China Business Luncheon." 5 September. https://www.pmo.gov.my/ucapan/index.php?m=p&p=najib tpm&id=3553.

Najib Abdul Razk (2014). "Speech at Georgetown University, Washington, DC." 23 September. https://www.pmo.gov.my/ucapan/index.php?m=p&p= najib&id=4262.

Najib Abdul Razak (2017). "Why Malaysia Supports China's Belt and Road." *South China Morning Post*, 12 May. https://www.scmp.com/comment/insight-opinion/article/2094094/why-malaysia-supports-chinas-belt-and-road.

Ngeow, Chow-Bing (2019a). "A 'Model' for ASEAN Countries? Sino-Malaysian Relations during the Xi Jinping Era." In Alvin Cheng-hin Lim and Frank Cibulka (eds.), *China and Southeast Asia in the Xi Jinping Era*, pp. 103–122. Lanham: Lexington Books.

Ngeow, Chow-Bing (2019b). "Malaysia-China Cooperation on the Belt and Road Initiative under the Pakatan Harapan Government: Changes, Continuities, and Prospects." In *NIDS ASEAN Workshop 2019: China's BRI and ASEAN*, pp. 25–42. Tokyo: National Institute for Defense Studies.

Ngeow, Chow-Bing (2021a). "Have Friendly Malaysia-China Relations Gone Awry?" *Carnegie Endowment for International Peace*, 16 July. https://carnegieendowment.org/2021/07/16/have-friendly-malaysia-china-relations-gone-awry-pub-84981.

Ngeow, Chow-Bing (2021). "Malaysia-China Defence Relations: Disruptions Amid Political Changes and Geopolitical Tensions." *ISEAS*, https://www.iseas.edu.sg/articles-commentaries/iseas-perspective/2021-57-malaysia-china-defence-relations-disruptions-amid-political-changes-and-geopolitical-tensions-by-ngeow-chow-bing/.

Ngeow, Chow-Bing (2023). "How Malaysia Views U.S. and Chinese Narratives About the World Order." *Carnegie Endowment for International Peace*, 21 August. https://carnegieendowment.org/2023/08/21/how-malaysia-views-u.s.-and-chinese-narratives-about-world-order-pub-90409.

Ngeow, Chow-Bing and Fan Pik Shy (2024). "China's Educational Soft Power: A View from Malaysia." In Leo Suryadinata (ed.), *Rising China's Soft Power in Southeast Asia: Impact on Education and Popular Culture*, pp. 139–160. Singapore: ISEAS.

Ngeow, Chow-Bing and Nur Shahadah Jamil (2022). "Malaysia's Relations with China under Mahathir 2.0: Reaffirming Bilateral Ties, Renegotiating Economic Collaboration, Reasserting Security Interests." *Issues and Studies*, Vol. 58, No. 2, 2251001.

Nur Shahadah, Jamil (2023). "Ten Years into the Belt and Road Initiative in Malaysia: Shift, Continuity and Way Forward." *East Asian Policy*, Vol. 15, No. 3, pp. 7–19.

Raja Nushirwan Zainal Abidin (2024). "Australia and Malaysia: Thinking Differently, Working Closely." *Asialink*, the University of Melbourne, 19 April. https://asialink.unimelb.edu.au/insights/australia-and-malaysia-thinking-differently,-working-closely.

Saravanamutu, John (2010). *Malaysia's Foreign Policy, the First Fifty Years: Alignment, Neutrality, Islamism.* Singapore: ISEAS.

Schuman, Michael, Jonathan Fulton, and Tuvia Gering. (2023). "How Beijing's Newest Global Initiatives Seek to Remake the World Order." *Atlantic Council*, Issue Brief, 21 June. https://www.atlanticcouncil.org/in-depth-research-reports/issue-brief/how-beijings-newest-global-initiatives-seek-to-remake-the-world-order/.

Shambaugh, David (2004). "China Engages Asia: Reshaping the Regional Order." *International Security*, Vol. 29, No. 3, pp. 64–99.

State Council Information Office (2023a). "Global Civilization Initiative Injects Fresh Energy Into Human Development." 19 March. http://english.scio.gov.cn/topnews/2023-03/19/content_85177312.htm.

State Council Information Office (2023b). "A Global Community of Shared Future: China's Proposals and Actions." http://english.scio.gov.cn/node_9004328.html.

Suehiro, Akira (2017). "China's Offensive in Southeast Asia: Regional Architecture and the Process of Sinicization." *Journal of Contemporary East Asia Studies*, Vol. 6, No. 2, pp. 107–131.

Sultan Nazrin Shah (2018). "Keynote Address by His Royal Highness Sultan Nazrin Muizzuddin Shah." *Asialink*, the University of Melbourne, 14 March. https://asialink.unimelb.edu.au/stories/archive/keynote-address-by-his-royal-highness-sultan-nazrin-muizzuddin-shah.

Syed Hamid Albar (2004/2005). "Speech at the 30th Anniversary Commemorative Reception Hosted by H. E. Wang Chungui, Ambassador of the People's Republic of China." In *Selected Foreign Policy Speech by Syed Hamid Albar*, pp. 509–513. Kuala Lumpur: Institute of Diplomacy and Foreign Relations.

Syed Hamid Albar (2005). "Speech at the International Conference on the Emerging East Asian Community: Economic and Security Issues." In *Selected Foreign Policy Speech by Syed Hamid Albar*, pp. 69–78. Kuala Lumpur: Institute of Diplomacy and Foreign Relations.

Syed Umar Ariff and Luqman Karim (2018). "Najib Unapologetic over Strong Malaysia-China Ties." *New Straits Times*, 27 February. https://www.nst.com.my/news/nation/2018/02/339469/najib-unapologetic-over-strong-malaysia-china-ties.

Wang, Jianwei (2018). "Xi Jinping's 'Major Country Diplomacy': A Paradigm Shift?" *Journal of Contemporary China*, Vol. 25, No. 115, pp. 15–30.

Wong, Sai Wan and Chow How Ban (2009). "Najib's Visit Heralds a New Era of Diplomatic Ties with China." *The Star*, 4 June.

Xi, Jinping (ed.) (2015/2017). "A New Partnership of Mutual Benefit and a Community of Shared Future." In *The Governance of China, Volume II*, pp. 569–575. Beijing: Foreign Languages Press.

Xi, Jinping (ed.) (2017a). "Toward a Community of Shared Future with Mankind." In *The Governance of China, Volume II*, pp. 588–601. Beijing: Foreign Languages Press.

Xi, Jinping (ed.) (2017b). "Work Together to Build the Belt and Road." In *The Governance of China, Volume II*, pp. 553–566. Beijing: Foreign Languages Press.

Yee, Herbert and Ian Storey (eds.) (2002). *The China Threat: Perceptions, Myths and Reality*. London: Routledge.

Zhao, Shuisheng (2022). *The Dragon Roars Back: Transformational Leaders and Dynamics of Chinese Foreign Policy*. Stanford: Stanford University Press.

Zheng, Bijian (2005), "China's 'Peaceful Rise' to Great-Power Status." *Foreign Affairs*, Vol. 84, No. 5, pp. 18–24.

Zunaira, Saieed (2023). "Malaysian PM Anwar Calls for Revived Push for China's Belt and Road Projects." *The Straits Times*, 30 March. https://www.straitstimes.com/asia/se-asia/malaysian-pm-anwar-calls-for-revived-push-on-china-s-belt-and-road-projects.

© 2025 World Scientific Publishing Company
https://doi.org/10.1142/9789819801350_0003

Chapter 3

The Future of Malaysia's China Policy: Factors Determining Small-State Hedging

Kuik Cheng-Chwee and Nur Shahadah Jamil

Introduction[1]

Since the late 1990s, numerous international relations scholars have described Malaysia's China policy as "hedging." Storey (1999, 2007), Liow (2005, 2009), Lee (2006), Kuik (2008, 2016), Suzuki and Lee (2017), Haacke (2019), and Gerstl (2020) have used "hedging" either as a verb or a concept to depict Malaysia's external policy posture toward the rising power. Most of these authors have focused on diplomatic and/ or defense dimensions and often frame the dynamics within the context of weaker-state alignment choices *vis-à-vis* the United States and China, the two competing superpowers in the 21st century (Kuik, 2021a, 2024a; Saravanamuttu, 2020; Abuza, 2020; Mishra and Wang, 2021; Lai and Kuik, 2021; Ngeow and Nur Shahadah Jamil, 2022a; Han, 2018). In recent years, some scholars have extended the term to cover developmental and political-economic aspects of Malaysia's relations with China (Lampton, Ho, and Kuik, 2020; Liu, 2021; Chin, 2021, 2023; Zhao 2024).

We define hedging as insurance-seeking behavior under conditions of high stakes and high uncertainties to mitigate risks, maximize returns, and

---

[1]This chapter is adapted from "The Feasibility and Future of Middle-State Hedging (2024)." *East Asian Policy* Vol. 16, No. 4.

maintain fallback positions, primarily via the concurrent adoption of active equidistance, inclusive diversification, and prudent offsets (Kuik, 2021a, 2024a). Malaysia's China policy entails all three attributes (Kuik and Lai, 2023; Kuik, 2024b). Indeed, the greater the external uncertainties (especially those surrounding the big powers' intentions and interactions), the greater Malaysia's and other similarly situated weaker states' tendencies to hedge by deepening all three behavioral traits. The fact that this tendency has persisted and deepened, even when Malaysia has undergone unprecedented changes in government since 2018, suggests that the traits are not entirely products of its leaders' personal likes or dislikes, but the results of a combination of structural and domestic factors. The hedging tendency and traits are likely to endure even beyond the current Anwar Ibrahim-led "Unity Government."

As scholarly literature on hedging grows, so do the skeptics and critics of this policy approach. There are growing voices that hedging is neither viable nor tenable (Chong, 2016; Mishra and Wang, 2021). This chapter assesses the feasibility and future of small-state hedging by focusing on the case of Malaysia's China policy. This chapter proceeds in three sections. The first is a brief overview and response to the skeptics and critics of Malaysian hedging. The second offers an analysis of the major factors determining the future of Malaysia's China policy and small-state hedging. The third presents the concluding analysis. We argue that while hedging is a logical and desirable position on the part of Malaysia and similarly situated smaller states under conditions of uncertainty, such desirability may not necessarily be matched by feasibility. This is because the prospect and possibility of hedging, like other forms of alignment choices, are always subject to factors at multiple levels, especially systemic ones.

A Response to the Critics of Malaysian (and Small-State) Hedging

Skeptics, naysayers, and opponents of hedging as a small-state alignment choice abound. Some analysts question the conceptual clarity and/or analytical utility of hedging as a term (Ciorciari and Haacke, 2019; Jones and Jenne, 2022), while some highlight the issues surrounding the effectiveness of hedging as a strategy (Ciorciari, 2019). Yet others express doubts, if not disapproval, about the logic of hedging, questioning the feasibility and even the desirability of hedging. Chong Ja Ian (2020), for instance, contends that hedging will exacerbate uncertainty and commitment problems for both Washington and Beijing, complicating their respective attempts to maintain or modify the international order, which will sharpen the security dilemma between the two powers, pushing them to compete even more and increasing their demand for allegiance from other regional actors, thereby diminishing the room for smaller states to maneuver.

In this section, we focus on the scholars who are skeptical and critical of Malaysia's hedging behavior. While some of their observations are valid and valuable, their main critiques and comments about Malaysian hedging reflect their misunderstanding of the following aspects.

Misconceiving What Hedging Is

Many critics of hedging (not just of Malaysia's hedging behavior but also of hedging as an alignment approach) do not provide their definition of the term, which makes it difficult to ascertain, let alone evaluate, how these critics conceptualize hedging. Based on these critics' comments and descriptions, however, we can infer their implicit understanding of hedging. In the article "How long can Malaysia keep hedging its bet," Mishra and Wang opine that Malaysia's new foreign policy framework — *Focus in Continuity: A Framework for Malaysia's Foreign Policy in a Post-Pandemic World* (Wisma Putra, 2021) — "like Malaysia's current defense policy" as outlined in Malaysia's inaugural *Defence White Paper* (Ministry of Defence, 2020), "essentially reflects a non-aligned policy with (albeit diminishing) elements of a hedging strategy." While they do not explicitly identify what these "elements" are, their subsequent sentences equate Malaysian hedging with "stay[ing] ambiguous vis-à-vis the competing superpowers," "keeping us all guessing," and adopting "opposite and counteracting measures along with a foolproof fallback position" (Mishra and Wang, 2021).

While such attributes as "opposite and [mutually] counteracting measures" and "fallback position" are accurate characterizations of hedging (consistent with Kuik, 2016, 2020, 2021a), others are flawed understandings. Yes, hedging inevitably involves "ambiguous" dynamics (as observed by Lim and Cooper, 2015). However, ambiguity is a by-product, not the intended and prioritized goal of hedging's mutually counteracting acts. And, no, hedging is not intended to "keep everybody guessing." In fact, "guessing" is merely the unavoidable result of ambiguity but it is neither an intended end nor a function of hedging. Yes, hedging is about a fall-back position, but it is not about being "foolproof." Given the uncertain nature of international life, nothing is foolproof, and there is no panacea in the real world, as will be elaborated shortly.

Some interpretations of hedging are on theoretical and conceptual grounds. Hong Liu (2021: 160), for instance, writes, "The strategic hedging thesis, in its own right, has provided some instrumental insights in explaining the rationality and choices of foreign policy behaviors of smaller powers such as those in Southeast Asia." However, "there is a need to consider other alternatives beyond Neo-realism and Neo-liberalism, which focus on the state's material power and serve as main theoretical foundation of strategic hedging." This observation can be contested, because most writers from the hedging school (Marston, 2024; Kuik, 2008) actually challenge, not concur with, the neorealist propositions which overemphasize structural factors and material drivers.

Zachary Abuza's 2020 article indicates how a conceptual gap can become a source of misunderstanding about what hedging is. Abuza (2020: 117) rightly notes that Malaysia's "classic hedging strategy" illustrates that "a small country" can "navigate the escalating rivalry between two superpowers with which it has deep economic relations," simultaneously embracing opportunities "while pushing back in small ways to hedge and maintain sovereignty." He also accurately observes that Malaysia's "cautious hedging strategy" consists not only of pragmatic approaches of partnering with China economically and adopting "a less confrontational position toward China" on the South China Sea but also concurrent efforts of selectively challenging China on certain principles, pursuing legal claims on its continental shelf, and maintaining traditional US ties. Nevertheless, his understanding of hedging is questionable. According to Abuza, Malaysia's hedging strategy involves a choice of "lean[ing] toward bandwagoning with China, despite the government's stated intentions to assert Malaysia's autonomy." This is a misconception as it equates hedging with "bandwagoning." Without making a clear distinction between the two policy choices, such a misconception obscures reality and complicates analyses. As has been argued in various articles (Kuik, 2008, 2024a), the two choices are distinguishable from each other in one small but significant aspect: Hedging entails *limited* bandwagoning — displaying deference (saying yes and showing respect;

pleasing China) — but only in a limited, partial, and selective manner, while a pure form of bandwagoning involves across-the-board and unlimited deference. The latter does not correctly depict Malaysia's China policy, as it insists on concurrently displaying selective deference *and* selective defiance (saying no and showing autonomy; displeasing China) on virtually all issues, including Beijing's Belt and Road Initiative (BRI) and the South China Sea (Kuik and Lai, 2023; Kuik, 2023b).

Misunderstanding What (and How) Hedging Does

Some critics misunderstand what hedging does and how it functions. To cite Mishra and Wang again, "Hedging strategies like Malaysia's can sometimes fail" and "Malaysia may eventually find itself having to make a choice between the superpowers. It has to decide too whether to act as an 'interlocutor for regional peace' or a 'smooth self-defense operator'" before adding that "Hedging is a luxury middle powers cannot afford for long, especially when the stakes are high, superpowers are pushy, and the rivalry is intensifying" (Mishra and Wang, 2021).

These observations are sharp and stimulating, but they are more faulty assumptions than accurate reflections of the nature and functions of hedging as an alignment choice. According to Mishra and Wang, hedging "can sometimes fail." Well, everything may fail and no sensible scholar would suggest that hedging, or any policy, would not fail. In addition, hedging is not an indecisive or undecided stance, as commonly but inaccurately assumed. In fact, for Malaysia and many other hedging states in Southeast Asia (and probably beyond), "not making a choice between the competing powers" is a choice, and it is a decisive and not a tentative choice. Hedgers do not view choices as either–or options: They see "choosing the US or choosing China" as a false and dangerous dichotomy and, indeed, a big-power bias that they must reject. Similarly, Malaysia and other hedgers do not see the roles of "an interlocutor for regional peace" and "a self-defense operator" as either–or incompatible tasks. Hedgers seek to do both and to do more, concurrently, even though and especially because they know some of their efforts may fail, but some may succeed. This is not being silly or stubborn because for smaller and weaker states, prudent hedging is never a "luxury," but an essential survival-seeking approach.

Finally, as we have noted earlier and elsewhere (Kuik, 2021a, 2023c): hedging is no panacea. Like any other policy or strategy, hedging entails its own limits, drawbacks, and shortcomings. In real-life international relations, there is *no* "foolproof" solution, no alliance, no institutional arrangement, and certainly no hedging. States choose to hedge, not because they see that hedging "would always be effective" or "would not fail" (such magic does not exist in the real world), but because they see hedging as a *more acceptable* or a *less unacceptable* option of a range of non-ideal options, especially under imperfect conditions of uncertainties (Kuik, 2024a). Consequently, hedging is not about a singular "fallback position," but more about plural measures, multiple positionings, and several Plans B, because the risks, trade-offs, and undesirable eventualities associated with uncertainties are always multiple, plural, and numerous.

Misinterpreting Malaysia's Actions

While Abuza's 2020 essay presents numerous nuanced observations, not all his points accurately interpret Malaysia's actions. For instance, he writes, "Malaysia has demonstrated a cautious hedging strategy that overall *tends to acquiesce toward China*, even in areas of tension [italic added]" (2020: 116). He later concludes, "The United States is looking for partners in the region who will *resist* Chinese actions aimed at undermining the current rules-based order, but *Malaysian interest in such a partnership is waning*" (2020: 133). He then adds, "Even as it pushes back against overreach, Malaysia *has already accepted de facto Chinese leadership in the region.* It will likely continue to embrace the deep economic interdependence between the two countries, *acquiesce to Chinese security interests*, and *do little to stand up to Chinese coercion in the South China Sea*" (2020: 133–134).

Each of the italicized points is problematic. Cumulatively, they misinterpret Malaysia's policy and position vis-à-vis the United States, China, and the South China Sea. Yes, Malaysia and the United States have been partners in many domains, including defense and security. But no, Malaysia has never been in the sort of "defending rules-based order partnership" with the US as described by Abuza, in large part because Malaysia has never viewed the "rules-based order" simplistically. Malaysia has never adopted a black-and-white outlook that a big power is "defending" while another is "undermining" the "rules-based order" (Ngeow, 2023). Besides, it is unclear why Abuza is under the impression that

Malaysia "has already accepted de facto Chinese leadership," "acquiesce to Chinese security interests," and "do little to stand up to Chinese coercion in the South China Sea." These are misinterpretations, as the observations confuse Malaysia's acceptance of "power asymmetry" as acceptance of "status hierarchy" and Malaysia's "selective and partial" deference as across-the-board deference (Kuik, 2023b). The observations narrowly define "stand up" defiance in terms of armed confrontation, while in reality small-state defiance can and often does take multiple forms, including legal means (as Abuza himself acknowledges) and other indirect approaches (Kuik and Lai, 2023; Kuik, 2024a). Finally, Abuza's conclusion also narrowly conceives of Malaysia's hedging as targeting only one specific risk, i.e., "domination," when in reality hedging (by Malaysia and other small states) is almost always about mitigating and offsetting multiple forms and sources of risks. In the current context, hedging targets not just Chinese domination and maritime aggression but also unpredictable U.S. commitment, uncertain US–China relations, and perhaps most importantly the dangers of military entrapment and big-power war (Kuik, 2023a, 2023c).

Factors Determining the Feasibility and Future of Hedging

No policy lasts forever. Policy evolves when conditions change. Malaysia's hedging policy, however logical and desirable, may neither be feasible nor sustainable should current circumstances change, i.e., if and when present structural uncertainties give way to certainties that profoundly reshape Malaysia's security environment. Three clusters of conditions, as elaborated shortly, are capable of stopping Malaysia from hedging and starting to pursue such non-hedging policies as balancing, bandwagoning, or other forms of alignment behavior. The three clusters represent conditions and factors at different levels as follows:

- *Structural-level conditions*: If and when US–China rivalry escalates into an all-out, across-the-board big-power confrontation and armed conflict, the maneuvering space for all regional states largely diminishes and the certainty of rigidly polarized bipolarity and possible wartime entrapment increases, rendering hedging extremely difficult and possibly untenable.

- *Unilateral- or bilateral-level conditions*: If and when China's actions become even more aggressive and directly threaten Malaysia's core interests, the certainty of China becoming Malaysia's principal threat increases, thereby rendering hedging undesirable and unfeasible.
- *Domestic-level conditions*: If internal identity politics worsen in Malaysia and if China is perceived more as a problem than a partner for the Malaysian elite's domestic legitimation, the utility of confronting China for domestic political gain increases, thereby rendering hedging undesirable.

Structural Factors: If and When US–China Rivalry Escalates into Big-power Conflict

Wanting to hedge is a matter of desirability, but whether a state is able to do so is an issue of feasibility (Kuik, 2023c). The feasibility and future of small-state hedging, to a large extent, depends on systemic, structural factors. Chief among these factors is whether, for how long, and to what extent the ongoing US–China rivalry can be mitigated, managed, or spiraled into direct, open, all-out military conflict involving the two superpowers.

For weaker states, the big powers' action–reaction and eventual intentions are a matter of structural, systemic-wide dynamics, which they can do little about. Smaller states can attempt to shape and reshape, but because of the vast power asymmetries, the weaker actors are hardly in a position to stop the stronger power(s) from making any undesired moves that might, or will, harm their interests. This is so during the present peacetime and especially so during possible wartime.

Although war is not imminent under current circumstances, few analysts would dismiss the possibility of US–China armed conflicts, especially in Asia. The Taiwan Strait and the South China Sea are viewed by many security experts as among the potential hotspots (for an illuminating analysis of the possible Taiwan contingency and how Southeast Asian countries might react, see Ngeow, 2024). If and when the two competing superpowers clash militarily over either of these hotspots, the wartime situation means that no matter how much Malaysia and other weaker states declare their desirability to be "neutral," it would not be up to any of the non-big powers to ensure that their declared neutrality will save them from being entrapped.

This is particularly so for such maritime Southeast Asian countries as Malaysia, whose location adjacent to both disputed waters and US military bases means that it is more affected by big-power action–reaction and wartime entrapment than other states. As military assets are mobilized around the Southeast Asian waters and northward to battle theaters, the likelihood that Malaysia and similarly situated states will be entrapped into the conflict increases, which makes any "neutral," "equidistant," or hedging position increasingly untenable.

Bilateral or Unilateral Factors: If and When China's Maritime Actions Directly Threaten Malaysia

A central component of Malaysia's hedging policy is its prudent "low-profile" approach of downplaying and de-emphasizing the security risks surrounding China over the South China Sea (Lai, Kuik, and Amy Azuan Abdullah, 2021). Such an approach has persisted even after China became more assertive regarding multination maritime territorial disputes since the 2010s (Hamzah, Leong and Forbes, 2020; Ngeow and Nur Shahadah Jamil, 2022b). Malaysia's low-key approach toward China is demonstrated through various incidents. One of the most recent ones took place in April 2020 when the Chinese survey vessel *Haiyang Dizhi* 8, accompanied by several coast guard and maritime militia vessels, was spotted following West Capella, an oil drilling ship under charter to Malaysian national oil company Petronas, near Malaysia's Exclusive Economic Zone (EEZ) (Ngeow, 2020). The Malaysian government's response was slow, mild, and non-confrontational, reflecting its long-standing preference to manage disputes via "behind the scene" diplomacy. After no official response for several days, the then Malaysian Foreign Minister Hishammuddin Hussein released a press statement calling for peaceful means to resolve the situation (Tang, 2020). Hishammuddin's remarks, which mentioned both China and the United States, while highlighting the risks of increased tensions and miscalculations, clearly indicated that the Malaysian authorities were more concerned about the dangers of big-power conflict than the presence of foreign vessels in the disputed waters (Lai and Kuik, 2021).

Malaysia's approach contrasts sharply with the Philippines' US-centric, alliance-based, confrontational policy toward China, especially under its current President Bongbong Marcos Jr. Malaysia's approach also differs from Vietnam's, which adopts an openly and directly defiant stance to push back Beijing, whenever it perceives China's maritime actions as undermining Vietnamese maritime and sovereign interests. As tensions have grown over the South China Sea since the 2010s, Malaysia (like Brunei, the other claimant country from the ASEAN region) has continued to adhere to its non-confrontational, diplomatic, alliance-allergic approach. This is so even though Malaysia has the option of turning its alliance-allergic stance to an alliance-centric approach, considering its decades-long defense partnership with the United States and the Five Powers Defence Arrangement (FPDA) (both partnerships predated the rise of China). Thus far, Malaysia has always maintained a deliberately low-key approach to its defense ties with the United States. This is because the Malaysian ruling elites are aware that making its defense alignment with the United States too high profile involves both external and internal risks. China may be provoked, while Malay Muslim majority voters, now increasingly critical of US support of Israel's actions in Gaza, would be displeased. But this may change if Malaysia faces a direct and immediate threat.

Indeed, Malaysia's current approach is justified by a moderate level of risk perception. Malaysian policy elites consider China's maritime actions as increasingly assertive, but not yet aggressive to the point of threatening Malaysia's sovereignty and maritime stakes in the South China Sea. While China's growing and near-permanent presence around Malaysia's maritime areas since 2013 has increased Malaysia's risk perception, it has not yet reached the level that leads Malaysia to view China as a clear-and-present threat that must be pushed back at all costs. This is primarily because thus far China's growing presence has not directly undermined Malaysia's core stakes in the South China Sea.

Malaysia's security establishments as well as the Sarawak and Sabah state governments — the frontline entities in the South China Sea — have, in recent years, become much more concerned about Beijing's maritime actions.[2] Nonetheless, this has not fundamentally altered the Malaysian government's policy judgment and stance at the federal level. Indeed, successive leaders from Najib Abdul Razak to Anwar Ibrahim have judged that any overaction or "preemptive move" (e.g., upgrading existing

---

[2]For an illuminating analysis of Sarawak and Sabah's perceptions of the South China Sea before 2021, see Ngeow and Nur Shahadah Jamil, 2022b.

alignments into anti-Beijing alliances) can be strategically counterproductive, turning a potential security concern into an immediate and more aggressive threat. Considering a range of now-and-here economic and political interests and the fact that risks are perceived as moderate, Malaysian leaders have judged that Malaysia's core interests in the South China Sea would be best served by continuing its decades-long policy of pragmatic, prudent hedging. Malaysia prioritizes using diplomatic channels as its principal platform for managing (albeit not necessarily solving) the overlapping claims and the deepening economic and regional interdependence to ensure stable and productive Malaysia–China relations, while simultaneously playing down but preserving military options as risk contingency measures in the background. While a diplomatic approach by itself will not resolve the South China Sea problem, it manages risk and gives peace a chance. This pragmatic and multipronged approach is deemed more acceptable and desirable under current conditions, as it allows Malaysia to preserve its sovereignty, exercise its agency to continue its energy exploration activities in the South China Sea, and concentrate on more pressing domestic challenges, while still mitigating and hedging against such multiple external risks as the dangers of military coercion and confrontation and the risks of abandonment and big-power entrapment.

This policy, however, might become unjustifiable and unsustainable if and when China's actions become more assertive and aggressive. This is a scenario that some Malaysian defense planners do not and would not dismiss, especially after 31 May 2021. On that day, 16 People's Liberation Army Air Force (PLAAF) aircraft flew towards Malaysian airspace 40–60 nautical miles off Malaysia's Sarawakian coast. The Chinese aircraft flew in tactical formation at up to 27,000 feet and ignored the instructions of regional air traffic control (Zack, 2021). The overflight prompted the Royal Malaysian Air Force (RMAF) to scramble *Hawk* light combat jets from its nearby Labuan Air Base to intercept the aircraft, which were identified as Ilyushin 11-76 and Xian Y-20 transport aircraft capable of performing various missions (*Reuters*, 2021). The RMAF issued a press release publicizing the incident the following day, a departure from Malaysia's typically quiet approach. The incident was widely reported in the local media. A mild surge of nationalist sentiment was witnessed among Malaysians, especially on social media.

Some in the Malaysian security establishment figured that the PLAAF overflight was aimed at testing Malaysia's air defense, testing its own plane operation performance, and demonstrating an ability to reach Beting Patinggi Ali (commonly called BPA in Malaysian defense circles or South Luconia Shoals in English, these reef complexes are about 84 miles off Sarawak's Miri, but claimed by China).[3] Some reckoned the overflight was also aimed at deterring Malaysia from undertaking operations in Kasawari, a giant offshore gas development project located 35 km from BPA. The project involves an area that contains approximately three trillion cubic feet of recoverable gas resources. Petronas Carigali, the project developer and a subsidiary of Malaysian petroleum company Petronas, was reportedly gearing up to install an offshore drilling platform at the Kasawari gas field in early June 2021. After the overflight, both Malaysia and China made efforts to prevent the incident from affecting the bilateral relations. However, for Malaysian defense planners, the PLAAF overflight signaled that China's years-long "show-of-presence" approach in the Malaysian maritime zone is now evolving into a "show of force." On 1 June 2021, a spokesperson for the Chinese Embassy in Malaysia said that the Chinese aircraft were on "routine flight training" conducted in international airspace, "did not target any country," and adhered to international laws, before emphasizing that "China is willing to continue bilateral friendly consultations with Malaysia to jointly maintain regional peace and stability" (Teh Athira Yusof, 2021).

Regardless of China's motives, the PLAAF incident has increased Malaysia's risk perception of China (Fikry Rahman and Abdul Razak Ahmad, 2022). Whether, when, and how the next "show of force" will or will not occur are all matters of conjecture and concern in the Malaysian security establishments. If and when the "show of force" escalates into "use of force" that directly and profoundly harms Malaysian maritime interests and sovereign rights (e.g., stopping Malaysia's energy exploration in the Kasawari oil field; occupying Malaysia's claimed features; causing loss of life), then dormant anti-China sentiments among Malaysians will ignite, rendering Malaysia's hedging policy unjustifiable and untenable. If and when a potential danger becomes an immediate threat, some within the defense and security establishments might advocate turning Malaysia's alliance-avoidant stance into an alignment-centric policy.

---

[3] Personal communication with Malaysian defense experts familiar with the incident, 19 July 2024, Kuala Lumpur.

Malaysia's Domestic Politics

In the absence of a direct external threat and/or big-power armed conflicts, lesser states are unlikely to abandon hedging. However, domestic political problems, especially those severe enough to undermine elite legitimation and regime security, might compel states to adjust their alignment postures. In Malaysia, such problems involve racial or religious sentiments at home, and/or Muslim solidarity emotions over external issues with spillover effects into the domestic political landscape.

Given Malaysia's multiracial and multicultural demographic structure, it is logical that inter-ethnic relations, especially those between the ethnic Malay majority and ethnic Chinese minority, will always be a crucial variable shaping the dynamics and complexities of Malaysia–China relations. The effects of this variable can be positive and profoundly productive, particularly on trade and investment partnerships, people-to-people ties, and civilizational exchanges, as well as sociopolitical values and regional connectivity cooperation. However, the effects can be negative as well, especially at moments when inter-racial relations are tense *and* when China pursues problematic policies (e.g., its practices during the Cold War: supporting the outlawed Malayan Communist Party which sought to overthrow the legitimate government in Malaysia, as well as treating Chinese Malaysians as its citizens) or when it makes inappropriate, insensitive moves and/or remarks. A controversial episode in 2015 involving the then Chinese Ambassador Huang Huikang during a visit to Petaling Street (the "Chinatown" of Kuala Lumpur) illustrates this point when Huang made a statement that was perceived by many in Malaysia as interfering with Malaysia's internal affairs (see Suryadinata, 2017: 111–120; Ngeow and Tan, 2018: 108–111).

For now, and the foreseeable future, the one identity-based issue most likely to impact Malaysia–China relations would be the Xinjiang issue. To be sure, Malaysia has long regarded Xinjiang as China's internal affairs. When meeting his Chinese counterpart Li Qiang during his official visit to China in 2023, Prime Minister Anwar Ibrahim made a statement: "Malaysia firmly adheres to the One-China policy and believes that Xinjiang-related issues are China's internal affairs" (Kader, 2023). However, over the past few years, as periodic but growing news about China's alleged mass detention policy toward Uighurs is reported, the saliency of the Xinjiang issue as a sensitive issue in Malaysia–China relations has increased. As a Muslim-majority country, Malaysia has always been concerned about the Muslim Ummah and the injustice faced by Muslim communities in other parts of the world. The religious sentiments of Malaysian Muslims, when heightened, might affect Malaysia's China policy.

Successive Malaysian governments have not opted for an openly critical and confrontational posture toward China on the Xinjiang issue. In October 2018, Malaysia did not accede to Beijing's request to repatriate 18 Uighurs (whom Beijing suspected of ties to extremism) back to China, but the then Prime Minister Mahathir Mohammad did so in a low-profile manner and refrained from openly criticizing Beijing (*Al Jazeera*, 2018; Chew, 2020). When Washington and its allies brought a draft decision targeting China to the UN Human Rights Council in September 2022, Malaysia was among the 11 nations that abstained from the UN vote to debate China's treatment of the Uighurs (*AFP*, 2022). Quietly, Malaysia has engaged with Beijing regarding its policy in Xinjiang. The Xinjiang issue is a complex matter. There are genuine violent, extremist, and separatist-inspired threats to China but also government measures that are deemed too heavy-handed.

The impact of the Xinjiang issue on Malaysia's China policy for now remains limited. However, if this issue is badly mishandled, resulting in emotional sympathy and solidarity among Malaysian Muslims for the Uighurs, the Malaysian ruling elites in Putrajaya, driven by both identity-based and electoral-based legitimation needs, will be pressured by Muslim voters to take a harder position vis-à-vis China on the Xinjiang issue. This might not be strong enough to push the Malaysian government to end its hedging policy, but it will make Putrajaya's defiance of Beijing much stronger and more open.

Concluding Analysis

To conclude, Malaysia's current hedging policy is primarily a product of structural and domestic imperatives. Structurally, the growing dangers of big-power entrapment and regional polarization will continue to push Malaysia, and other smaller states, to avoid siding with either the United States or China and insist on active neutrality, inclusive diversification, and prudent offsets to keep a fallback position. Domestically, crucial political reasons drive the ruling elites to adopt a pragmatic approach to foster the strongest and the most productive cooperation possible with both powers. Such an approach is closely linked to the ruling elites' desire to mitigate multiple risks and balance major trade-offs to preserve authority and remain in power.

For current Prime Minister Anwar, proactive, inclusive, and prudent hedging is required not only to mitigate the multiple systemic risks surrounding the US–China rivalry but also to maximize the concrete benefits to boost his Unity Government's political survival at home, with an eye to winning Malaysia's next general election. To win the hearts and minds of different segments of an increasingly polarized multiethnic, multireligious Malaysia, Anwar's ruling coalition has relied on two major cards: development-based performance and identity-based mobilization. On the one hand, the performance card constantly requires the Anwar government to pragmatically adapt to and leverage fast-changing geopolitical and geoeconomics realities (e.g., viewing the "China Plus One" trend as a window of opportunity to push Malaysia's semiconductors up the value chain, while concurrently embracing China's BRI and US's Indo-Pacific Economic Framework), while simultaneously hedging the multi-level, multi-domain risks by pursuing inclusive diversification with old and new partners, including Japan, South Korea, and the European powers. On the other hand, the mobilization card induces Anwar to take a high-profile, personal, and passionate position on the Palestinian cause, as the deepening suffering and deteriorating humanitarian crisis in Gaza fuel strong anger among Malaysians, especially the Muslim community. While the former pathway compels a pragmatic, cool-headed policy, the latter calls for an emotionally charged confrontational posture on selective issues, especially those central to identity-based sentiments. Hence, the politics of survival in a multicultural, middle-income, medium-sized nation involves a painful struggle to balance often-conflicting policy goals and means, amid uncertainties.

As an instance of small-state hedging, Malaysia's China policy is dynamic, not static. Like other dynamic policies, hedging emerges and evolves according to circumstances, and hedging will end when the conditions that gave rise to it disappear. While empirical observations and scholarly works suggest that Malaysia has hedged continuously throughout the post-Cold War decades, this continuity does not mean that Malaysia's China policy is set in stone. Rather, when circumstances and conditions alter, Malaysia's China policy and its wider hedging behavior will be adjusted and adapted as well. Our preceding analysis identified three factors and possible scenarios that will most likely alter Malaysia's China policy and its hedging tendency: structural, unilateral/bilateral, and domestic. Future studies should concentrate on comparative cases, perhaps beyond Malaysia and Southeast Asia, that illuminate not only the logic of hedging but also its limits and underlying constraints, compared to other alignment choices.

References

Abuza, Zachary (2020). "Malaysia: Navigating between the United States and China." *Asia Policy*, Vol. 15, No. 2, pp. 115–134.

AFP (2022). "Malaysia among 11 Nations That Abstained from UN Vote on Debate about China's Treatment of Uyghur Muslims." *The Malay Mail*, 7 October. https://www.malaymail.com/news/world/2022/10/07/malaysia-among-11-nations-that-abstained-from-un-vote-on-debate-about-chinas-treatment-of-uyghur-muslims/32202.

Al Jazeera (2018). "Malaysia Ignores China's Request; Frees 11 Ethnic Uighurs." 12 October. https://www.aljazeera.com/news/2018/10/12/malaysia-ignores-chinas-request-frees-11-ethnic-uighurs.

Chew, Amy (2020). "Malaysia Stands Firm on Not Deporting Uygurs, Risking Beijing's Anger." *South China Morning Post*, 15 November. https://www.scmp.com/week-asia/politics/article/3109885/malaysia-stands-firm-uygur-deportations-risking-chinas-wrath-and?campaign=3109885&module=perpetual_scroll_0&pgtype=article.

Chin, Kok Fay (2021). "Malaysia's Perception and Strategy toward China's BRI Expansion: Continuity or Change?" *The Chinese Economy*, Vol. 54, No. 1, pp. 9–19.

Chin, Kok Fay (2023). "Malaysia in Changing Geopolitical Economy: Navigating Great Power Competition between China and the United States." *The Chinese Economy*, Vol. 56, No. 4, pp. 321–329.

Chong, Ja Ian (2016). "America's Asia-Pacific Rebalance and the Hazards of Hedging: A Review of Evidence from Southeast Asia." In David W. F. Huang (ed.), *Asia Pacific Countries and the US Rebalancing Strategy*, pp. 155–173. New York, NY: Palgrave Macmillan.

Chong, Ja Ian (2020). "How Hedging Made US-China Tensions Worse: Order, Strategic Competition, and Aggregated Security Dilemmas in Asia and the Pacific." Video, Lieberthal-Rogel Center for Chinese Studies (LRCCS), 28 January. https://www.youtube.com/watch?v=KLmh7lKN8Cc.

Ciorciari, John D (2019). "The Variable Effectiveness of Hedging Strategies." *International Relations of the Asia-Pacific*, Vol. 19, No. 3, pp. 523–555.

Ciorciari, John D. and Jürgen Haacke (2019). "Hedging in International Relations: An Introduction." *International Relations of the Asia-Pacific*, Vol. 19, No. 3, pp. 367–374.

Fikry Rahman and Abdul Razak Ahmad (2022). "Bolster Overall Strategy, Territorial Integrity in South China Sea." *New Straits Times*, 27 July. https://www.nst.com.my/opinion/columnists/2022/07/817020/bolster-overall-strategy-territorial-integrity-south-china-sea.

Gerstl, Alfred (2020). "Malaysia's Hedging Strategy Towards China Under Mahathir Mohamad (2018–2020): Direct Engagement, Limited Balancing, and Limited Bandwagoning." *Journal of Current Chinese Affairs*, Vol. 49, No. 1, pp. 106–131.

Haacke, Jürgen (2019). "The Concept of Hedging and Its Application to Southeast Asia: A Critique and a Proposal for a Modified Conceptual and Methodological Framework." *International Relations of the Asia-Pacific*, Vol. 19, No. 3, pp. 375–417.

Hamzah, B. A., Adam Leong, and Vivian Louis Forbes (eds.) (2020). *Malaysia and South China Sea: Policy, Strategy and Risks*. Kuala Lumpur: Centre for Defence and International Security Studies (CDiSS), National Defence University of Malaysia.

Han, David (2018). "China-Malaysia Relations and the Malaysian Election." *The Diplomat*, 8 May. https://thediplomat.com/2018/05/china-malaysia-relations-and-the-malaysian-election/.

Jones, David Martin, and Nicole Jenne (2022). "Hedging and Grand Strategy in Southeast Asian Foreign Policy." *International Relations of the Asia-Pacific*, Vol. 22, No. 2, pp. 205–235.

Kader, Anne (2023). "Malaysian PM Anwar Accused of Betraying Uyghurs: States Xinjiang-Related Issues Are China's Internal Affairs." *Uyghur Times*, 1 April. https://uyghurtimes.com/malaysian-mp-anwar-accused-of-betraying-uyghurs-states-xinjiang-related-issues-are-chinas-internal-affairs/.

Kuik, Cheng-Chwee (2008). "The Essence of Hedging: Malaysia and Singapore's Response to a Rising China." *Contemporary Southeast Asia*, Vol. 30, No. 2, pp. 159–185.

Kuik, Cheng-Chwee (2016). "Malaysia Between the United States and China: What Do Weaker States Hedge Against?" *Asian Politics and Policy*, Vol. 8, No. 1, pp. 155–177.

Kuik, Cheng-Chwee (2021a). "Getting Hedging Right: A Small-State Perspective." *China International Strategy Review*, Vol. 3, No. 2, pp. 300–315.

Kuik, Cheng-Chwee (2023a). "Shades of Grey: Riskification and Hedging in the Indo-Pacific." *The Pacific Review*, Vol. 36, No. 6, pp. 1181–1214.

Kuik, Cheng-Chwee (2023b). "Malaysian Conceptions of International Order: Paradoxes of Small-State Pragmatism." *International Affairs*, Vol. 99, No. 4, pp. 1477–1497.

Kuik, Cheng-Chwee (2023c). "Southeast Asia Hedges between Feasibility and Desirability." *East Asia Forum*, 4 July. https://www.eastasiaforum.org/2023/07/04/southeast-asia-hedges-between-feasibility-and-desirability/.

Kuik, Cheng-Chwee (2024a). "Explaining Hedging: The Case of Malaysian Equidistance." *Contemporary Southeast Asia*, Vol. 46, No. 1, pp. 43–76.

Kuik, Cheng-Chwee (2024b). "Southeast Asian Responses to U.S.-China Tech Competition: Hedging and Economy-Security Tradeoffs." *Journal of Chinese Political Science*, Online First Article, pp. 1–30.

Kuik, Cheng-Chwee, and Lai Yew Meng (2023). "Deference and Defiance in Malaysia's China Policy: Determinants of a Dualistic Diplomacy." *International Journal of Asian Studies*, Online First Article, pp. 1–20.

Lai, Yew Meng, and Kuik Cheng-Chwee (2021). "Structural Sources of Malaysia's South China Sea Policy: Power Uncertainties and Small-State Hedging." *Australian Journal of International Affairs*, Vol. 75, No. 3, pp. 277–304.

Lai, Yew Meng, Kuik Cheng-Chwee, and Amy Azuan Abdullah (2021). "Pulau Layang-Layang in Malaysia's South China Sea Policy." *International Journal of China Studies*, Vol. 12, No. 2, pp. 189–222.

Lampton, David M., Selina Ho, and Cheng-Chwee Kuik (2020). *Rivers of Iron: Railroads and Chinese Power in Southeast Asia*. Oakland, CA: University of California Press.

Lee, John (2006). "Malaysia's Two-Step Hedging Strategy: Bilateral and Regional Activism." *Strategic Insights*. No. 24, 20 April. https://www.aspi. org.au/report/strategic-insights-24-malaysias-two-step-hedging-strategy-bilateral-and-regional-activism.

Liow, Joseph Chinyong (2005). "Balancing, Bandwagoning, or Hedging?: Strategic and Security Patterns in Malaysia's Relations with China, 1981-2003." In Ho Khai Leong and Samuel C. Y. Ku (eds.), *China and Southeast Asia: Global Changes and Regional Challenges*, pp. 281–306. Singapore: Institute of Southeast Asian Studies.

Liow, Joseph Chinyong (2009). "Malaysia's Post-Cold War China Policy: A Reassessment." In Jun Tsunekawa (ed.), *The Rise of China: Responses from Southeast Asia and Japan*, pp. 47–79. Tokyo: The National Institute for Defense Studies.

Liu, Hong (2021). "Beyond Strategic Hedging: Mahathir's China Policy and the Changing Political Economy of Malaysia, 2018–2020." In Felix Heiduk (ed.), *Asian Geopolitics and the US–China Rivalry*, pp. 159–176. London: Routledge.

Marston, Hunter S. (2024). "Navigating Great Power Competition: A Neoclassical Realist View of Hedging." *International Relations of the Asia-Pacific*, Vol. 24, No. 1, pp. 29–63.

Ministry of Defence (2020). *Defence White Paper: A Secure, Sovereign, and Prosperous Malaysia*. Kuala Lumpur, Malaysia: Ministry of Defence.

Mishra, Rahul, and Peter Brian M. Wang (2021). "How Long Can Malaysia Keep Hedging Its Bets?" *The Strategist*, 22 December. https://www.aspistrategist. org.au/how-long-can-malaysia-keep-hedging-its-bets/.

Ngeow, Chow-Bing (2020). "South China Sea Tensions: Malaysia's Strategic Dilemma." *South China Sea Strategic Situation Probing Initiative*, 3 June. http://www.scspi.org/en/dtfx/1591153812.

Ngeow, Chow-Bing (2023). "How Malaysia Views U.S. and Chinese Narratives About the World Order." *Carnegie Endowment for International Peace*, 21 August. https://carnegieendowment.org/research/2023/08/how-malaysia-views-us-and-chinese-narratives-about-the-world-order?lang=en.

Ngeow, Chow-Bing (2024). "How Southeast Asia Might React in a Potential Military Conflict Over Taiwan." *Carnegie Endowment for International Peace*, 17 June. https://carnegieendowment.org/research/2024/06/how-southeast-asia-might-react-in-a-potential-military-conflict-over-taiwan?lang=en&center=china.

Ngeow, Chow-Bing, and Nur Shahadah Jamil (2022a). "Malaysia's Relations with China under Mahathir 2.0: Reaffirming Bilateral Ties, Renegotiating Economic Collaboration, Reasserting Security Interests." *Issues & Studies*, Vol. 58, No. 2, 2251001.

Ngeow, Chow-Bing, and Nur Shahadah Jamil (2022b). "Malaysia's layered Nationalism and the South China Sea Dispute." In Nien Peng and Chow-Bing Ngeow (eds.), *Populism, Nationalism and South China Sea Dispute: Chinese and Southeast Asian Perspectives*, pp. 59–77. Singapore: Springer.

Ngeow, Chow-Bing, and Tan Chee-Beng (2018). "Cultural Ties and State Interests: Malaysian Chinese and China's Rise." In Bernard P. Wong and Tan Chee-Beng (eds.), *China's Rise and the Chinese Overseas*, pp. 96–116. New York, NY: Routledge.

Reuters (2021). "Malaysia Scrambles Fighter Jets after 16 Chinese Military Aircraft Fly toward Borneo." 1 June. https://edition.cnn.com/2021/06/01/asia/malaysia-china-air-force-flight-intercept-intl-hnk/index.html.

Saravanamuttu, Johan (2020). "Mahathir 2.0 and China: Hedging in a Fluid World." *RSIS Commentary*, 20 January. https://www.rsis.edu.sg/rsis-publication/rsis/mahathir-2-0-and-china-hedging-in-a-fluid-world/.

Storey, Ian (1999). "Living with the Colossus: How Southeast Asian Countries Cope with China." *Parameters*, Vol. 29, No. 4, pp. 111–125.

Storey, Ian (2007). "Malaysia's Hedging Strategy with China." *China Brief*, Vol. 7, No. 14. https://jamestown.org/program/malaysias-hedging-strategy-with-china-2/.

Suryadinata, Leo (2017). *The Rise of China and the Chinese Overseas: A Study of China Beijing's Changing Policy in Southeast Asia and Beyond*. Singapore: ISEAS.

Suzuki, Ayame, and Poh Ping Lee (2017). "Malaysia's Hedging Strategy, a Rising China, and the Changing Strategic Situation in East Asia." In Lowell

Dittmer and Ngeow Chow Bing (eds.), *Southeast Asia and China: A Contest in Mutual Socialization*, pp. 113–129. Singapore: World Scientific.

Tang, Ashley (2020). "Malaysia Calls for Calm and Stability in South China Sea after 'Tagging' Incident Involving Chinese, M'sian Vessels." *The Star*, 23 April. https://www.thestar.com.my/news/nation/2020/04/23/malaysia-calls-for-calm-and-stability-in-south-china-sea-after-039tagging039-incident-involving-chinese-m039sian-vessels.

Teh Athira Yusof (2021). "Chinese Embassy: Aircraft Were on 'Routine Flight Training', Adhered to International Laws." *New Straits Times*, 1 June. https://www.nst.com.my/news/nation/2021/06/695092/chinese-embassy-aircraft-were-routine-flight-training-adhered.

Wisma Putra (2021). *Focus in Continuity: A Framework for Malaysia's Foreign Policy in a Post-Pandemic World*. Putrajaya: Ministry of Foreign Affairs.

Zhao, Xinlei (2024). "Economic Hedging by Small-State Firms in Great Power Strategic Competition: The Case of Malaysian Rail Link (MRL) (2013-2020)." *Journal of Social and Political Sciences*, Vol. 7, No. 2, pp. 63–81.

Zack, Justin (2021). "RMAF: 16 China Military Aircraft Detected near Malaysian Airspace." *The Star*, 1 June. https://www.thestar.com.my/news/nation/2021/06/01/rmaf-16-foreign-military-aircraft-detected-near-malaysian-airspace.

© 2025 World Scientific Publishing Company
https://doi.org/10.1142/9789819801350_0004

Chapter 4

A Chinese Perspective on Managing the South China Sea Issue: The Roles of ASEAN and the United States, and the Lessons of China–Malaysia Interactions in the South China Sea

Zhang Mingliang

From China's point of view, China's claims in the South China Sea are legitimate, legal, and reasonable, and these claims are well documented in both Chinese and foreign sources. But China's claims are not universally accepted by the littoral countries in the South China Sea, which are all member states of the Association of Southeast Asian Nations (ASEAN). Hence, pending the final agreement or a solution to the dispute, the South China Sea issue can only be managed. The crucial body for managing this issue is ASEAN. The South China Sea issue has been mentioned and discussed in many meetings of ASEAN and also mentioned in the documents issued by ASEAN. However, the Chinese government has been arguing that the South China Sea issue is not an issue between China and ASEAN, but only between China and some ASEAN states, although China recognizes that ASEAN remains a viable platform for discussions on this issue. In managing the South China Sea issue, China has also argued that this is a matter to be resolved by countries directly concerned only, and the interference or involvement of external powers is not welcome and will only create more problems. The role of the United States is particularly concerning and, from China's point of view, unhelpful and problematic, to say the least. Nevertheless, despite China's insistent objection, the United States' involvement in the South China Sea issue has only increased.

Among all the littoral countries of Southeast Asia that have disputes with China in the South China Sea, Malaysia is a unique case, where the disputes are well managed and have not resulted in a major decline in the good relationship between China and Malaysia. Malaysian specialists on the South China Sea issue can help in narrowing the gap between China and ASEAN states in understanding the roles of ASEAN and even of the United States.

The Role of ASEAN in the South China Sea Issue: China's Ambiguity

Formally speaking, in the past decade or so, China has been refusing to acknowledge the formal role of ASEAN in the South China Sea issue. Since 2010, China has insisted that the South China Sea issue is not one between China and ASEAN, but only an issue between China and some ASEAN states, and China is willing to work with ASEAN states to safeguard the peace of the South China Sea. This has been the formal position of China about the role of ASEAN in the South China Sea issue. The active role of ASEAN with regard to the South China Sea issue has also been encouraged and supported by the United States (Gittings, 1999; Shirk, 2023: 16–17), but China has been questioning this stance for a long time.

China's position however was only clarified after 2010. Before that, China was more willing to accept a legitimate role of ASEAN in managing the South China Sea issue. However, since 2010, especially with the United States' very public announcement of its involvement in the issue in Hanoi in July, China has reformulated its position and has been insisting that the South China Sea issue is not an issue between ASEAN and China. In China's view, this issue needs a lot of dialogue and consultation between China and the concerned ASEAN states, but not ASEAN *per se*.

ASEAN as a group, of course, has long been in talks with China and other parties about the South China Sea (Severino, 2013). The ASEAN states that are embroiled in the South China Sea dispute are Vietnam, the Philippines, Malaysia, and Brunei. Indonesia and China do not have overlapping claims over maritime features or islands but have disputes over maritime areas in the South China Sea, despite the fact that Indonesia refuses to acknowledge that it has any dispute with China. One of the key approaches of the ASEAN states in dealing with the South China Sea issue is to unite under the umbrella of ASEAN in coping with China's claims. In 1992, the ASEAN states were successful in uniting for the South China Sea issue, without China's objections. The same approach was followed after the Mischief Reef incident in 1995. In March 1995, the Philippines objected to China's occupation of Mischief Reef (Branigin, 1995). As a reaction, ASEAN foreign ministers issued a statement expressing their "serious concern over recent developments which affect peace and stability in the South China Sea." Although ASEAN was not able to reach a consensus in 2012 on the South China Sea issue, over the decades, it has mostly been able to uphold basic unity concerning the issue.

Before 2010, it was not clear whether China was agreeable to the participation of "ASEAN' or "ASEAN states" in managing the South China Sea issue together with China. For some time, China did not definitely object to ASEAN having a role in managing the South China Sea issue. China's early reactions concerning ASEAN's declarations on the South China Sea in the 1990s, as produced in official and authoritative newspapers such as the *People's Daily*, indicated that China did not question ASEAN playing a role in this issue (*Renmin Ribao*, 1992). Jiang Zemin, former president and general secretary of the Communist Party of China, said in a speech delivered in the United States in October 2002 that China and ASEAN (not *ASEAN states*) were committed to the negotiation of a Code of Conduct (COC) in the South China Sea (*Renmin Ribao*, 2002). A few days later, in early November 2002, the Declaration of Conduct of Parties in the South China Sea (DOC) was signed by China and all ten ASEAN member states in Cambodia.

Then, in July 2010, China continued to be consistent in its formulation concerning ASEAN and the South China Sea issue. On 23 July 2010, Chinese Foreign Minister Yang Jieci said in a speech that the South China Sea issue was not one between ASEAN and China but one between some ASEAN states and China. On 19 November 2011, the then Chinese Premier Wen Jiabao elaborated China's position at the Sixth East Asia Summit in Bali, Indonesia. According to Wen, the DOC in 2002 was signed by China and the ASEAN states, not ASEAN *per se*. Moreover, Wen also said that promoting pragmatic cooperation and working toward a Code of Conduct are common goals of both China and the *ASEAN states*, not ASEAN *per se* (Embassy of the People's Republic of China in the Republic of the Philippines, 2011). This was a different stance compared to Jiang's speech back in 2002 when he said that China and *ASEAN* were negotiating the COC.

In 2014, China advanced its now standard formula known as the "dual-track approach." The dual-track approach means "that any relevant dispute will be addressed by the countries directly concerned through friendly consultations and negotiations and in a peaceful way. And for issues like the South China Sea, peace and stability should be jointly maintained by China and the ASEAN countries" (*China Daily*, 2014). Whether for "consultations and negotiations" regarding the dispute or the "maintenance of the peace and stability of the South China Sea," the dual-track approach suggests that only the "countries directly concerned" and "ASEAN countries" have a role to play in this process. This has been China's consistent position ever since.

China's position, nonetheless, is contentious in Southeast Asia. ASEAN has worked well as a group on the South China Sea issue for a long time. China's preference to accept only ASEAN states but not ASEAN in the South China Sea issue contradicts the reality of ASEAN's long-term active role in the South China Sea issue. Since its first statement on the South China Sea issue in 1992, ASEAN has discussed the South China Sea many times and produced several documents on the South China Sea issue in the last three decades. Nearly half of the ASEAN states have claims to the disputed features and/or maritime areas in the South China Sea; most of these involved states are important and/or founding members of ASEAN. The South China Sea issue is an important element of their policies toward China. Almost all of them have been looking forward to ASEAN having a major role in the South China Sea issue. Hence, it is impossible for ASEAN not to be involved in the South China Sea issue in its dialogue with China.

Rejecting the Involvement of the United States in the South China Sea Issue

Due to the importance of the South China Sea for the United States and its allies, the United States has been keeping a close watch on the developments in the South China Sea for decades. The position of the United States however has fluctuated over the decades since the end of the

Second World War. Depending on how the South China Sea affected its national interests, the United States modified its position from time to time. In the early Cold War years, especially in the 1950s and during the process of drafting the San Francisco Peace Treaty, the United States was actually not very supportive of the claims of the Philippines in the South China Sea and was more supportive of the Chiang Kai-shek authorities (the Republic of China), and its main goal was to prevent the islands in the South China Sea from falling under the authority of the People's Republic of China. In the 1970s and 1980s, the United States was beginning to have a good relationship with China and was not interested in being involved when China and Vietnam fought two naval battles in 1974 and 1988 in the South China Sea (Zhang, 2011a). After the end of the Cold War, the United States continued to generally maintain a neutral position regarding the different claims from different countries. In July 1995, the then United States Secretary of State Warren Christopher emphasized that the United States had consistently urged the claimants to the resources in the South China Sea to resolve their differences through dialogue and not through any military confrontation (Christopher, 1995). In July 1999, the then Secretary of State Madeline Albright said in an ASEAN meeting in Singapore that "the US is concerned about rising tensions in the South China Sea" since "several nations have sought recently to bolster their claims in the area by building or upgrading outposts." The primary concern of the United States was certainly China in the wake of its occupation of Mischief Reef (Gittings, 1999). Still, overall, the United States maintained a relatively disinterested distance from the issue in most of the decades before the 2010s.

The United States made a landmark change that had long-term consequences in 2010. On 23 July 2010, Hillary Clinton, the then US secretary of state, made a landmark speech in Hanoi that marked a significant change in the United States' policy toward the South China Sea, signaling the more active involvement of the United States in this issue (Chang, 2010). The South China Sea was now defined as a core national interest of the United States. Clinton asserted that "the US supports a collaborative diplomatic process by all claimants for resolving the various territorial disputes without coercion," and "opposes the use or threat of force by any claimant" (Landler, 2010). China sensed the changed posture of the United States beyond this rhetoric, which it felt was targeted against China's interests. Yang Jiechi characterized Clinton's comments as "an attack on China" (Chang, 2010). In November 2010, China's Assistant

Foreign Minister Hu Zhengyue said in an interview that "forces from outside the region" should not be involved in the disputes (Embassy of the People's Republic of China the Lao People's Democratic Republic, 2010). Since then, "forces from outside the region" and "countries outside the region" have become popular references to the United States in China's public statements regarding the South China Sea issue. China has been frequently voicing its objections to the active role and involvement of the United States in the South China Sea issue.

In China's eyes, the United States has also gradually taken a more hardened stance against China's claims. Before February 2014, the United States had not taken a position on the territorial disputes in the South China Sea, while emphasizing the importance of adhering to international law, including the United Nations Convention on the Law of the Sea (UNCLOS). US Assistant Secretary of State for East Asian and Pacific Affairs Danny Russel said the following in a testimony before the House Committee on Foreign Affairs on 5 February 2014: "Under international law, maritime claims in the South China Sea must be derived from land features. Any use of the 'nine-dash line' by China to claim maritime rights not based on claimed land features would be inconsistent with international law. The international community would welcome China to clarify or adjust its nine-dash line claim to bring it in accordance with the international law of the sea." It was the first time that United States government came out publicly with an explicit statement against China's "nine-dashed line" claims in the South China Sea (Bader, 2014). In July 2020, the then United States Secretary of State Mike Pompeo came out with a stronger statement, claiming that China's maritime claims "are completely unlawful, as is its campaign of bullying to control them" (Hansler, 2020).

The involvement of the United States in the South China Sea and the departure from its previous neutral stance regarding the dispute would only make managing and resolving the dispute more difficult, as the United States and China are in a rivalry or competition. China will see the United States as having an agenda in using and politicizing this issue to undermine China's relationship with the claimant states in ASEAN. This is why China has been saying that external interference will only create a more complex situation. With external interference, the South China Sea issue will become embroiled in the tensions between the United States and China will not stay as a manageable dispute between China and the claimant states.

Hence, China often argues that "certain countries outside the region would hype up certain particular issues and they should stop driving a wedge between China and ASEAN countries by making use of these issues" (State Council of the People's Republic of China, 2019). On different occasions, China's top officials (such as Foreign Minister Wang Yi) have often stated that "not making a distinction between countries in and outside the region" (when it comes to which countries should have a more important voice in the South China Sea matter) disregards the justified and legitimate rights and interests of coastal states of the South China Sea. In China's view, the use and abuse of the pretext of "freedom of navigation" by "countries outside the region" to interfere in the South China Sea issue should be resisted by countries in the region because "freedom of navigation" is never really an issue but is meant to create provocation and challenge the national security and interests of the coastal states of the South China Sea (Embassy of the People's Republic of China in the Socialist Republic of Vietnam, 2021). As expressed by Wang Yi, countries from outside the region should respect the efforts made by China and ASEAN, play a positive role in maintaining regional stability, and should stop sending military assets to flex their muscles in the South China Sea, stop provoking and exploiting the differences between regional countries for their own geopolitical interests and selfish gains, and stop making groundless comments without understanding the realities (Mission of the People's Republic of China to ASEAN, 2023). In a conversation in December 2023 between Wang Yi and Philippines Secretary of Foreign Affairs Enrique Manalo, Wang used the phrase "ill-intentioned external forces" in referring to the involvement of the United States in the South China Sea issue (*Xinhua*, 2023).

China–Malaysia Interactions in the South China Sea Issue

Admittedly, China's arguments about ASEAN and the United States with regard to the South China Sea issue are at odds with many in Southeast Asia and beyond would look at these issues. A majority of ASEAN claimant states will likely prefer the United States to continue to have a strong role and also for ASEAN as a whole to have an active role in the South China Sea issue.

Malaysia has been unique among the claimant states of ASEAN due to its cordial relations with China. Malaysia was the first among the original ASEAN states (before the enlargement of ASEAN) to form diplomatic relations with China. In 1974, Malaysia's Prime Minister Abdul Razak visited China and signed a Joint Communique that established formal diplomatic ties with China. This was a very important move as Malaysia played the leading role in ASEAN's relations with China. The good relationship formed the foundation for future heights, such as the elevation of Malaysia–China relations to a Comprehensive Strategic Partnership in 2013; in 2023, Malaysia and China also agreed to jointly build a community of shared future.

In addition, it was Malaysia, and not the other ASEAN states, that invited China to attend the ASEAN meetings in the early 1990s. Malaysia managed to convince ASEAN to extend an invitation to China to attend the annual ASEAN Ministerial Meeting, a move that eventually saw China become one of ASEAN's Dialogue Partners (Liow, 2000). In July 1991, the then Chinese Foreign Minister Qian Qichen attended the 24th ASEAN Foreign Ministers Meeting in Kuala Lumpur, Malaysia, which marked the beginning of the dialogue process. Malaysia also maintained a substantial economic relationship with China. Malaysia used to be the largest trade partner of China among the ASEAN states for many years before Vietnam took over that position in 2018 (*Jakarta Post*, 2018). Since 2009, China has been Malaysia's largest trading partner, generally accounting for close to 20 percent of the total trade of Malaysia. At the same time, due to stable and friendly ties between the two countries, more and more Chinese investors have confidence in investing in Malaysia. China's foreign direct investment in Malaysia reached a record high in 2021 (*The Star*, 2022).

The South China Sea issue undeniably remains an issue between China and Malaysia. Ever since Malaysia started to assert its claims in the South China Sea in the 1970s, China and Malaysia have been in dispute, but over the decades, the two countries have handled their dispute in a very moderate way (Zhang, 2011b: 266–280). Many foreign and also Malaysian observers argue that China has violated Malaysian rights in the disputed area in the South China Sea with the patrol of China's ships in recent years. Nevertheless, China's main purpose is only to protect its claims in the disputed area, which China feels should be seen as an acceptable practice. China has no intention to harm Malaysia's national interests and welcomes a peaceful solution to the dispute with dialogue, consultation, and finally negotiation. China appreciates that Malaysia also maintains a rational and moderate attitude toward the South China Sea issue and that both countries, despite the issue, can manage to continue to have good relations for mutual benefits. Malaysia is a good example to show that the existence of a dispute should not be an obstacle to good and friendly relations.

On the role of ASEAN, Malaysia has strongly insisted on the multi-lateral role and platform of ASEAN, so there is a gap between China and Malaysia on this point. Nevertheless, on the role of the United States, Malaysia actually feels that the involvement of extra-regional countries may not be very helpful. In 1999, during a visit to China, the then Malaysian Prime Minister Mahathir Mohammad said that the South China Sea issue should be handled and settled peacefully by countries directly involved without interference by external players (cited in Zhang, 2011b: 278). In a 2016 Joint Statement between China and Malaysia, in Article 26, both countries also stated that the involvement of parties not directly concerned in the South China Sea issue could be counterproductive (Ministry of Foreign Affairs of the People's Republic of China, 2016). Nonetheless, Malaysia has not always insisted very strongly on this point. This same point is not always mentioned in speeches or statements by Malaysian leaders, unlike China's leaders. Understandably, Malaysia has its own considerations and wants to maintain some space and flexibility.

Malaysia can be a bridge between ASEAN and China. Many Chinese specialists in the South China Sea issue often find that their Malaysian counterparts are moderate and can have frank discussions albeit with dis-agreements between the two sides. Malaysian specialists also understand sentiments in ASEAN well. They can play a leading role in broadening China's perception and understanding of how the region sees the South China Sea issue, which can help create common ground on the issue.

Conclusion

From China's point of view, China has maintained its claims in the South China Sea in accordance with historical facts and international law for many decades, but it does not intend to use force to settle the dispute. China wants to peacefully settle the dispute with all directly concerned countries through consultation and negotiation. Pending the final settle-ment, China has often proposed "shelving the dispute, engaging in joint development." This was a proposal from Deng Xiaoping, but

64 *Zhang Mingliang*

unfortunately no claimant countries in Southeast Asia have agreed to it. China hopes that the claimant countries can agree to this joint development proposal and feels that Malaysia is probably in the best position to do so, given their cordial relations. Nevertheless, this has not happened yet, which shows that Malaysia has not agreed with China. Still, China and Malaysia can maintain good relations even with the existence of the dispute and without joint development.

References

Bader, Jeffrey A. (2014). "The U.S. and China's Nine-Dash Line: Ending the Ambiguity." *Brookings Institution*, 6 February. https://www.brookings.edu/articles/the-u-s-and-chinas-nine-dash-line-ending-the-ambiguity/.

Branigin, William (1995). "China Takes Over Philippine-Claimed Area of Disputed Island Group." *The Washington Post*, 10 February. https://www.washingtonpost.com/archive/politics/1995/02/11/china-takes-over-philippine-claimed-area-of-disputed-island-group/6babb62d-2154-4856-be1f-9befd-a00bd63/.

Chang, Gordon (2010). "Hillary Clinton Changes America's China Policy." *Forbes*, 28 July. https://www.forbes.com/2010/07/28/china-beijing-asia-hillary-clinton-opinions-columnists-gordon-g-chang.html.

China Daily (2014). "Foreign Minister Encourages a 'Dual Track' Approach to Sea Issue." 11 August. https://www.chinadaily.com.cn/china/2014-08/11/content_18282602.htm.

Christopher, Warren (1995). "U.S. National Interest in the Asia-Pacific Region." Address before the National Press Club, Washington, DC, U.S. Department of State. 29 July. https://1997-2001.state.gov/regions/eap/950728.html.

Embassy of the People's Republic of China in the Lao People's Democratic Republic. (2010). "Assistant Foreign Minister Hu Zhengyue's Remarks on China's Asia Policy." 11 November. http://la.china-embassy.gov.cn/eng/news/201011/t20101111_1546733.htm.

Embassy of the People's Republic of China in the Republic of the Philippines (2011). "Premier Wen Jiabao Elaborates China's Position on South China Sea." 20 November. http://ph.china-embassy.gov.cn/eng/zt/ASEAN/201201/t20120112_1334715.htm.

Embassy of the People's Republic of China in the Socialist Republic of Vietnam (2021). "Wang Yi: Interference by Countries Outside the Region Has Constituted the Biggest Threat to Peace and Stability in the South China

Sea." 7 August. http://vn.china-embassy.gov.cn/eng/xwdt/202108/t20210807_8912626.htm.

Gittings, John (1999). "Albright Makes Waves in Chinese Waters, US Risks Beijing's Anger with Warnings on Spratly Isles Claims." *The Guardian*, 27 July 27. https://www.theguardian.com/world/1999/jul/27/china.johngittings.

Hansler, Jennifer (2020). "US Declares 'Most' of China's Maritime Claims in South China Sea Illegal." *CNN*, 13 July. https://edition.cnn.com/2020/07/13/politics/south-china-sea-pompeo-announcement/index.html.

Jakarta Post (2018). "Vietnam Overtakes Malaysia, Becomes China's Biggest Trading Partner in ASEAN." 27 July. https://www.thejakartapost.com/seasia/2018/07/27/vietnam-overtakes-malaysia-becomes-chinas-biggest-trading-partner-in-asean-.html.

Landler, Mark (2010). "Offering to Aid Talks, U.S. Challenges China on Disputed Islands." *The New York Times*, 23 July. https://www.nytimes.com/2010/07/24/world/asia/24diplo.html.

Liow, Joseph (2000). "Malaysia-China Relations in the 1990s: The Maturing of a Partnership." *Asian Survey*, Vol. 40, No. 4, pp. 672–691.

Ministry of Foreign Affairs of the People's Republic of China (2016). "Zhonghua renmin gongheguo yu Malaixiya lianhe xinwen shengming (Joint Press Statement between the People's Republic of China and Malaysia)." 3 November. https://www.mfa.gov.cn/web/gjhdq_676201/gj_676203/yz_676205/1206_676716/1207_676728/201611/t20161103_7985412.shtml.

Mission of the People's Republic of China to ASEAN (2023). "Wang Yi Makes Clear China's Principled Position on the South China Sea Issue." 19 July. http://asean.china-mission.gov.cn/eng/stxw/202307/t20230719_11115198.htm.

Renmin ribao (1992). "Zhongguo zhuzhang heping jiejue Nansha zhengduan, dui Dongmeng xuanyan yixie jiben yuanze biaoshi zanshang (China Advocates for the Peaceful Resolution of the South China Sea Dispute and Expresses Appreciation for Some Basic Principles in the ASEAN Declaration)." 23 July.

Renmin ribao (2002). "(Jiang Zemin zhuxi) Zai qiaozhi·bushi zongtong tushuguan de yanjiang ([Chairman Jiang Zemin Chairman] Speech at George H.W. Bush Presidential Library)." 30 October.

Severino, Rodolfo (2013). "How Much Can ASEAN do for a South China Sea Code of Conduct?" *East Asia Forum*, 30 October. https://eastasiaforum.org/2013/10/30/how-much-can-asean-do-for-a-south-china-sea-code-of-conduct/.

Shirk, Susan (2023). *Overreach: How China Derailed Its Peaceful Rise*. New York, NY: Oxford University Press.

State Council of the People's Republic of China (2019). "State Councilor Says Consultations on COC in South China Sea Can be Concluded in Time."

1 August. https://english.www.gov.cn/statecouncil/wangyi/201908/01/content_WS5d427e00c6d0c6695ff7e10a.html.

The Star (2022). "King Grants Audience to Chinese Foreign Minister Wang Yi." 12 July. https://www.thestar.com.my/news/nation/2022/07/12/king-grants-audience-to-chinese-foreign-minister-wang-yi.

Xinhua (2023). "Philippines Urged to Decide Rationally, Work with China to Manage Situation at Sea." 21 December 21. https://english.news.cn/202312 21/0258c18dc4f348f6a335d151cc25cfe2/c.html.

Zhang, Mingliang (2011a). *Chaoyue hangxian: Meiguo zai nanhai de zhuiqiu* (Beyond Navigation: The United States' Choices in the South China Sea). Hong Kong: Xianggang shehui kexue chubanshe.

Zhang, Mingliang (2011b). *Choayue jiangju: Zhongguo zai nanhai de xuanze* (Breaking the Deadlock: China's Choices in the South China Sea). Hong Kong: Xianggang shehui kexue chubanshe.

© 2025 World Scientific Publishing Company
https://doi.org/10.1142/9789819801350_0005

Chapter 5

Dissecting Malaysia's Low-Profile Posture in the South China Sea Dispute

Lam Choong Wah

Introduction

The dispute over the South China Sea is known for its longevity, persisting since the era of colonial expansion in Southeast Asia in the late 19th century until today. A retrospective view suggests that Britain, China, France, and Japan were the initial claimants to the hydrocarbon-rich Spratly archipelago, subsequently followed by Vietnam, the Philippines, Malaysia, and Brunei. Following the withdrawal of colonial powers such as Britain, France, and Japan, China emerged as the most potent, albeit distant, claimant (Carty, 2019a, 2019b). The South China Sea dispute also goes beyond the dimension of territorial and maritime dispute, with the United States, Japan, and Australia also consistently emphasizing the importance of freedom of navigation in the South China Sea for global trade and regional security. This has led to a rivalry among the great powers in the disputed area (Leong, 2017). Given the complexity of the claims and the involvement of these powers, Malaysia has developed a unique posture in response to the challenges posed by the dispute. Malaysia maintains a low-profile posture and seldom sensationalizes confrontations in the disputed area, whether involving Malaysia or other claimants.

Tracing Malaysia's Claims

On 21 December 1979, Malaysia officially claimed a maritime zone in the South China Sea and several features of the Spratly archipelago by gazetting the map showing the territorial waters and continental shelf boundaries of Malaysia. This action positioned Malaysia as one of the latest claimants to the features of the South China Sea, subsequently followed by Brunei. As anticipated, Malaysia's claim elicited protests from China, Vietnam, the Philippines, and the United Kingdom on behalf of Brunei. In response to these protests, Malaysia expressed its willingness to engage in bilateral negotiations over the overlapping sovereign claims in the South China Sea with Vietnam and the Philippines, but not China (Haller-Trost, 1998). While Malaysia acknowledges the disputes that exist between Kuala Lumpur, Hanoi, and Manila, it does not recognize Beijing's claims and asserts that there is no need to involve China in any bilateral negotiations (Liow, 2009).

Malaysia began deploying troops to the disputed features, such as Swallow Reef, from 1983 onward and constructed sovereign monuments to reinforce its claims. In 1988, the first armed conflict in the Spratly dispute erupted when the naval forces of China and Vietnam clashed over the control of several features of the Spratly Islands. Militarily, this incident prompted Malaysia to allocate 7 million ringgit to enhance military facilities at Swallow Reef, including the construction of a 10,000-gallon diesel storage tank for the Malaysian Air Force (Parlimen Malaysia, 1988: 2890–2891). Politically, however, Malaysia dismissed allegations that these efforts were a response to the clash between China and Vietnam. A minister responded that the actual situation in the South China Sea was not as tense as perceived and was manageable because the government believed that negotiations conducted by the relevant ministry would progress smoothly (Parlimen Malaysia, 1988: 2911). The remark was consistent with the soft approach and optimistic stance being maintained over the subsequent decades.

Why has Malaysia adhered to a soft approach in the dispute? While various explanations have been proposed, this chapter aims to present an alternative interpretation that stems from the nature of Malaysia's claim. While the true motivations that propelled Malaysia into the disputes remain unclear, it is understood that Malaysia would have forfeited significant maritime interests had Kuala Lumpur not intervened (Valencia, 1991: 87). This chapter attempts to provide an examination of why

Malaysia chose to participate in the disputes and how its soft approach has enabled Malaysia to deftly navigate anticipated objections.

This chapter is structured into five sections. The first section examines the prevailing interpretations of Malaysia's response pattern. The following three sections analyze respectively three pivotal events that reflected the nature of Malaysia's claims. The fifth section concludes with a summary of the discussion and proposes that the nature of Malaysia's claim has contributed to the adoption of the soft approach.

Conceptualizing the Low-Profile Approach

Malaysia's conduct in the South China Sea disputes, particularly its responses to maritime confrontations and its relations with China, has often raised puzzling questions, especially in comparison to the responses by other claimants in Southeast Asia, such as Vietnam and the Philippines. There are several leading hypotheses: light hedging, trust in China as a benign power, economic interests, acceptance of power hierarchy, and Malaysia's domestic policy process.

The theory of light hedging suggests that structural conditions, such as "geopolitical dynamics of power asymmetry," compel Malaysia to "hedge lightly" in the context of significant regional strategic uncertainties (Lai and Kuik, 2021; Kuik and Lai, 2023). Under the light hedging strategy, Malaysia deliberately adopts opposing positions or contradictory measures to counterbalance the multiple risks arising from the high uncertainty created by the asymmetric regional power structure and the rivalry between the US and China. While Malaysia places high value on the hydrocarbon deposits in the South China Sea, it is more concerned about "the dangers of being entrapped in big-power conflict than the encroachment of foreign vessels into its EEZ *per se*." Moreover, it is the "domestic dynamics that determine how and why" Malaysia adopts this hedging strategy (Lai and Kuik, 2021).

Hamzah is a pioneering scholar in Malaysia on the South China Sea dispute. His earlier work tended to argue that China was not an aggressive power and Malaysia need not undertake a high-profile approach in asserting its claims in the South China Sea. He had claimed that China should be given a prominent role in the consultation and negotiations among all the claimant states (Hamzah, 1990: 23). Lately, Hamzah has adopted a more critical perspective on China, observing that China has become more assertive in pressing its claims. Moreover, Hamzah observed that Malaysia had been reluctant to react strongly to China's assertiveness in the disputed areas in the South China Sea, as a more moderate approach served Malaysia's strategic interests. Hamzah also argued that China could shape into a benign power, while the existing regional security architecture, guaranteed by the preeminent US military force, could deter China from acting aggressively (Hamzah, 2020). James Chin also made a similar observation that Malaysia's established policy elites tended to have a "benign" perception of China, even when confronted with the growing assertiveness of China in the South China Sea (Chin, 2023: 48).

Another popular explanation relates to the economic interests that Malaysia has garnered from having a good relationship with China. Given the fact that Malaysia's economic ties with China are closely integrated, and with a relatively weaker military compared to China's military, Mohammad Zaki Ahmad and Mohd Azizuddin Mohd Sani posited that Malaysia's soft approach has served pragmatic purposes. It is necessary to maintain a low-profile, cautious posture in the South China Sea dispute since a high-profile, confrontational approach will generally destabilize bilateral relations and will affect economic exchanges and benefits (Mohammad Zaki Ahmad and Mohd Azizuddin Mohd Sani, 2017).

Anthony Milner's moral balance approach offers an insightful explanation, suggesting that Malaysia's soft response to Chinese assertions is something "more than balance of power or hedging thinking…The Malaysian approach seems to incorporate a moral and even an aesthetic sense of balance" (Milner, 2017). The concept of moral balance is derived from the historical experiences of the Malay leadership in dealing with regional powers such as China and Siam. The fundamental principles are that the Malay leadership is willing to adopt a long-term perspective on territorial ownership, accepts power hierarchy, and is "relatively comfortable with overlapping sovereignty" claims (Milner, 2017). Furthermore, the Malay leadership believes that safety was derived from engagement and entanglement, which helped the old Malay sultanates ensure their survival. By practicing engagement and entanglement, or the moral balancing strategy, the old Malay sultanates managed to navigate around major powers like China, Siam, the Dutch, the French, and the British when they encroached into this region. Milner's thesis has inspired scholars to revisit Malay strategic culture in order to understand Malaysia's foreign policy, including its China policy.

Ngeow Chow Bing, in examining the China policy of the administration of Najib Abdul Razak (2009–2018), argued that the domestic policy process played a role in shaping the outcome of Malaysia's policy toward China and the South China Sea dispute. The argument was that Malaysia's China policy during the Najib administration was bifurcated into two channels, one dealing with cooperation and the other dealing with the security aspect (the South China Sea issue); the bifurcation allowed the insulation of the dispute from the overall bilateral relations (Ngeow, 2019).

Despite the existing differences among the aforementioned explanations, they all aim to explain why Malaysia has used a soft approach or a low-profile posture toward the South China Sea issue. This chapter does not invalidate these explanations, but suggests an additional explanation in order to enhance our understanding of the essence of Malaysia's low-profile approach. Undeniably, the low-profile approach is a deliberate strategy intended to serve a purpose. But what is the most significant purpose that Malaysia aims to serve? This chapter argues that Malaysia does not want its claim to be scrutinized and challenged, and the deliberate strategy is designed in such a way as to prevent Malaysia from being targeted by other stronger claimants.

Expansion of Maritime Jurisdiction during Oil Crisis

It is crucial to understand that Malaysia's entry into the South China Sea dispute occurred during the peak of the international oil crisis. The 1970s presented significant challenges for Malaysia, particularly as the outbreak of the international oil crisis imposed substantial external and internal pressures on Kuala Lumpur. On the one hand, the Arab oil embargo of 1973 resulted in skyrocketing international oil prices, which had severe implications for Malaysia's economic well-being. On the other hand, the government resorted to subsidizing essential items, including fuel, to stabilize the deteriorating economic situation. Conversely, the surge in international oil prices provided an incentive for Malaysia, which had been a net exporter of crude oil since 1973, to explore more hydrocarbon resources (Lam, 2021). During this challenging period, a viable mitigation plan was to capitalize on the rise in oil prices and use the resulting revenues to alleviate the problems caused by the oil price hike and offset the rapidly increasing subsidy burden. Consequently, this led the Malaysian government to have a greater interest in expanding its maritime jurisdiction in the South China Sea area, especially with the proclamation of the *New Malaysia Map* in late 1979 (Lam, 2022). By proclaiming this new map, Malaysia also staked claim on several contested features and maritime areas in the South China Sea. In hindsight, the strategy of capitalizing on the rise in international oil prices proved effective in reducing the implications of the oil crisis and significantly increased federal revenue, although Malaysia also effectively became a party in the protracted, uncertain, and potentially dangerous South China Sea dispute.

Nonetheless, Malaysia's entry into the dispute was not without contention. As confirmed in the memoir of former Prime Minister Mahathir Mohammad, when Malaysia began to make the move to claim and occupy the features in the South China Sea, it was aware that these features of the South China Sea were claimed by Vietnam, China, and the Philippines. In his memoir, Mahathir recounted an episode when he was Deputy Prime Minister serving under the then Prime Minister Hussein Onn (1976–1981). In this episode, Mahathir disagreed with Hussein Onn in terms of how boldly Malaysia should undertake action to occupy the South China Sea features now claimed by Malaysia as shown in the New Malaysia Map. Regarding the basis of the claim, Mahathir believed that "by right all those adjacent islands and the many atolls should belong to us because they lie within our continental shelf" (Mahathir Mohammad, 2011: 317). Initially, Hussein Onn agreed to Mahathir's plan to claim Amboyna Cay (Pulau Kecil Amboyna), which was the only feature with natural trees and sufficient land for an airstrip. However, Hussein Onn later changed his mind, "believing that [Malaysia's] claim might provoke a confrontation with the other countries." Mahathir was greatly disappointed by Hussein Onn's changed decision. He contended that

> *[T]he issue may seem a small one but it was most important, especially in the light of subsequent debates about the finite and diminishing nature of the world's available natural resources. We don't know what resources may lie beneath Amboyna Cay and its vicinity, especially now that we have developed the technology to drill deeper into the seabed. Some people have since claimed there is oil there... By claiming it as part of our territory, we also lay a claim to a large part of the sea around it* (Mahathir Mohammad, 2011: 317).

Following the loss of Amboyna Cay to Vietnam, Malaysia then shifted its focus to Swallow Reef (Terumbu Layang-layang). Mahathir continued in his memoir,

"It was agreed that we put men there. One week the Cabinet agreed, and the next week Tun Hussein again decided that we should not make this claim, for fear of war with Vietnam. That same year, when I became Prime Minister, the first thing I did was to put people on Layang-layang..." (Mahathir Mohammad, 2011: 318).

Formally, Malaysia asserted its claims on the features as grounded in the Convention on the Territorial Sea and the Contiguous Zone 1958, the Convention on the Continental Shelf 1958, bilateral and border agreements, laws established by colonial powers, the Continental Shelf Act 1966, and the Emergency (Essential Powers) Ordinance, No. 7, 1969 (Haller-Trost, 1998: 13–22). These claims by Malaysia elicited criticism not only from neighboring countries such as Singapore, Indonesia, Thailand, Brunei, and China but also from academic circles.

Firstly, the New Malaysia Map was declared without first clarifying Malaysia's baselines. As per Article 76(1) of UNCLOS, "The continental shelf of a coastal State comprises the seabed and subsoil of the submarine areas that extend beyond its territorial sea throughout the natural prolongation of its land territory to the outer edge of the continental margin, or to a distance of 200 nautical miles from the baselines from which the breadth of the territorial sea is measured where the outer edge of the continental margin does not extend up to that distance." Ideally, Malaysia should have first declared the baselines of the maritime zone, followed by the proclamation of the maritime zone, which includes the territorial sea, exclusive economic zone, and continental shelf. The absence of a proclamation of the maritime zone's baselines has resulted in Malaysia's declaration of the boundary of the continental shelf being inconsistent with the provision of UNCLOS, potentially jeopardizing Malaysia's claims on the Spratly features (Rizal Zamani Idris, Razali Dollah, and Marja Azlima Omar, 2010: 48).

Secondly, UNCLOS does not confer or establish any legal entitlement for a coastal state to assert a claim of sovereignty, title, or rights on a maritime feature. The implication by Mahathir that Malaysia can possess any islands or atolls as long as they are within its continental shelf has been widely criticized by scholars. Greg Austin argued that "international law, until now at least, has been based on the notion that it is demonstrable jurisdiction over land that gives right to jurisdiction over water not vice versa" (Austin, 1998: 159). Austin's contention was similarly noted by Haller-Trost, who noted that Malaysia has conflated the terms "sovereign rights" and "sovereignty," with the former not encompassing the rights of "full sovereignty" (Haller-Trost, 1998: 324). Haller-Trost further added that it was problematic for Malaysia to claim the features of the Spratly Islands which lie beyond the 200-nautical-mile limit measured from the inferred baselines, as this was only permissible under certain circumstances which Malaysia could scarcely justify (Haller-Trost, 1998: 325). Christopher Joyner contended that Malaysia's claims were "ill-founded" because the "geological affinity of a coastal state to island formations arising from continental shelves" did not entitle a state to acquire "sovereign title over an island formation" (Joyner, 1998). Malaysian analysts and scholars such as Sutarji Kasmin, Ismail Ali, and Rizal Zamani Idris have also similarly recognized the issues related to Malaysia's claim (Sutarji Kasmin, 1996; Rizal Zamani Idris, Razali Dollah, and Marja Azlima Omar, 2010; Ismail Ali, Baszley Bee Basrah Bee, and M. Malik Awang Rasin, 2019). While Malaysia is not oblivious to the nature of its claim, any further explanation by Malaysia could be counterproductive and could potentially exacerbate the situation.

San Francisco Treaty and Terra Nullius

In response to inquiries from parliamentarians about the dispute, the Foreign Ministry of Malaysia consistently provides a general response, reiterating that "The position of Malaysia concerning overlapping claims in the South China Sea is clear and consistent. All claims and resolutions regarding issues related to the South China Sea shall be based on international law, including the United Nations Convention on the Law of the Sea 1982 (Parlimen Malaysia, 2024)." Undoubtedly, UNCLOS is a significant piece of international law that regulates global maritime affairs. Nonetheless, it should also be considered that there are areas of international law other than UNCLOS which are relevant to the South China Sea dispute.

Specifically, the Treaty of Peace with Japan (San Francisco Peace Treaty) and the Treaty of Peace between the Republic of China and Japan (Taipei Treaty), which came into effect on 28 April 1952 and 5 August 1952, respectively, are relevant to the status of the Paracel and Spratly Islands. Clause F of Article 2 of the San Francisco Peace Treaty stipulates that "Japan renounces all right, title, and claim to the Spratly Islands and to the Paracel Islands." Article 2 of the Taipei Treaty states that "it is recognized that under Article 2 of the Treaty of Peace with Japan, signed at the city of San Francisco in the United States of America on September 8,

1951 (hereinafter referred to as the San Francisco Treaty), Japan has renounced all right, title, and claim to Taiwan (Formosa) and Penghu (the Pescadores), as well as the Spratly Islands and the Paracel Islands."

Both provisions addressed the renouncement by Japan of the right, title, and claim to the Spratly Islands and Paracel Islands, but there was no specific mention of which country would be designated as the legal recipient after Japan's renouncement. The Republic of China government (based in Taiwan) asserted that although the San Francisco Treaty did not specify the recipient of the Spratly and Paracel Islands, Japan's willingness to negotiate exclusively with the Republic of China regarding the arrangement of both island groups in the Taipei Treaty suggested that the Republic of China was the intended recipient (Lin, 2018). However, since the Republic of China is not recognized by any claimant states involved, and since the People's Republic of China claims to be the legitimate successor to the Republic of China, the claim asserted by the Republic of China on Taiwan continues to be ignored by all the parties involved. The People's Republic of China was not a party to the San Francisco Treaty and the Taipei Treaty, but in 1951, in reaction to the San Francisco Treaty, Premier Zhou Enlai made a statement reaffirming that, after Japan's surrender, the sovereignty of the island groups in the South China Sea (including the Paracel and Spratly Islands) had now reverted back to China (Wu, 2000: 45). In contrast, Vietnam and the Philippines have leveraged the Japanese renouncement to advance their claims for the features in the South China Sea. The Philippines claimed that following the Japanese renouncement, the Spratly Islands were reduced to *terra nullius* status and open for other countries to claim (Austin, 1998: 152–153). On the other hand, Vietnam asserted that after the Japanese renouncement, the Spratly and Paracel Islands should be returned to their original owner, which Vietnam claimed to be (Austin, 1998: 120–121). Given that both treaties are significant international legal documents, how has Malaysia responded to them?

In 1959, Malaysia's first foreign minister, Ismail, highlighted that when the San Francisco Peace Treaty was signed in 1951, Malaya (now Malaysia) had not yet achieved independence and thus lacked the authority to sign international treaties. Consequently, the British government represented both itself and Malaya in signing the treaty and pursued war reparations from Japan based on that treaty (Parlimen Malaysia, 1959: 104). The subsequent question is whether Malaysia recognized the San Francisco Peace Treaty or the Taipei Treaty. In 2016, a parliamentarian posed an oral question, requesting the Ministry of Foreign Affairs to interpret the legal status of the South China Sea islands as referenced in the 1951 San Francisco Peace Treaty and the 1952 Taipei Treaty, and to determine whether these two treaties resulted in the South China Sea islands becoming terra nullius. In response, the then Foreign Minister Anifah stated, "Since Japan is not a claimant state to the South China Sea, and Malaysia and ASEAN countries do not recognize China's sovereignty claims, there is no issue of interpretation regarding the 1951 San Francisco Peace Treaty and the 1952 Treaty of Peace between the Republic of China (Taiwan) and Japan. Furthermore, neither of these treaties mentions the term *terra nullius*" (Parlimen Malaysia, 2016). Again, in 2018, in response to a question about the legality of the San Francisco Peace Treaty in addressing the South China Sea dispute, the then Foreign Minister Saifuddin Abdullah replied that the treaty was an agreement for Japan to compensate Allied countries and Malaysia had already resolved the compensation issue with Japan in an agreement signed on 21 September 1967, rendering any further compensation issues between Malaysia and Japan obsolete (Parlimen Malaysia, 2018). Additionally, in dismissing a further parliamentary question about the treaty, the then Speaker of the House of Representatives (Dewan Rakyat) justified the dismissal by stating, "Malaysia's position is that all the geographical or maritime features within the maritime zone of Malaysia belong to Malaysia. Thus, the Peace Treaty between China and Japan, which was signed in 1951 and 1952, and the issue of the South China Sea is not an issue because Japan is not a claimant and Chinese claims are not recognized by Malaysia and other ASEAN claimants" (Pandikar Amin Mulia, 2017).

As these treaties are established international instruments, they might be invoked if the dispute is presented before an arbitration court (Loja, 2016) and implicates Malaysia's claims. It should be noted that some Malaysian scholars have argued that the terms of the San Francisco Peace Treaty regarding the Spratly Islands should be interpreted as indicating the Spratly Islands being reverted back to the state of *terra nullius* after Japanese renunciation (an interpretation similar to that of the Philippines, as mentioned earlier), and hence Malaysia's occupation of those features should be regarded as legal and consistent with the terms of the San Francisco Peace Treaty (Kuik, Lai and Amy Azuan Abdullah, 2021). This interpretation however is not the formal position of the Malaysian government. Instead, while recognizing the significance and implications of these treaties, Malaysia's official position is to limit the scope of the

Dissecting Malaysia's Low-Profile Posture in the South China Sea Dispute 77

treaties to legal instruments for settling war reparations to Malaysia and nothing more. Hence, by maintaining a low profile and remaining silent when discussions about these treaties arise, Kuala Lumpur can potentially avoid any unnecessary complications.

The Occupation of Reefs and Rocks

While it is widely known that Malaysia officially staked its claims to the maritime economic zone and features in the South China Sea in 1979, it is less commonly known that the idea was first proposed in 1974, following the official visit of the late Prime Minister Tun Abdul Razak to China. In a revealing book chapter, retired officers of the Royal Malaysian Navy who played a direct role in Malaysia's occupation of some Spratly features recounted that the Malaysian government decided not only to assert its claims but also dispatched the warship *KD Sri Langkawi* in 1975 to install markers on the "Spratly features identified to be within Malaysia's claimed territory, including Amboyna Cay," in an operation codenamed Ops Terumbu (Mat Taib Yasin, Azhar Abdul Rahman, and Johari Ramzan Ahmad, 2020: 12). It was further disclosed that, in 1978, Malaysian naval hydrographers were sent to conduct reconnaissance and surveys of the features. The task group discovered that Malaysia's marker, installed on Amboyna Cay in 1975, was missing, prompting the installation of a replacement marker to reaffirm Malaysia's claim over the feature. Subsequently, it was found that the marker was once again destroyed by Vietnam in 1979, and Amboyna Cay was then occupied by Vietnam (*ibid.*).

On 13 June 1979, Malaysia resolved to install more robust 25-foot monuments on Commodore Reef (Terumbu Laksamana), Swallow Reef (Terumbu Layang-Layang), Royal Charlotte Reef (Terumbu Semarang Barat Besar), and Louisa Reef (Terumbu Semarang Barat Kecil) in Operation Tugu (*ibid.*). However, the monument on Commodore Reef was discovered to have been destroyed by the Philippines in June 1980. The loss of Amboyna Cay and Commodore Reef to Vietnam and the Philippines, respectively, prompted Malaysia to decide to occupy Swallow Reef on 21 August 1981 (Mat Taib Yasin, Azhar Abdul Rahman, and Johari Ramzan Ahmad, 2020: 13). Following extensive preparations, on 5 May 1983, an 11-member team of the Special Naval Force, led by Lieutenant Johari Ramzan Ahmad, boarded *KD Mutiara*, a naval

78   *Lam Choong Wah*

hydrographic survey ship that was part of the naval task force involved in Exercise PAHLAWAN, and landed on Swallow Reef (Mat Taib Yasin, Azhar Abdul Rahman, and Johari Ramzan Ahmad, 2020: 16). *KD Mutiara* was selected because it "has been seen in the vicinity of [Terumbu Layang-Layang] in the past conducting 'routine' hydrographic surveys" and its presence "would likely be construed as just carrying out its routine tasks" (*ibid.*). The planners of the occupation operation were highly praised, as "deception plan worked so well that the landing and first permanent occupation of Terumbu Layang-layang transitioned from a tactical landing into an administrative landing instead" (*ibid.*).

There are some discrepancies between what was disclosed by Mat Taib Yasin and his co-authors and other accounts of this episode. Firstly, an official account states that on 11 October 1977, Malaysian troops first set foot on Amboyna Cay and discovered that "Vietnam had placed a monument there in 1976." The troops did not destroy the monument but instead erected a sign reading "Pulau Kecil Amboyna" (Royal Malaysian Navy, 2018: 22). Subsequently, the troops conducted marking and surveys at Dallas Reef, Ardasier Reef, Swallow Reef, Royal Charlotte Reef, Louisa Reef, Seahorse Breakers, Hayor Reef, and South Luconia Shoals. The official account does not mention the marking operation conducted in 1975 and indicates that the first landing was carried out in 1977 instead of 1975. Secondly, contrary to Mat Taib Yasin and his co-authors' claim that this occurred in 1979, the official account states that Malaysia discovered that Vietnam had "physically occupied and armed Amboyna Cay on 2 June 1978" (*ibid.*).

Despite these discrepancies between different accounts, the story revealed here is indeed interesting. What was disclosed by Mat Taib Yasin and other officers indeed suggests that the occupation operations were conducted clandestinely to evade unwelcome international interventions and to ensure the safety of military personnel from potential intimidation by troops from other claimant states. This reinforces the impression that Malaysia was fully aware that it was asserting claims over features and a maritime zone that were already contested by other countries.

Conclusion

This chapter does not aim to invalidate existing explanations of Malaysia's response to the dispute but rather seeks to expand the discussion. There is a consensus that Malaysia has consistently maintained a low profile in the dispute, striving to avoid interventions from major powers and becoming entangled in large-scale power rivalries. However, scholars have often overlooked the significance of the nature of Malaysia's claim in their analyses. This is confirmed by the fact that the expansion of Malaysia's maritime jurisdiction was based on economic interests, rather than purely legal grounds. Furthermore, Malaysia intentionally disregarded the San Francisco Peace Treaty and the Taipei Treaty, which are the only two international instruments related to the general settlement of the title of the Spratly and Paracel Islands. The occupation operations were conducted in secret, as Kuala Lumpur was aware that it was asserting its claims over contested features. This chapter argues that all these factors both reflect and contribute to the low-profile stance. After all, Malaysia has limited capacity and national power to confront other larger claimants; Malaysia is particularly worried about being embroiled in big-power rivalry involving China and the United States. Malaysia's low-profile posture has led not only other claimants but also scholars to overlook the basis of its claims. If this is the case, then the policy has indeed served its purpose and enabled Malaysia to maintain friendly relations with China though both have sharply different sovereignty claims in the South China Sea.

References

Austin, Greg (1998). *China's Ocean Frontier: International Law, Military Force and National Development.* Sydney: Allen and Unwin.

Carty, Anthony (2019a). "Archives on Historical Titles to South China Sea Islands: The Spratlys." *Jus Gentium: Journal of International Legal History*, Vol. 4, No. 1, pp. 7–76.

Carty, Anthony (2019b). "British and French Archives Relating to the Ownership of the Paracel Islands 1900–1975." *Jus Gentium: Journal of International Legal History*, Vol. 4, No. 2, pp. 301–350.

Chin, James (2023). "Malaysia Between China and the West: Don't Rock the Boat." *Georgetown Journal of Asian Studies*, No. 9, pp. 43–49.

Haller-Trost, R. (1998). *The Contested Maritime and Territorial Boundaries of Malaysia: An International Law Perspective.* London: Kluwer Law International.

Hamzah, B. A. (1990). *The Spratlies: What Can Be Done to Enhance Confidence.* Kuala Lumpur: Institute of Strategic and International Studies.

Hamzah, B. A. (2020). "China's Excessive Maritime Claims in the South China Sea: A Malaysian Perspective." In B. A. Hamzah, Adam Leong, and Vivian Louis Forbes (eds.), *Malaysia and South China Sea: Policy, Strategy and*

Risks, pp. 131–150, Kuala Lumpur: Centre for Defence and International Security Studies, Universiti Pertahanan Nasional Malaysia.

Ismail Ali, Baszley Bee Basrah Bee, and M. Malik Awang Rasin (2019). "Hubungan Malaysia-Vietnam dan Pertindihan Wilayah di Kepulauan Spratly: Pendekatan Pembangunan Bersama Dalam Pengurusan Konflik." In Ramli Dollah, Wan Shawaluddin Wan Hassan, and Rizal Zamani Idris (eds.), *Isu-Isu Terpilih Dalam Hubungan Malaysia Dengan Negara Serantau Asia Tenggara*, pp. 237–248. Kuala Lumpur: Dewan Bahasa dan Pustaka.

Joyner, Christopher C. (1998). "The Spratly Islands Dispute: Rethinking the Interplay of Law, Diplomacy, and Geo-politics in the South China Sea." *The International Journal of Marine and Coastal Law*, Vol. 13, No. 2, pp. 193–236.

Kuik, Cheng-Chwee and Lai Yew Meng (2023). "Deference and Defiance in Malaysia's China Policy: Determinants of a Dualistic Diplomacy." *International Journal of Asian Studies*, First View, pp. 1–20.

Kuik, Cheng-Chwee, Lai Yew Meng, and Amy Azuan Abdullah (2021). "Pulau Layang-Layang in Malaysia's South China Sea Policy: Sovereignty Meets Geopolitical Reality amid China–U.S. Rivalry." *International Journal of China Studies*, Vol. 12, No. 2, pp. 189–222.

Lai, Yew Meng and Cheng-Chwee Kuik (2021). "Structural Sources of Malaysia's South China Sea Policy: Power Uncertainties and Small-State Hedging." *Australian Journal of International Affairs*, Vol. 75, No. 3, pp. 277–304.

Lam, Choong Wah (2021). *1974 nian yilai de Malaixiya duihua zhengce yanjiu: jiyu Malaixiya guohui shijiao* (*A Study of Malaysia's China Policy since 1974: From the Perspective of Malaysia's Parliament*). Unpublished Doctoral Thesis, Xiamen University.

Lam, Choong Wah (2022). "Malaysia's Expansion of Its Maritime Jurisdiction and the World Oil Crisis, 1973–80." *Journal of Southeast Asian* Studies, Vol. 53, No. 1–2, pp. 309–338.

Leong, Adam Kok Wey (2017). "A Small State's Foreign Affairs Strategy: Making Sense of Malaysia's Strategic Response to the South China Sea Debacle." *Comparative Strategy*, Vol. 3, No. 5, pp. 392–399.

Lin, Man-houng (2018). "A Neglected Treaty for the South China Sea." In Tsu-Sung Hsieh (ed.), *The South China Sea Disputes Historical, Geopolitical and Legal Studies*, pp. 1–13. Singapore: World Scientific.

Liow, Joseph Chin Yong (2009). "Malaysia's Post Cold War China Policy: A Reassessment." In Jun Tsunekawa (ed.), *The Rise of China: Responses from Southeast Asia and Japan*, pp. 43–79. Tokyo: The National Institute for Defense Studies.

Loja, Melissa H. (2016). "The Spratly Islands as a Single Unit Under International Law: A Commentary on the Final Award in Philippines/China

Arbitration." *Ocean Development and International Law*, Vol. 47, No. 4, pp. 309–326.

Mahathir Mohamed (2011). *A Doctor in the House: The Memoirs of Tun Dr Mahathir Mohamed.* Petaling Jaya: MPH.

Mat Taib Yasin, Azhar Abdul Rahman, and Johari Ramzan Ahmad (2020). "Malaysia's Occupation of Spratly Features: A Special Operation by PASKAL." In B. A. Hamzah, Adam Leong and Vivian Louis Forbes (eds.), *Malaysia and South China Sea: Policy, Strategy and Risks*, pp. 12–33. Kuala Lumpur: Centre for Defence and International Security Studies, Universiti Pertahanan Nasional Malaysia.

Mohammad Zaki Ahmad and Mohd Azizuddin Mohd Sani (2017). "China's Assertive Posture in Reinforcing its Territorial and Sovereignty Claims in the South China Sea: An Insight into Malaysia's Stance." *Japanese Journal of Political Science*, Vol. 18, No. 1, pp. 67–105.

Milner, Anthony (2017). "Sovereignty and Normative Integration in the South China Sea: Some Malaysian and Malay Perspectives." In Lowell Dittmer and Ngeow Chow Bing (eds.), *Southeast Asia and China: A Contest in Mutual Socialization*, pp. 229–246, Singapore: World Scientific.

Ngeow, Chow-Bing (2019). "Malaysia's China Policy and the South China Sea Dispute Under the Najib Administration (2009–2018): A Domestic Policy Process Approach." *Asian Politics and Policy*, Vol. 11, No. 4, pp. 586–605.

Pandikar Amin Mulia (2017). Letter from Tan Sri Datuk Seri Panglima Pandikar Amin bin haji Mulia to Yang Berhormat Tuan Oscar Ling Chai Yew, *Ucapan Di Bawah Usul Berkenaan Perkara Tadbir Kerajaan (Peraturan Mesyuarat 17 Baharu)*, YDPR.08/4/1/11(22), 24 July.

Parlimen Malaysia (1959). Parliamentary Debates: Dewan Rakyat, Vol. 1, 25 November.

Parlimen Malaysia (1988). Penyata Rasmi Parlimen: Dewan Rakyat, Vol. 11, 28 June.

Parlimen Malaysia (2016). Pemberitahuan Pertanyaan Lisan No. 28, Dewan Rakyat, 16 May.

Parlimen Malaysia (2018). Pemberitahuan Pertanyaan Bukan Lisan No. 116, Dewan Rakyat, 16 July–16 August.

Parlimen Malaysia (2024). Pemberitahuan Pertanyaan Lisan: Dewab Rakyat, No. 73, 4 March.

Rizal Zamani Idris, Razali Dollah, and Marja Azlima Omar (2010). *Isu Keselamatan Persempadanan Negeri Sabah dan Tuntutan Terhadap Kepulauan Spratly.* Kota Kinabalu: Penerbit Universiti Malaysia Sabah.

Royal Malaysian Navy (2018). In Fadhil Abdul Rahman (ed.), *Gugusan Semarang Peninjau: Guardian of the Frontier.* Kuala Lumpur: Sea Power Centre, Royal Malaysian Navy.

Sutarji Kasmin (1996). "Tuntutan Malaysia Ke Atas Kepulauan Spratly: Apakah Implikasinya Terhadap Dasar Negara." *Pemikir*, No. 4, pp. 86–113.

Valencia, Mark (1991). *Malaysia and the Law of the Sea: The Foreign Policy Issues, the Options and Their Implications*. Kuala Lumpur: Institute of Strategic and International Studies.

Wu, Shicun (2000). *Nanhai wenti wenxian huibian (Compilation of Documents Regarding the South China Sea Issue)*. Haikou: Hainan chubanshe.

© 2025 World Scientific Publishing Company
https://doi.org/10.1142/9789819801350_0006

Chapter 6

From Bilateral Trade to Supply Chain Integration: Evolving Patterns of Malaysia–China Economic Relations

Zhang Miao and Li Ran

Introduction

China's emergence on the world stage has been phenomenal, with the pivotal milestone being the initiation of China's reform and opening-up policy in the late 1970s. Diplomatic relations between China and Malaysia were formally established on 31 May 1974, marking the beginning of five decades of bilateral relations. Over these decades, economic and trade cooperation has become a cornerstone and a major driving force behind the development of bilateral relations between the two countries. Trade has served as the most predominant and basic form of economic and commercial exchanges between the two countries. Factors such as geographical proximity, people-to-people ties, and a complementary trade structure have continuously elevated the level of trade interdependence. In 2023, China retained its position as Malaysia's largest trading partner for the 15th consecutive year. Additionally, Malaysia held the position of China's largest trading partner within ASEAN for a long period (2009–2019). The vibrant, young, and diverse population of Malaysia and China's growing middle class and large domestic consumer market indicate that economic relations between China and Malaysia will continue to thrive in the future, with immense potential.

The advent of economic globalization in the 21st century has catalyzed a profound shift in the international division of labor, transitioning from inter-industry trade to intra-industry and intra-product dynamics. This transformation has notably influenced the economic and trade landscape between China and Malaysia. Formerly dominated by raw material-based commodity trade, this trade relationship has evolved into a comprehensive integration of supply chains, propelled primarily by trade in intermediate products and, significantly, foreign direct investment (FDI). Since the 2010s, there has been a sharp increase in Chinese FDI in Malaysia, and increasingly the investment has covered or encompassed a wide range of sectors including manufacturing, services, construction, and real estate.

Compared to the traditional form of trade, the current pattern of trade is characterized by the emerging role of multinational corporations (MNCs) and their international operations, which entail the strong growth of trade volume of intermediate products and cross-border flow of other factors such as capital technology and human resources. MNCs embed various production factors in different countries, forming a transnational network of production and exchange, influenced by the interaction and competition of multiple forces and actors including the market, governments, and international organizations and regimes.

Standing at the 50th anniversary of the establishment of diplomatic relations between China and Malaysia, it is pertinent to examine the of drivers and evolving patterns of the economic relations between the two countries. Existing literature has made many fruitful attempts to capture the general trends and new features of economic relations between China and Malaysia (Yeoh, 2019; Yeoh, Chang, and Zhang, 2018; Zhang and Li, 2018; Tham, Kam, and Tee, 2019). While the literature has undoubtedly made substantial contributions, there is still a need to look into and address an emerging key feature, notably the evolving landscape of comprehensive cooperation and integration within the global value chain.

Therefore, this chapter will address the increasing complexity of Malaysia–China trade and economic relations, considering the globalization of supply chains over the past few decades and the investments made by MNCs from and between both countries. The chapter will not only use conventional measurement methods such as trade balance, total trade volume, investment flows, and stocks but also employ more advanced measurement methods, including value-added trade, to provide a more comprehensive, objective, and accurate study to reflect the circumstances and latest developments of the China–Malaysia economic relations more comprehensively. Macro quantitative data will be sourced from the United Nations Commodity Trade Statistics Database (Comtrade), the Trade in Value-Added (TiVa) Database by OECD, and the United Nations Development Indicators (UNDIs). In addition, other important information obtained from official reports from relevant departments of China and Malaysia, as well as international organizations, such as ASEAN, the World Trade Organization (WTO), and the United Nations, will also be used.

Following the introduction in this section, the second part primarily discusses the trade structure and trade-related institutional arrangements. The third and fourth parts, respectively, focus on the current status and development of FDI and financial cooperation between the two countries. The final section provides a conclusion and some policy recommendations.

Bilateral Trade: Structure, Value-Added, and Free Trade Agreements

Trade Volume and Balance

Bilateral trade has consistently played a pivotal role in the economic collaboration between China and Malaysia. Since the establishment of diplomatic ties in 1974, both nations have nurtured a robust exchange, characterized by frequent interactions among trade delegations. This dynamic engagement has yielded significant results, exemplified by the pivotal trade agreements negotiated between 1975 and 1980, in particular those pertaining to the trade of rubber and rice. Throughout the 1970s to the 1980s, Malaysia primarily exported traditional products such as rubber, palm oil, and timber to China, later diversifying into industrial goods like plywood and polyester. On the other hand, China's exports to Malaysia mainly comprised primary products like grains, oils, and medicinal herbs, along with light industrial goods such as textiles and glassware.

Prior to the 1980s, Malaysia struggled with significant trade deficits in its dealings with China. However, following the conclusion of several meticulously arranged trade negotiations after the establishment of diplomatic relations, the trade dynamic between the two countries gradually shifted, achieving equilibrium from the mid-1970s onward (see Table 1). According to Chinese customs data, China has consistently maintained a

Table 1.   Trade between China and Malaysia, 1972–2022.

Year	China Export to Malaysia	China Import from Malaysia	Total Volume of China–Malaysia Trade	Trade Balance of China–Malaysia Trade	China–ASEAN Total Volume of Trade	% of Malaysia in China–ASEAN Total
1972	0.41	0.03	0.44	0.38	N/A	N/A
1973	1.25	0.01	1.26	1.24	N/A	N/A
1974	1.55	0.04	1.59	1.51	N/A	N/A
1975	1.09	0.51	1.60	0.58	N/A	N/A
1976	0.87	0.49	1.36	0.38	N/A	N/A
1977	0.94	1.05	1.99	−0.11	N/A	N/A
1978	1.63	1.11	2.74	0.52	N/A	N/A
1979	1.72	1.89	3.61	−0.17	N/A	N/A
1980	1.84	2.40	4.24	−0.56	20.64	20.5
1981	1.88	1.17	3.05	0.71	19.65	15.5
1982	1.76	1.53	3.29	0.23	21.53	15.3
1983	1.85	2.14	3.99	−0.29	18.27	21.8
1984	1.65	1.67	3.32	−0.02	28.62	11.6
1985	1.82	1.86	3.68	−0.04	38.41	9.6
1986	2.03	1.80	3.83	0.23	33.81	11.3
1987	2.55	3.02	5.57	−0.47	42.79	13.0
1988	3.08	5.68	8.76	−2.60	56.74	15.4
1989	3.52	6.92	10.44	−3.40	66.39	15.7
1990	3.41	8.35	11.76	−4.94	71.72	16.4

From Bilateral Trade to Supply Chain Integration 87

1991	5.28	8.04	13.32	-2.76	78.63	16.9
1992	6.45	8.30	14.75	-1.85	87.47	16.9
1993	7.04	10.84	17.88	-3.80	112.62	15.9
1994	11.20	16.20	27.40	-5.00	141.33	19.4
1995	12.81	20.70	33.51	-7.89	199.70	16.8
1996	13.71	22.43	36.14	-8.72	211.68	17.1
1997	19.22	24.95	44.17	-5.73	251.53	17.6
1998	15.96	26.74	42.70	-10.78	236.45	18.1
1999	16.74	36.05	52.79	-19.31	272.08	19.4
2000	25.65	54.79	80.44	-29.14	394.25	20.4
2001	32.21	62.04	94.25	-29.83	416.13	22.6
2002	49.74	92.96	142.70	-43.22	547.70	26.1
2003	61.41	139.86	201.27	-78.45	782.55	25.7
2004	80.86	181.75	262.61	-100.89	1,058.67	24.8
2005	106.06	200.93	306.99	-94.87	1,303.61	23.5
2006	135.37	235.72	371.09	-100.35	1,608.38	23.1
2007	177.44	287.23	464.67	-109.79	2,025.33	22.9
2008	214.55	321.01	535.56	-106.46	2,313.20	23.2
2009	196.32	323.31	519.63	-126.99	2,130.13	24.4
2010	238.02	504.30	742.32	-266.28	2,928.66	25.3
2011	278.86	621.36	900.22	-342.50	3,630.85	24.8
2012	365.26	583.05	948.31	-217.79	4,001.42	23.7

(Continued)

Table 1. (*Continued*)

Year	China Export to Malaysia	China Import from Malaysia	Total Volume of China–Malaysia Trade	Trade Balance of China–Malaysia Trade	China–ASEAN Total Volume of Trade	% of Malaysia in China–ASEAN Total
2013	459.31	601.53	1,060.84	−142.22	4,436.17	23.9
2014	463.53	556.52	1,020.05	−92.99	4,801.32	21.2
2015	439.80	532.77	972.57	−92.97	4,721.65	20.6
2016	376.60	492.69	869.29	−116.09	4,522.13	19.2
2017	417.12	544.26	961.38	−127.14	5,154.53	18.7
2018	453.76	632.05	1,085.81	−178.29	5,876.04	18.5
2019	521.42	719.10	1,240.52	−197.68	6,416.93	19.3
2020	563.01	751.74	1,314.75	−188.73	6,853.12	19.2
2021	764.04	979.83	1,743.87	−215.79	8,784.20	19.9
2022	937.11	1,098.79	2,035.90	−161.68	9,644.72	21.1
Average annual growth (%)	16.73	23.39	18.39		15.76	

Note: In hundred million USD.
Source: *China Foreign Economic and Trade Yearbook* (various years), UN Comtrade.

From Bilateral Trade to Supply Chain Integration 89

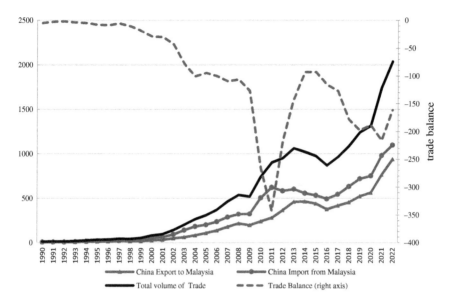

Figure 1. China–Malaysia Trade Volume and Balance, 1990–2022.
Note: In hundred million USD.

trade deficit since the 1990s, driven by the increasing imports from Malaysia, as evidenced by the annual average growth rate of 23.4% (see Figure 1).

Since the beginning of the new century, bilateral trade has consistently represented approximately one-fourth of China's total trade volume with ASEAN constituents. Remarkably, from 2009 to 2019, Malaysia emerged as China's biggest trading partner within the ASEAN. Similarly, China retained its status as Malaysia's biggest trading partner for the 15th consecutive year in 2023. Overall, bilateral trade has exhibited an upward trajectory, growing 16.6% annually on average and surging from USD159 million in 1974 to USD203.5 billion in 2022.

As shown in Figure 2, the Trade Intensity Index(TII) between the two countries remained below 1 from 1989 to 2001. However, it exceeded this threshold after 2002 and has continued to do so up to the present. This signified a heightened level of trade integration and complementarity between the two countries compared to the global average. It is noteworthy that the TII's peak in the 1970s was followed by a decline in the 1980s. However, a steady uptrend of the TII has been observed since the turn of the millennium. The gradual rise of the TII after the 2000s, albeit relatively modest, is attributed to China's strategic diversification of

Figure 2. Trade Intensity Index (TII), China and Malaysia, 1970–2022.
Source: UN Comtrade Database.

global trading partners after its WTO accession. During the nascent stages of diplomatic ties, Malaysia held a pivotal status as China's foremost trading partner. While Malaysia's prominence may have waned in recent times, bilateral trade relations have consistently thrived, with the TII persistently exceeding 1 since the dawn of the new century.

Trade Structure

Following the establishment of diplomatic relations in 1974, Malaysia primarily exported traditional products such as rubber, palm oil, and timber to China until the 1980s, when Malaysia gradually diversified into industrial goods like plywood and plastic-related products. On the other hand, China's exports to Malaysia mainly comprised primary products like grains, oils, and medicinal herbs, along with light industrial goods such as textiles and glassware. In the late 1980s, China significantly boosted its exports of heavy industrial products to Malaysia, expanding beyond steel, agricultural machinery, and metalworking machines to include telecommunications equipment. For instance, between 1987 and 1990, China's exports of metal-cutting machines to Malaysia surged from USD341,000 to USD4.753 million, marking a nearly 13-fold increase. Similarly, exports of telecommunications equipment grew from USD143,000 to USD297,000, more than doubling during the same period.

The bilateral trade structure underwent notable transformations in the 1990s. Previously dominated by China's exports of grains, food, agricultural products, and light textiles in exchange for Malaysia's primary products like rubber, timber, palm oil, and plywood, the trade dynamic shifted toward an increasing proportion of electromechanical products exported from China to Malaysia. By 1997, electromechanical products accounted for 36.2% of China's exports to Malaysia, with industrial manufactured goods comprising over 70% of the total export value. Concurrently, Malaysia's industrial manufactured goods began penetrating the Chinese market, demonstrating strong competitiveness. The proportion of Malaysia's industrial manufactured goods rose from 8% in 1988 to 23.9% in 1992 and further to 54.8% in 1997. This shift signifies the advancement of the China–Malaysia trade toward higher levels with greater diversification across various sectors.

The trade composition of these key commodities is delineated in Table 2, revealing a progressive increase in the share of high-tech manufactured goods in bilateral trade, coupled with a simultaneous decline in products with lower technological content. As evidenced by the data in Table 2, the proportion of high-tech electronic appliances in China's exports to Malaysia has steadily risen from 8% in 1992 to 28% in 2022. Concurrently, the share of electronic appliances in China's imports from Malaysia has experienced even more rapid growth, surging from 2% in 1992 to 28% in 2022. In stark contrast, products with lower technological content such as animal and plant oils, with palm oil representing a significant portion, have witnessed a substantial decline in their share of imports from Malaysia to China, plummeting from 22% in 1992 to 2% in 2022. This trend underscores the ongoing upgrading of manufacturing industries in both countries and the continual optimization of the bilateral trade structure.

Amid the wave of globalization, the value-added trade of intermediate goods[1] has emerged as a critical barometer of a country's trade and production dynamics within the intricate web of global supply chains.

---

[1] According to Broad Economic Categories (version 4). See https://unstats.un.org/unsd/trade/classifications/bec.asp for details. Based on the sections of the Standard International Trade Classification (SITC), intermediate goods include food and beverages processed for industry (121), industrial supplies (processed) (22), fuels and lubricants (processed) (322), parts and accessories of capital goods (42), and parts and accessories of transport equipment (53).

Table 2.   China–Malaysia Trade Structure, 1992 to 2022.

	Electronic Machinery				Animal and Plant Oils			
Year	China's Export to Malaysia	% in Total Export to Malaysia	China's Import from Malaysia	% in Total Import from Malaysia	China's Export to Malaysia	% in Total Export to Malaysia	China's Import from Malaysia	% in Total Import from Malaysia
1992	0.523	8.112	0.178	2.141	0.012	0.181	1.842	22.192
1994	1.282	11.451	0.965	5.954	0.036	0.319	5.833	36.003
1996	3.053	22.268	3.043	13.568	0.040	0.291	4.628	20.633
1998	4.304	26.967	6.405	23.954	0.087	0.544	4.842	18.106
2000	9.268	36.131	20.970	38.274	0.034	0.134	3.964	7.235
2002	16.314	32.798	45.675	49.134	0.021	0.042	6.813	7.329
2004	21.754	26.904	99.884	54.957	0.092	0.114	13.847	7.619
2006	34.323	25.355	145.135	61.571	0.151	0.112	16.374	6.946
2008	51.666	24.081	172.203	53.644	0.170	0.079	38.734	12.066
2010	58.874	24.735	286.267	56.765	0.097	0.041	30.854	6.118
2012	73.536	20.132	333.062	57.124	0.116	0.032	38.281	6.566
2014	93.099	20.085	321.680	57.802	0.167	0.036	26.729	4.803
2016	80.118	21.274	319.036	64.754	0.087	0.023	14.442	2.931
2018	125.252	27.603	337.596	53.413	0.897	0.198	14.175	2.243
2020	162.923	28.938	388.235	51.645	1.312	0.233	20.021	2.663
2022	269.439	28.752	407.171	37.056	2.262	0.241	24.224	2.205

Note: In 100 million yuan.

Figure 3 offers insights into the value-added trade structure between China and Malaysia. Evidently, the proportion of intermediate goods in total trade has been consistently higher than the weight of final products, maintaining a high position between 60% and 80% from 1995 to 2020. Conversely, the share of final products remained low and witnessed a gradual decline from 35% in 1995 to 21% in 2020. This prevalence of intermediate goods trade underscores the profound integration of both China and Malaysia within the regional production network of East Asia, aligning seamlessly with the earlier analysis of heightened trade of technological sophistication. Products demanding advanced technical expertise, such as electronics, electrical products, and transport equipment, entail intricate production processes, necessitating frequent engagement in intermediate goods trade activities. Therefore, the prominence of intermediate goods trade in value-added terms, as a significant gauge of the deepening international division of labor, indicates a substantial entrenchment of both countries within the global value chain.

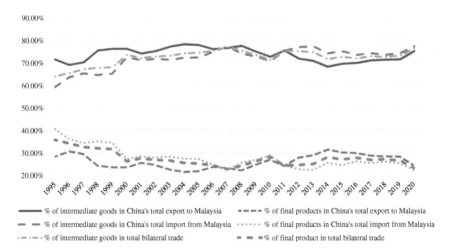

Figure 3. China–Malaysia Trade Structure in Value-Added, According to BEC, 1995–2022.

Source: TiVA Database (1995–2020).

Free Trade Agreements

A comprehensive examination of bilateral trade between China and Malaysia necessitates an exploration of their trade-related institutional frameworks. Notably, the impacts of CAFTA (China–ASEAN Free Trade Area) and RCEP (Regional Comprehensive Economic Partnership) stand out as pivotal and multifaceted determinants. CAFTA represents China's inaugural foray into formal participation in a regional economic integration initiative following its accession to the WTO in 2001. The ratification of CAFTA marked a pivotal shift toward institutionalized and heightened economic integration, transcending the confines of WTO parameters. This integrative framework injected fresh momentum into the China–Malaysia trade collaboration. The empirical evidence underscores the significance of CAFTA's early harvest program, as it engendered a notable increase in trade dependency between China and Malaysia. The negotiations for the CAFTA 3.0 commenced in February 2023, while ASEAN has evolved into a more tightly integrated entity. CAFTA, initiated at the beginning of the 21st century, has transformed over the past three decades from a mere FTA into a crucial instrument and platform for constructing political mutual trust between China and ASEAN.

Expanding upon the groundwork laid by CAFTA, the introduction of RCEP unveiled several innovative features that transcend traditional trade frameworks.[2] Firstly, alongside conventional measures like tariff reduction, a pivotal aspect is the adoption of the accumulation of origin principle within RCEP member states, which facilitates the seamless flow of products, services, and factors of production across a vast regional terrain. This principle incentivizes the efficient allocation of resources within a broader geographic expanse, thereby optimizing production processes and enhancing economic efficiency. Scholars anticipate that the total trade effect of RCEP on all goods for Malaysia and China will increase by USD4.05 billion and USD665 million, respectively (Jiang and Hartini Husin 2023).[3] In a scenario of complete tariff elimination, Malaysia experiences greater trade and welfare effects compared to China.

An illustrative example is Japan's inclusion within the ambit of RCEP. Historically, the absence of a Free Trade Agreement (FTA) between Japan

---

[2]RCEP was initiated by ASEAN in 2012, but it was not until 18 March 2023 that it officially came into effect in Malaysia.

[3]The stipulation in the agreement is that RCEP would ultimately eliminate over 90% of tariffs on goods among participating countries.

and China was notable prior to the establishment of RCEP, although Japan assumes a pivotal role as a substantial trading partner for both China and Malaysia. Trade between the two countries and Japan is characterized by intricate trade structures primarily dominated by the exchange of intermediate goods. The introduction of the cumulative rule of origins within RCEP holds the promise of bolstering Malaysia–China trade relations. This enhancement stems from the integration of Japan into regional production networks facilitated by intertwined supply chain linkages and the complementary nature of the industrial and trade structures of the three countries.

Secondly, the provisions within RCEP pertaining to e-commerce serve as a catalyst for bolstering trade relations between China and Malaysia, in particular the trade of intermediate and component goods, thereby strengthening their industrial chain cooperation. By facilitating seamless electronic transactions and data flow, RCEP creates a conducive environment for micro, small, and medium enterprises (MSMEs) to engage in cross-border trade of parts and components. It does so by streamlining supply chain logistics and reducing transaction costs, thereby promoting greater efficiency in the trade of intermediate goods crucial for manufacturing processes. Additionally, RCEP's provisions for reducing barriers to digital trade, such as eliminating tariffs and non-tariff barriers on electronic transactions, further incentivize businesses to engage in the trade of intermediate and component goods. As a result, enhanced trade facilitation through e-commerce provisions fosters deeper integration of the industrial chains between China and Malaysia, promoting collaboration and mutual benefit in the manufacturing and production sectors.

Moreover, RCEP also extends its purview to encompass areas of agricultural and government procurement, underscoring its comprehensive and forward-looking approach toward economic integrations. By addressing previously overlooked sectors and modernizing trade regulations, RCEP will continue to harmonize regional trade practices and enhance intra-regional cooperation, thereby further benefiting trade relations between China and Malaysia.

Bilateral Investment

Malaysia's OFDI in China

Malaysia's OFDI in China began in the 1980s. In 1984, Kuok Brothers invested $300 million in building the China International Trade Center and Shangri-La Hotel in Beijing, marking the entry of the Malaysian–Chinese enterprise venture into the Chinese market. Subsequently, Malaysia's investments in China witnessed steady growth. Initially concentrated in regions like Guangdong and Fujian along the coastal south, the investments focused on industries such as rubber, food, cosmetics, furniture, and machinery manufacturing, with a strong presence in processing industries. With the further liberalization of China's reform and opening-up policies after 1992, Malaysia saw a surge in FDI into China, marking the fastest growth phase. In 1992, there were 169 Malaysian-funded projects in China, with an agreement value of $209 million. By 1993, this figure had increased to 442 with an agreement value of $759 million, reflecting an impressive annual growth rate of 262.8%. The investment landscape expanded beyond manufacturing to encompass energy, transportation, real estate, wholesale and retail, and service industries in the 1990s. While Malaysian investments gradually moved inland, coastal regions remained the primary investment destination, accounting for about 87.36% of the total Malaysian investments utilized in China. Moreover, there was a notable transition from a focus on small and medium-sized enterprises to larger companies actively engaging in China, with major conglomerates like Sime Darby and the Sunway Group assuming pivotal roles in investment endeavors. As depicted in Figure 4, the significant uptick in

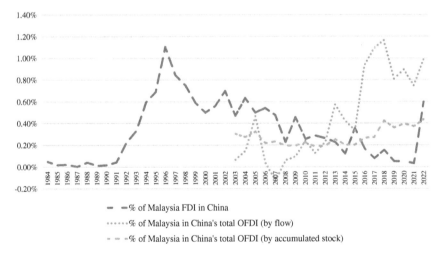

Figure 4. Share of FDI from Malaysia in China's Total FDI, 1984–2022.

Source: *China Foreign Economic and Trade Yearbook*, *China Outward Foreign Direct Investment Statistical Bulletin* (various years).

Malaysia-funded projects after the 1990s aligned with the substantial increase in Malaysia's share of total FDI in China from 1991 to 1997, until challenges emerged when the Asian Financial Crisis hit the Southeast Asian countries terribly (Table 3).

Table 3. Malaysian OFDI in China, 1984–2022.

Year	Total FDI in China	FDI from Malaysia in China	% of Malaysian FDI in China
1984	12.58	0.006	0.05
1985	16.58	0.003	0.02
1986	18.75	0.004	0.02
1987	23.14	0.001	0.00
1988	31.94	0.013	0.04
1989	33.92	0.004	0.01
1990	34.87	0.006	0.02
1991	43.66	0.019	0.04
1992	110.08	0.247	0.22
1993	275.15	0.914	0.33
1994	337.66	2.01	0.60
1995	375.21	2.59	0.69
1996	417.26	4.6	1.10
1997	452.57	3.82	0.84
1998	454.63	3.41	0.75
1999	403.19	2.38	0.59
2000	407.15	2.03	0.50
2001	468.77	2.63	0.56
2002	527.43	3.68	0.70
2003	535	2.51	0.47
2004	606.31	3.85	0.63
2005	724.1	3.61	0.50
2006	727.2	3.93	0.54
2007	835.2	3.97	0.48
2008	1083.1	2.47	0.23
2009	940.6	4.29	0.46

(Continued)

98 *Zhang Miao & Li Ran*

Table 3. *(Continued)*

Year	Total FDI in China	FDI from Malaysia in China	% of Malaysian FDI in China
2010	1147.3	2.94	0.26
2011	1239.9	3.58	0.29
2012	1210.7	3.18	0.26
2013	1239.1	2.81	0.23
2014	1285	1.57	0.12
2015	1355.8	4.8	0.35
2016	1337.1	2.21	0.17
2017	1363.2	1.08	0.08
2018	1383.1	2.12	0.15
2019	1412.2	0.71	0.05
2020	1493.4	0.78	0.05
2021	1809.6	0.58	0.03
2022	1891.32	11.27	0.60

Note: In 100 Million USD.
Source: *China Foreign Economic and Trade Yearbook, China Outward Foreign Direct Investment Statistical Bulletin* (various years).

In the first decade of the 21st century, Malaysian FDI in China continued to flourish, with numerous Malaysian–Chinese companies expanding their ventures in the country. A standout example is the Lion Group, which made significant strides in the retail sector by establishing Parkson department stores nationwide. By 2010, it had successfully opened over 40 shopping malls across China. Additionally, since 2005, the Lion Group diversified into the hotel industry, with a strong presence in cities like Qingdao and Hangzhou, boasting over 30 chain hotels nationwide by 2010. Following the initiation of the Belt and Road Initiative (BRI) in 2013, the Malaysian business community actively engaged in it. Notably, industrial park collaboration emerged as a key focus of bilateral investment cooperation during this period. Noteworthy projects such as the "two countries, twin parks" — the China–Malaysia Qinzhou Industrial Park and the Malaysia–China Kuantan Industrial Park (MCKIP) — pioneered a novel model of value chain cooperation under the BRI. By the conclusion of 2023, the Qinzhou Industrial Park had developed an industry cluster centered on bird's nest, palm oil, biomedicine, electronic information, and new energy sectors. In the foreseeable future, the Qinzhou Industrial Park is strategically positioned to attract investments in the field of advanced technological equipment manufacturing, encompassing sectors such as engineering machinery, automotive industry, information and communication technology, biotechnology, innovative materials, as well as ancillary services like education and cultural enrichment experiences. The enduring establishment of Malaysian enterprises within the Chinese market serves as a testament to the enduring and mutually beneficial economic partnership between the two countries, albeit somewhat eclipsed by the disproportionate surge of Chinese outbound foreign direct investment (OFDI) into Malaysia (Table 4).

China's OFDI in Malaysia

When Malaysia experienced significant FDI in the 1980s from Japan and Western countries, China was still a very insignificant player. By the end of 1988, China had two joint venture plans in Malaysia, one in manufacturing bicycle tires and another in ceramic tiles. However, Chinese enterprises increasingly became more active. By early 1994, China had invested in more than 100 companies in Malaysia and injected more than 200 million USD. Most of these companies were joint ventures with local enterprises, mainly engaged in manufacturing, construction, hospitality, trading, catering services, and medical services. By the end of 1996, China had set up about 150 enterprises and institutions in Malaysia, with investment concentrated in the four major industries of construction, manufacturing, trade, and services, of which the investment in manufacturing alone had reached 214 million USD. After the Asian Financial Crisis, Chinese investment in Malaysia continued to grow, and by the end of 1998, there were more than 160 approved trade and non-trade enterprises in Malaysia in which China had invested, with actual investment exceeding USD300 million (Huang, 2000; Wang, 2004; Ma, 1999).

In addition to direct investment in Malaysia, Chinese enterprises in Malaysia also actively participated in local project bidding. Chinese companies started to cooperate on contracting projects in Malaysia in 1990s. In 1992, the amount of this type of cooperation and among this type of cooperation in ASEAN countries. By the beginning of 1995, the two sides had signed 381 agreements on contracting projects and labor service

Table 4. China's OFDI in Malaysia, 2002–2022.

	Total (Billion $)[a]	State Enterprises OFDI (Stock, %)[b]	No. of State Enterprises (%)	Malaysia (Million $)[c]
2022	163.12	52.4	5.6	1,610.00
2021	178.82	51.6	5.7	1,336.25
2020	153.71	46.3	5.3	1,374.41
2019	136.91	50.1	5.0	1,109.54
2018	143.04	48.0	4.9	1,662.70
2017	158.29	49.1	5.6	1,722.14
2016	196.15	54.3	5.2	1,829.96
2015	145.67	50.4	5.8	488.91
2014	123.12	53.6	6.7	521.34
2013	107.84	55.2		616.38
2012	87.80	59.8		199.04
2011	74.65	62.7		95.13
2010	68.81	66.2		163.54
2009	56.53	69.2		53.78
2008	55.91	69.6		34.43
2007	26.51	71	19.7	−32.82
2006	21.16	81	26	7.51
2005	12.26			56.72
2004	5.50		35	8.12
2003	2.85		43	1.97
2002	2.70			

Notes: [a]2002–2005 is non-financial data; [b]Non-financial data; [c]2003–2006 is non-financial data.
Source: Ministry of Commerce of the People's Republic of China, National Bureau of Statistics and State Administration of Foreign Exchange, Statistical Bulletin of China's Outward Foreign Direct Investment 2002–2022.

cooperation, with a total value of USD860 million, of which USD834 million was from agreements on contracting projects and USD26 million from contracts on labor service cooperation. By the end of 1998, the two sides had signed more than 900 agreements on contracting projects with a total contract value of USD1.886 billion. Overall, at the end of the last century, Chinese companies had established a good reputation in the Malaysian project contracting market, and the key areas of cooperation between the two sides included power generation equipment, substations, port dredging, road expansion, real estate development, and building construction (Ma, 1999; Jin, 1997; Huang, 2000).

Entering the 21st century, China's direct investment in Malaysia has grown linearly. According to statistics from the Malaysian Industrial Development Authority (MIDA), China invested RM134 million in Malaysia's manufacturing sector in 2006, accounting for only 0.38% of the country's total foreign investment. By 2007, China's manufacturing investment in Malaysia had jumped to RM1.88 billion, making it the seventh largest source of foreign investment in Malaysia. In addition to direct investment, the cooperation between the two countries on contracting projects has developed well. According to the statistics of the Department of Foreign Investment and Economic Cooperation of the Ministry of Commerce of China, in 2007, Chinese enterprises signed agreements on contracting projects, labor cooperation, and design and consulting in Malaysia with a total value of USD1.42 billion and a turnover of USD649 million. By the end of 2007, Chinese enterprises had signed a total of USD6.203 billion in contracts on labor service cooperation in Malaysia, with a turnover of USD3.156 billion. During this period, the key projects in Malaysia included the Penang Second Bridge, a pulp and paper manufacturing plant in Sarawak, the construction of a national high-speed broadband network, and Bakun Dam (Zhou and Chen, 2015).

Since 2013, with the promotion of the BRI, the cooperation between China and Malaysia in manufacturing, real estate, infrastructure, and other fields has become more and more substantial. In the manufacturing sector, MIDA statistics show that, in 2016, Malaysia approved a total of 33 Chinese-led projects, with a total investment of about RM4.8 billion, a year-on-year increase of 60.4%, and China became the largest annual source of foreign investment in Malaysia's manufacturing industry for the first time in history. In the field of real estate, Real Capital Analytics data showed that from 2014 to 2016, Chinese real estate developers such as Greenland and R&F invested a total of more than US$2.1 billion in real estate projects in Malaysia. In the field of infrastructure construction, China launched major projects in Malaysia such as the East Coast Railway Link and Kuantan Port. The East Coast Railway project, with an investment of USD13 billion, is the largest single transportation infrastructure project undertaken by Chinese enterprises overseas (Li and Huang, 2018; Zhang, 2018; Liu, 2015; Guo, 2016).

In recent years, the areas and entry points of Chinese investment in Malaysia have become increasingly diversified, and more and more Chinese enterprises have set up production bases, regional headquarters, and other important institutions in Malaysia. There is a clear trend of industrial chain cooperation between the two countries, based on manufacturing investment in major trade products. Electronics, mechanical equipment, and chemical products have become the main avenues of Chinese investment in Malaysia. The production capacity cooperation between China and Malaysia represents a natural progression driven by the concurrent industrial upgrading in both countries, as evidenced by the vertical integration and expansion of critical manufacturing sectors. With the implementation of RCEP and strategic planning, the Malaysian authorities encouraged capital-intensive, high value-added, and high-tech enterprises to expand their business in Malaysia, including companies engaged in automated mechanical manufacturing, aerospace, biopharmaceutical and medical devices, advanced information technology, and new energy vehicles, to promote the transformation and upgrading of Malaysia's industry.

China's trade with Malaysia used to be dominated by low- and medium-technology manufactured goods (textiles, food, plastic products, etc.), but now the proportion of high-tech products (electronic products, optical components, mechanical and electrical equipment, etc.) has increased significantly. Investment has also followed a similar trend. The sectors in which Chinese enterprises have invested are expanding from the previous concentration on daily necessities and textiles to new areas such as the Internet of Things, the digital economy, new energy, green development, automobiles and technical equipment, and biotechnology (Cheng and Zhou, 2024).

In the future, China should continue to expand investment in advanced manufacturing industries, such as alternative energy, critical mineral resources, biotechnology, semiconductor materials, aerospace, electronics and electrical appliances, artificial intelligence, and new energy vehicles, which will all become key areas of the future industrial chain cooperation between the two countries.

Supply Chain Cooperation for Mutual Benefit

China is committed to enhancing comprehensive cooperation in trade and investment with Malaysia, with the aim of utilizing Malaysia as a regional hub to expand into the broader ASEAN region. ASEAN represents a pivotal arena for global economic advancement, with the International Monetary Fund (IMF) forecasting a growth rate of 4.7% in 2023 and the Asian Development Bank (ADB) projecting a growth rate of 5% in 2024 (Liu, 2024). In terms of purchasing power parity, ASEAN accounted for 5.3% of the global economy in 2022, positioning it as the fifth largest economy following China, the United States, the European Union, and India (Zhong, 2023). Investors from China are driven by resource-seeking and policy-seeking motives, drawn to Malaysia's abundant reservoir of raw materials, notably rubber products, metals, petroleum, and petrochemical products. Malaysia also boasts a high-quality pool of human resources. Malaysia's openness and friendly attitude have allowed China's companies to invest in sectors in which they enjoy a comparative advantage, such as infrastructure construction and management. Kuantan Port, the largest port on Malaysia's east coast, plays a pivotal role in supporting the MCKIP. In 2013, China's Guangxi Beibu Gulf International Port Group made significant investments in Kuantan Port (Zhang and Liu, 2023), enhancing its capacity and transforming it into a key gateway to China and a regional shipping hub (Malaysia–China Kuantan Industrial Park, 2024). The BRI focuses on infrastructure projects, bolstering Malaysia's domestic infrastructure development. Chinese greenfield investments in the manufacturing sector enhance Malaysia's production capabilities, elevating its position in the global supply chain and paving the way for future investments. This not only fosters the growth of new industries but also scales up existing ones, stimulating economic activity and generating employment opportunities.

Of paramount significance is China's contribution of technology to Malaysia through economic cooperation. Developing countries typically acquire advanced technology through two primary channels: technology innovation and technology transfer. For nations with lower levels of economic development, industrial upgrading and structural adjustments rely heavily on access to advanced foreign technologies. Multinational corporations and their FDI serve as crucial conduits for host countries to access advanced technologies. In the realm of international technology transfer, multinationals primarily utilize two approaches: internalized technology transfers within their subsidiaries through FDI and externalized technology transfers to other enterprises through various means such as technology sales, licensing, and collaborative research and development. To safeguard their technological advantages, multinationals often refrain from transferring core technologies to external entities. Technology spillover typically occurs through three main avenues: human resource development; forward and backward linkages; and imitating, learning, and competition. Local employees in MNCs acquire the knowledge and skills essential for mastering advanced technologies, which are subsequently disseminated through changing employment or entrepreneurial endeavors. Technical information from multinationals permeates local upstream and downstream enterprises, fostering industrial support systems and catalyzing the formation of industrial clusters. By imitating and learning from multinationals, local enterprises enhance their technological capabilities and stimulate innovation. Market competition pressures from MNCs prompt technological advancements among local enterprises.

In the context of the integrated steel project by Alliance Steel in MCKIP, technology spillover has been observed but remains limited due to substantial capacity and technology gaps. Alliance Steel, established in 2014 with investments from Guangxi Beibu Gulf Port International Group and Guangxi Shenglong Metallurgical, focuses on long steel and H-beam production, boasting an annual output of 3.5 million tons. The local labor market's inadequacy in providing skilled workers necessitated the recruitment of Chinese technicians initially, with a gradual shift toward local employment. However, the lack of comparable local enterprises impedes the dissemination of technology among skilled workers. The importation of raw materials from countries like Australia and Indonesia underscores Malaysia's insufficient supply of domestic resources for steel production. While Alliance Steel engages local enterprises for construction and logistics, technology spillover remains limited along the supply chain, hindering the formation of new industrial chains. In short, while technology spillover exists in the case of Alliance Steel, its impact is also limited by significant capacity and technology differentials. Malaysia's pursuit of independent research and innovation stands as the fundamental pathway forward.

Conclusion

This chapter provides a concise overview of the economic relations between China and Malaysia since the establishment of diplomatic ties in 1974, with a focus on trade and investment. It highlights the notable features of the evolution of China and Malaysia's economic relations in the past fifty years. The economic relations have evolved from a singular mode characterized by the trade of raw materials and finished products into a triumvirate mode, dominated by trade in intermediate goods and services, complemented by substantial growth in two-way FDI. As of 2023, China maintained its status as Malaysia's leading trading partner for the 15th consecutive year, while Malaysia continued to rank among China's top trading partners within the ASEAN bloc, with the bulk of bilateral trade being semi-finished products and parts and components. The increasing proportion of intermediate goods and the declining share of raw materials in the overall bilateral trade signify the concurrent sophistication of both economies and their deepening integration into the global value chain. Remarkably, China has emerged as a substantial investor in Malaysia's manufacturing sector and plays a prominent role in contractual services within Malaysia's infrastructure and real estate sectors. It is noteworthy that Malaysia also once took the lead in investing in China during the initial phases of China's economic reforms from the 1970s to the 1990s. The sustained two-way investment underscores the enduring and mutually beneficial economic partnership between the two countries. However, since the 2010s, the rapid growth of Chinese OFDI into Malaysia has notably outpaced the flow of Malaysian FDI into China.

What accounted for the resilience and momentum of the China–Malaysia economic relations over the past fifty years? Firstly, both countries prioritize economic development. The implementation of export-oriented industrialization strategies made both countries important members of the East Asian production network. Although their development timelines and trajectories differ, the manufacturing capability and technological levels of both countries have continued to develop and upgrade over the past fifty years. Secondly, both countries have maintained strategic communication and dialogue from the very beginning. This dialogue appears in an institutionalized form at the government level (e.g., ASEAN+3, CAFTA, and RCEP), as well as in an informal form at the grassroots level where exchanges between peoples and between the corporate sectors are vibrant at all levels of society in both countries. Finally, both countries uphold a shared vision of prosperity in Asia (Anwar Ibrahim, 1996). Although their social and cultural backgrounds differ, the common vision for rejuvenation, prosperity, and peace transcends occasional disagreements between the two countries. The leaders from both sides, over the decades, have worked to consolidate bilateral

106 *Zhang Miao & Li Ran*

relations while rationally managing differences so that these differences will not negatively impact bilateral relations. By establishing a strong foundation in trade and investment, fostering enhanced technological cooperation, and championing sustainable development practices, China and Malaysia are poised to collaboratively steer the course of development of Malaysia and China's economic and trade relations in the next five decades.

References

Anwar Ibrahim (1996). *The Asian Renaissance*. Singapore: Times Books.

Cheng, Aiping, and Zhou Huaming (2024). "Zhongqi dui Malaixiya touzi ridian (Hot Spots for Chinese Enterprises to Invest in Malaysia)." *Hezuo jingji yu keji* (*Co-operative Economy and Science*), No. 3, pp. 58–60.

Guo, Ming (2016). *Zhongguo qiye zai Malaixiya zhijie touzi yanjiu* (*A Study on Chinese Enterprises' Direct Investment in Malaysia*). Unpublished Master Thesis, Central China Normal University.

Huang, Huicheng (2000). *Jiushiniandai Zhongma guanxi de fazhan yu Malaixiya huaren* (*The Development of Sino-Malaysian Relations and Malaysian Chinese in the 1990s*). Unpublished Master Thesis, Jinan University.

Jiang, Yang, and Hartini Husin (2023). "Assessing the Economic Impact and Welfare Effects of RCEP: A Case Study of Malaysia's Progress in the ASEAN-China Free Trade Agreement." *The Journal of International Trade & Economic Development*, Online First Article. https://doi.org/10.1080/096 38199.2023.2285861.

Jin, Ge (1997). "Malaixiya huanying Zhongguo qiyejia qu touzi (Malaysia welcomes Chinese Entrepreneurs to Invest)." *Zhongwai qiyejia* (*Chinese and Foreign Entrepreneurs*), No. 5, pp. 17–18.

Li, Hao and Huang Xiaoyu (2018). "Dui Malaixiya de touzi: Zhongguo de jiyu yu fengxian (Investing in Malaysia: Opportunities and Risks for China)." *Duiwai jingmao shiwu* (*Practices in Economic Relations and Trade*), No. 1, pp. 22–25.

Liu, Hui (2024). "Dongmeng jingji shixian chixuwenbu zengzhang (ASEAN to Achieve Steady Growth)." *Renmin Ribao*, 28 February. http://paper.people. com.cn/rmrb/html/2024-02/28/nw.D110000renmrb_20240228_1-15.htm.

Liu, Shiyi (2015). "Zhongguo dui Malaixiya zhijie touzi xianzhuang ji fazhan qianjing fenxi (Current Situation and Development Prospect of China's Direct Investment in Malaysia)." *Tongji yu guanli* (*Statistics and Management*), No. 3, pp. 56–59.

Ma, Yong (1999). "Zhongma guanxi de xianzhuang yu qianjing: Jinian Zhongma jianjiao 25 zhounian (Current Situation and Prospects of China-Malaysia

Relations: Commemorating the 25th Anniversary of the Establishment of Diplomatic Relations between China and Malaysia." *Nanya Dongnanya yanjiu (South and Southeast Asian Studies)*, No. 4, pp. 35–40.

Malaysia–China Kuantan Industrial Park (2024). "General Overview of Malaysia-China Kuantan Industrial Park." http://zmqzcyyq.gxzf.gov.cn/zmhz/gdygk/t3190648.shtml.

Tham, Siew Yean, Andrew Kam Yi Jia, and Tee Beng Ann (2019). "U.S.–China Trade War: Potential Trade and Investment Spillovers into Malaysia." *Asian Economic Papers*, Vol. 18, No. 3, pp. 117–135.

Wang, Wangbo (2004). *Gaige kaifang yilai dongnanya huashang zai Zhongguo dalu de touzi yanjiu (A Study of the Investment of Southeast Asian Chinese Business in Mainland China since the Reform and Opening Up)*. Xiamen: Xiamen University Press.

Yeoh, Emile Kok-Kheng (2019). "Malaysia: Perception of Contemporary China and Its Economic, Political and Societal Determinants." *The Pacific Review*, Vol. 32, No. 3, pp. 395–418.

Yeoh, Emile Kok-Kheng, Chang Le, and Zhang Yemo (2018). "China–Malaysia Trade, Investment, and Cooperation in the Contexts of China–ASEAN Integration and the 21st Century Maritime Silk Road Construction." *The Chinese Economy*, Vol. 51, No. 4, pp. 298–317.

Zhang, Miao (2018). "Malaixiya daxuanhou de jingjing xinshi jidui woguo zai ma touzi de yingxiang (Malaysia's Economic Situation after the General Election and Its impact on China's Investment in Malaysia)." *Yatai anquan yu haiyang yanjiu (Asia-Pacific Security and Maritime Affairs)*, No. 6, pp. 109–119.

Zhang, Miao, and Li Ran (2018). "The Impact of China's Economic Restructuring on Southeast Asia: An Investment Perspective." *International Journal of China Studies*, Vol. 8, No. 2, pp. 1–30.

Zhang, Niansheng, and Liu Hui (2023). "Xieshou tuidong Mazhong Guandan chanyeyuan zouxiang xinhuihuang (Join Hands to Promote Malaysia-China Kuantan Industrial Park to New Glory)." *China Belt and Road Portal*, 4 April. https://www.yidaiyilu.gov.cn/p/08OEEB92.html.

Zhong, Feiteng (2023). "Zhongguo zhuli Dongmeng dazao jingji zengzhang zhongxin (China to Help ASEAN Build an Economic Growth Center)." *Guangmingwang*, 9 September. https://theory.gmw.cn/2023-09/09/content_36820796.htm.

Zhou, Kun and Chen Bingxian (2015). "2004–2013 Malaixiya Zhongzi qiye de touzi jiqi yingxiang (Investment and Impact of Chinese Enterprises in Malaysia from 2004 to 2013)." *Dongnanya zongheng (Crossroads: Southeast Asian Studies)*, No. 4, pp. 69–73.

© 2025 World Scientific Publishing Company
https://doi.org/10.1142/9789819801350_0007

Chapter 7

Malaysia's Trade and Investment Links with China: An Update

Andrew Kam Jia Yi and Tham Siew Yean

Introduction

Foreign direct investment (FDI) and international trade have always been important for Malaysia as it is a small, open, developing economy that depends on FDI for capital, technology, and exports while imports provide sources of inputs that are needed for FDI in the manufacturing sector. FDI peaked at 8.8% of gross domestic product (GDP) in 1992. This percentage dropped substantially over the years, reaching a new peak at 5.4% of GDP in 2021 before falling to 3.6% in 2022. Likewise, international trade has been over 100% of GDP since 1979, peaking at 220% in 2000 before dropping to 147% in 2022.[1]

China has been Malaysia's largest trading partner since 2009 with bilateral trade growing continuously over time. This bilateral trade is boosted through different channels. It is linked through the multinationals operating in the region, including in China, due to the global fragmentation of production, especially in the electrical and electronics (E&E) industry. Although Malaysia does not have a bilateral trade agreement with China, it is a member of trade agreements that also involve China, via the Association of Southeast Asian Nations (ASEAN) and

---

[1] These are data available from the World Bank (https://data.worldbank.org/indicator/ BX.KLT.DINV.WD.GD.ZS?locations=MY).

ASEAN-Plus agreements, including the Regional Comprehensive Economic Partnership (RCEP) agreement. Malaysia also has a Comprehensive Strategic Partnership with China that fosters cooperation between the two countries in various areas, including trade and investments.

The launch of the Belt and Road Initiative (BRI) in 2013 increased China's investment interest in Malaysia. However, despite the strong links in trade in the E&E sector, the sectors of interest for China's investors in Malaysia are diverse, with no particular focus on the E&E sector. This raises an important question: What is the impact of the increase in Chinese investments in Malaysia on the merchandise trade between the two countries? This chapter aims to investigate if the nature of merchandise trade between the two countries has changed with the increase in Chinese investments in Malaysia since the BRI was launched.

China's Investments in Malaysia

In the 1980s and 1990s, Japanese direct investments (JDI) garnered the largest share as a source country for inflows of FDI into Malaysia due to the significant increase in the value of the yen after the Plaza Accord in 1985 that triggered the outflows of JDI in search of lower production costs (Tham, 2005). On the other hand, outward FDI from China was formally promoted in China's "Go Overseas" Policy in 2001 (Cheng and Ma, 2010). Although natural resources attracted Chinese FDI to Africa, Central Asia, Southeast Asia, and Australia, Malaysia was not listed among the top ten recipients of China's FDI stock by the end of 2006. Thus, within Southeast Asia, China invested mostly in the natural resources of Indonesia and Cambodia. Malaysia was not a significant host economy for China before the BRI was launched in 2013.

Overall Pattern of Chinese Investments in Malaysia

It should be noted at the outset that published data on Chinese investments in Malaysia are fragmented and incomplete at the macro level, while micro-level data are not available. Despite this data challenge, it is still possible to identify the major Chinese investments and the main sectors receiving these investments.

As shown in Figure 1, in 2012, just before the launch of the BRI, Chinese investments constituted 0.34% of the total net inflows of FDI into

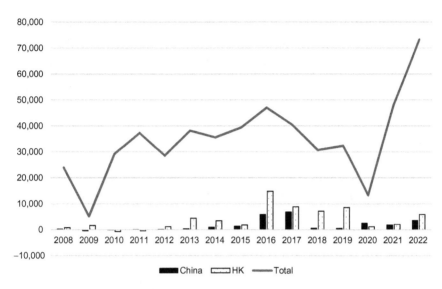

Figure 1. Net Inflows of Chinese Investments, 2008–2022 (RM million).
Source: Bank Negara Malaysia.

Malaysia. The launch of the BRI represented a watershed in the history of China's investments in Malaysia as the Najib administration was quick to embrace the initiative (Nur Shahadah Jamil, 2023). This attracted the attention of China's investors who were eager to follow the call of the BRI to Malaysia. At the same time, there were changes within China such as saturation of the domestic market and increasing costs (including labor costs) that created market-seeking and efficiency reasons for China's outward investments. China's subsequent investments abroad also sought to seek knowledge and strategic assets. These push-and-pull factors led to a jump of more than tenfold in the net inflows into Malaysia from China, albeit from a low base of a mere RM96 million to RM975 million in the span of one year after the launch of the BRI.

This number then grew rapidly to peak at RM6,886 million in 2017 or 17% of the total net inflows for that year. It was reported that Malaysia and China signed 14 Memorandums of Understanding (MoUs) worth RM143.6 billion in defense, economy, agriculture, education, finance, and construction during Najib's visit to China in late 2016. However, the general elections in 2018 led to a change in administration from Najib Abdul Razak to Mahathir Mohammad, who had used rhetoric critical of the

China-related investment projects during the election campaign. The Mahathir administration also paused the East Coast Rail Link (ECRL) project, which is China's flagship infrastructure project in Malaysia. The uncertainty over the Mahathir administration's receptivity toward Chinese investments led to a sharp drop in Chinese investments in 2018, which fell to RM562 million or 1.8% of the total net inflows for that year.

After the ECRL project was reinstated in 2019, investments from China rebounded in 2020 despite the emergence of the COVID-19 pandemic and the negative impact of the subsequent lockdowns on the global and national economies. Investments from China climbed to RM2,521 million or 20% of the total net inflows, even as the total net inflows nosedived from RM32,364 million in 2019 to RM13,281 million in 2020. China's prolonged lockdown and zero-COVID policy affected outward investments. Investments from China to Malaysia fell to RM1,819 million in 2021; subsequently, with the opening of China's economy, the investments from China to Malaysia increased to RM3,615 million in 2022.

Sectoral Distribution

Although services garnered a bigger share of total inflows of net FDI from China from 2015–2017, the situation was reversed from 2018 and 2021–2022 (Figure 2). In 2019, the manufacturing sector had negative net

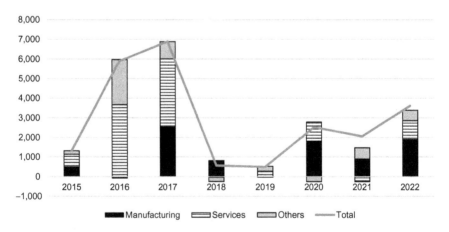

Figure 2. Chinese Investments by Sectors, 2015–2022 (RM million).
Source: Department of Statistics Malaysia (DOSM).

inflows, implying that at least one of the components of net FDI was negative and it was not offset by positive amounts in the remaining components. Since the focus of this chapter is on merchandise trade, investments in the manufacturing sector are examined in the following.

Manufacturing

As shown in Figure 3, the approved investments in manufacturing indicate that a diverse range of sub-sectors is involved, including basic metal products, petroleum products, non-metallic products, E&E (mainly solar), paper, printing and publishing, and transport equipment. Since detailed micro data are not available, it is not possible to examine all the sub-sectors involved. Instead, based on the availability of firm-level data, the first two largest recipients (namely, steel and solar) and textile and textile products are discussed in the following as well as in the trade section to investigate the possible impact on international trade.

Steel Investments

Basic metal products have garnered the largest share of approved investments in manufacturing since 2013. This sector provides crucial input for

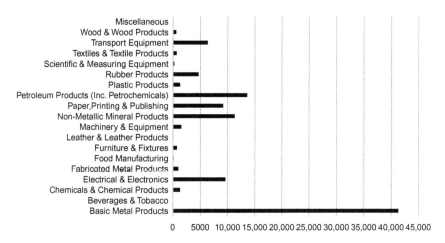

Figure 3. Total Approved Investments in Manufacturing, 2013–2023 (RM million).
Source: Malaysian Investment Development Authority.

114 Andrew Kam Jia Yi & Tham Siew Yean

Table 1. Chinese Investments in the Steel Industry in Malaysia as of 2024.

State	Name of Company
Kedah	ZXT Ruifeng Trading Sdn Bhd
Selangor	Xin Lon Sdn Bhd
Pahang	Alliance Steel Sdn Bhd
	Ji Kang Dimensi Sdn Bhd
	De Long Global Group (M) Sdn Bhd
Johor	Esteel Enterprise Pte Ltd
Kelantan	Xin Sheng Industries Sdn Bhd
Terengganu	Eastern Steel Sdn Bhd
	JXR Manufacturing Sdn Bhd
Sabah	Esteel Enterprises Labuan Sdn Bhd
	Esteel Enterprises Labuan Sdn Bhd (green steel at another location in Sabah which is in the planning stage)
Sarawak	Wenan Steel (Malaysia) Sdn Bhd (under construction)

Source: Malaysian Iron and Steel Federation (unpublished).

other manufacturing sectors like machinery and equipment (M&E), transport equipment, medical devices, energy, communication devices, and scientific equipment. Consequently, China has identified Southeast Asia, including Malaysia, as a potentially large demand market for steel (Tham and Yeoh, 2020). The region's high demand for infrastructure such as urban railway train lines, highways, bridges, roads, flyovers, dams, and power plants matches BRI aims and fuels the demand for steel. This demand also matches China's excess production capacity for steel and the increasingly difficult export market for steel made in China, as it is facing more anti-dumping probes launched in Western countries.

Chinese steel investments are distributed over numerous states in the Malay Peninsula as well as East Malaysia (Table 1). Of these investments, Alliance Steel is the most publicized project, due to its size and scale, as well as its location within the Malaysia–China Kuantan Industrial Park (MCKIP), which is the first national industrial park in the country. Alliance Steel is a state-owned joint-stock foreign investment enterprise into which Guangxi Beibu Gulf Port International Group Co. Ltd. and Guangxi Shenglong Metallugical Co. Ltd have jointly invested. The reported investment value of Alliance Steel is USD1.4 billion, and the factory covers 710 acres of the park. It produces high-speed wire rods, bar rods, and H-beam steel with an annual production of 3.5 million tons. It has been operating since 2018.

The investment by Alliance Steel, however, has not been free from controversy as it posed challenges to the domestic steel sector even though Alliance Steel is producing long steel. Operationally, it is required to export 50% of its steel but there have been allegations to the contrary by local producers which claim that the domestic market has been impinged upon by Alliance Steel's production and sale (*The Edge*, 2024).

Since MCKIP and Alliance Steel were established to provide traffic for Kuantan Port, the data on the port's throughput provides some indication of the impact of Alliance Steel on trade. Although there is no firm-level data available, the trade going through Kuantan Port indicates some changes that can be attributed to the construction of Alliance Steel at MCKIP. While the port was used primarily to export natural resources and resource-based products from the east coast region, with few imports due to the lack of manufacturing activities prior to the establishment of the park (Tham, 2019), the construction of Alliance Steel in 2017 and 2018 led to a jump in imports, specifically in machinery and transport equipment that were needed for the construction of Alliance Steel's factory. All the equipment and major inputs needed were imported from China in order to expedite the construction.

Solar Investments

The next largest recipient in manufacturing is the E&E sub-sector. Of particular importance are solar investments from China since Malaysia has aspired to develop an entire solar industry ecosystem — from research and development and design to the production of metal silicon, polysilicon/ ingots, solar wafer/cells, and solar modules — since the Eighth Malaysia Plan (2001–2005) (Malaysia, 2011). Therefore, the Malaysian Investment Development Authority (MIDA) has been targeting FDI for the development of the solar ecosystem, using fiscal incentives (such as tax holidays, investment tax allowances, reinvestment allowances, and import duty exemptions) and non-fiscal incentives (such as a feed-in tariff scheme and a green technology funding scheme). Malaysia's relatively low electricity and labor costs add to the locational advantages of this type of investment.

In 2008, Malaysia received RM12 billion in photovoltaic (PV) industries. Four well-known solar companies, First Solar, Q-Cells, SunPower, and Tokuyama (from the US, Taiwan, Germany, and Japan, respectively), invested in Malaysia. Malaysia was the fourth country in the world in the production of PV cells after China, Germany, and Japan in that year. By 2009, due to FDIs, Malaysia became the third largest producer of PV cells after China and Germany, overtaking Japan in just a year. All these developments predated the BRI.

Externally, in 2014, the US raised tariffs up to 165% on crystalline solar products imported from China. The imposition of these duties on the import of Chinese solar panels instigated the relocation of Chinese manufacturers to other countries such as Malaysia, Korea, and Taiwan to circumvent the tariffs as well as to lower costs by seeking out lowest-cost markets. These push-and-pull factors led to the relocation of solar investments out of China into Southeast Asia, including in Malaysia. Penang in Malaysia benefited from the relocation as the state hosted factories run by China's JA Solar (2015) and Jinko (2015). Subsequently, Xian Longi invested in Kuching Sarawak in 2016 (Zhang, 2021).

China also announced a shift toward green infrastructure, green investment, and green financing at the 2019 Second Belt and Road Forum for International Cooperation (Pike, 2019). This led to another round of solar investment in Peninsular Malaysia as well as East Malaysia (Table 2).

Table 2. Chinese Investments in the Solar Industry in Malaysia as of 2024.

Before 2019		After 2019	
Name of Company	Year of Establishment	Name of Company	Year of Establishment
Xinyi Solar Holdings (Melaka)	2015	Risen Energy (Kedah)	2021
JA Solar (Penang)	2015	SBH Kibing Solar New Materials and SBH Kibing Silicon Materials (Sabah)	2022
Jinko (Penang)	2017	Consortium of Haitai Solar, China Machinery Engineering Corp (CMEC), Adam Digital Assets Sdn Bhd and Solar Pulse Sdn Bhd (Sarawak)	2023
Longi (Sarawak)	2017	Longi Green Energy (Selangor)	2023

Source: Compiled by the Authors.

Since the PV cells produced by Chinese investment are exported to the international market, including to the US market, there have been investigations undertaken by the US on the domestic value-added (DVA) content of the plants in Malaysia. For example, the US Department of Commerce investigated the use of assembly in Malaysia and export to the US for circumventing anti-dumping and countervailing duties and found that circumvention did occur (Bond *et al.*, 2023). This would imply that the production of these PV cells depended on imports from China for its assembly operations in Malaysia.

Textiles and Textile Products

The enterprise D&Y Textile (Malaysia) Sdn. Bhd. is one of China's earlier investments in Malaysia. A total of USD200 million in green field investment was planned to build a world-class modern textile industrial park at Sendai Industrial Park in Johor (Gomez *et al.*, 2020). Good infrastructure, investment incentives, and relatively low energy prices attracted the company to Malaysia in 2014. In addition, duty-free import of raw cotton for the fabrication of yarn in the Malaysian factory was another additional pull factor. At that time, Malaysia was also negotiating to join the Trans-Pacific Partnership (TPP) Agreement, which included the US as a participating member until it pulled out in 2017. The TPP also had a yarn forward rule which required yarn used in the manufacture of clothing for export to member countries to be sourced from within member countries. Production in Malaysia would have benefitted D&Y greatly had the US remained in the TPP. Production at D&Y started in 2018.

Summary of the Three Sectors

Since Malaysia is a relatively small country, it is inevitable that investments must have an export component. The government also imposed export conditions for investment incentives such as pioneer status. In terms of domestic sourcing, there is a tendency to depend on imports from China for quality and cost reasons as well as the need to assist Chinese suppliers to internationalize their operations through exports. Malaysian small and medium firms may not be able to compete with the scale, efficiency, and costs of Chinese suppliers, leading the factories in Malaysia to be import dependent for their exports.

118 Andrew Kam Jia Yi & Tham Siew Yean

Malaysia–China Trade

Trade Trends

China holds significant importance in Malaysia's trade landscape across various dimensions. As one of Malaysia's largest trading partners, China's economic ties have proliferated over the years, underscoring a robust bilateral trade relationship. This partnership spans a diverse array of sectors, encompassing iron and steel, electronics, machinery, and chemicals, as well as key commodities such as palm oil and rubber. The substantial volume of goods flowing between the two nations underlines the pivotal role China plays in Malaysia's export-oriented economy. Since 2012, Malaysia has consistently experienced a trade deficit with China, indicating that its imports from China have exceeded its exports to the country (Figure 4). This deficit persisted and even widened until 2016, reflecting a sustained period of imbalanced trade relations. However, starting in 2017, there was a noticeable improvement in Malaysia's trade balance with China, characterized by a gradual narrowing of the deficit. This positive trend continued until 2020, as Malaysia implemented strategies to enhance export

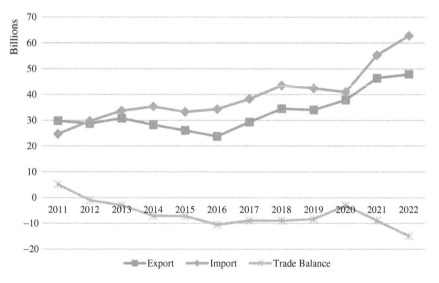

Figure 4.   Malaysia's Total Trade with China (2011–2022).

Note: In USD billions.
Source: UN Comtrade.

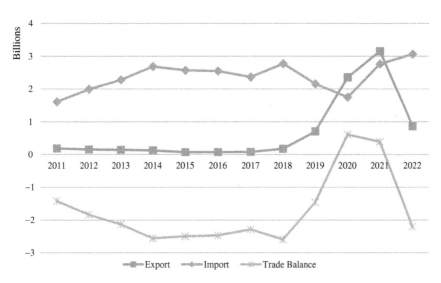

Figure 5. Malaysia's Trade with China in Iron and Steel (2011–2022).
Note: In USD billions. See Appendix 1 for product codes.
Source: UN Comtrade.

competitiveness and diversify its trade portfolio. Nevertheless, this progress was interrupted as the trade balance took a sharp downturn from 2021 onward, plunging into deficit once more by 2022. This abrupt reversal may be attributed to several factors, including shifts in global demand patterns, fluctuations in commodity prices, and the impact of external shocks such as the COVID-19 pandemic.

As one of the top approved investment sectors (see Figure 3), the iron and steel sector of Malaysia grappled with a widening deficit in its trade of iron and steel, signaling an imbalance where imports surpassed exports (Figure 5). However, a shift occurred in 2018 when the trade balance began to improve, largely attributed to the imposition of anti-dumping taxes on iron and steel imports from China and Vietnam. These protective measures aimed to shield local producers from the influx of cheaper imports, thereby fostering a more level playing field. Consequently, Malaysia witnessed trade surpluses in iron and steel in both 2020 and 2021, reflecting newfound competitiveness and resilience within the domestic industry. Despite these gains, the trade balance reverted to a deficit in 2022, likely influenced by global demand fluctuations, commodity price volatility, and ongoing challenges posed by the

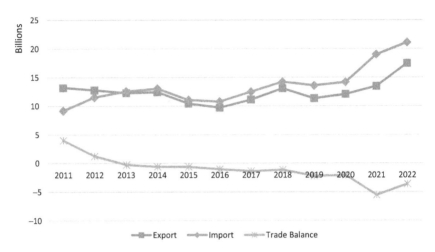

Figure 6. Malaysia's Trade with China in Overall E&E (2011–2022).
Note: In USD billions. See Appendix 1 for product codes.
Source: UN Comtrade.

pandemic. Trade in the other key manufacturing products is shown in Figure 6 (E&E), Figure 7 (Solar), and Figure 8 (Textile and Textile articles).

Figure 6 shows Malaysia's trade with China in one of the largest export sectors, the E&E [in both final and parts and components (PNC)] sector. Before 2013, Malaysia had enjoyed a surplus in the trade of E&E products. However, from 2013 onward, this surplus gradually eroded, giving way to a deficit as imports of E&E products began to outpace exports. Several factors likely contributed to this shift, including evolving market demands, intensifying global competition, and changes in supply chain dynamics as Chinese semiconductor suppliers began experiencing immense growth. One important product of the semiconductor sector is the production of solar-related products. Initially, Malaysia enjoyed a trade surplus in solar products, only to face deficits in 2014 and 2015 (Figure 7). However, a significant turnaround occurred in 2016, marked by an improvement in the trade balance, which transitioned back to a surplus. This positive momentum persisted into 2017, with Malaysia once again boasting a surplus in its trade of solar products with China. However, from 2018 to 2021, the sector experienced a reversal, returning to deficits. The US–China trade war may have contributed to this trend, as

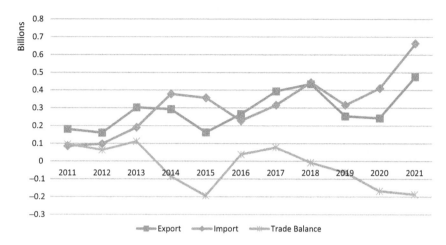

Figure 7. Malaysia's Trade with China in Solar Products (2011–2022).
Note: In USD Billions. See Appendix 1 for product codes.
Source: UN Comtrade.

mentioned in the earlier section. The production of these PV cells, involving assembly operations in Malaysia, has depended increasingly on imports from China as Malaysian small and medium enterprises (SMEs) are unable to compete with suppliers from China. SMEs in China are bigger in terms of size and are more competitive as they have economies of scale on their side since they supply to a much larger domestic economy.

Finally, Figure 8 shows that the trade relationship between Malaysia and China in the textile and textile articles sector has been characterized by a persistent deficit spanning the years 2011 to 2022. Despite ongoing trade activities, Malaysia consistently imported more textile goods from China than it exported during this period. However, a significant shift occurred between 2014 and 2016, marked by a sudden and notable widening of the trade deficit. One potential factor is increased competition from other low-cost textile-producing countries. During this period, countries like Vietnam and Bangladesh emerged as strong competitors in the global textile market, offering lower production costs and more competitive pricing compared to Malaysia. To examine the competitiveness of Malaysia's exports to China, we use the comparative advantage indicator and to identify the extent to which countries trade similar products both ways, we use the intra-industry indicator.

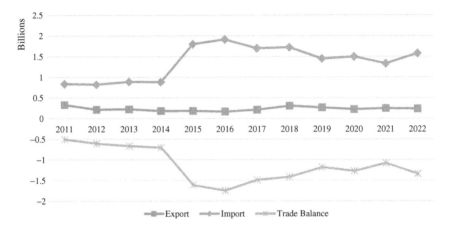

Figure 8. Malaysia's Trade with China in Textile and Textile Articles (2011–2022).
Note: In USD billions. See Appendix 1 for product codes.
Source: UN Comtrade.

Trade Competitiveness and Intra-Industry Trade

Bilateral revealed comparative advantage (RCA) between Malaysia and China indicates the degree to which Malaysia specializes in and holds a comparative advantage in producing specific goods relative to China. In essence, it measures Malaysia's comparative advantage in exporting certain products to China. Apart from assessing the competitiveness of Malaysia's exports to China, the level of mutual reliance or interdependence between industries is also evaluated using the intra-industry trade (IIT) index, known as the Grubel–Lloyd (GL) index.[2] Figure 9 further illustrates the competitiveness of Malaysia's products in the Chinese market while also indicating mutual dependency, highlighting the two-way trade dynamics between China and Malaysia. This interdependence is influenced by factors such as shared global supply chains. This is particularly prevalent for the E&E sector whereby both the RCA and GL indicators are high, as can be seen in Figure 9(a). However, when decomposing E&E exports into PNC and final goods, the trends are rather contrasting.

As shown in Figure 9(b), PNC E&E exports from Malaysia continued to maintain their competitiveness in the Chinese market throughout the analyzed period. Despite experiencing a temporary decline below a

---

[2] See Appendix 2 for further descriptions on the bilateral RCA index and the GL IIT index.

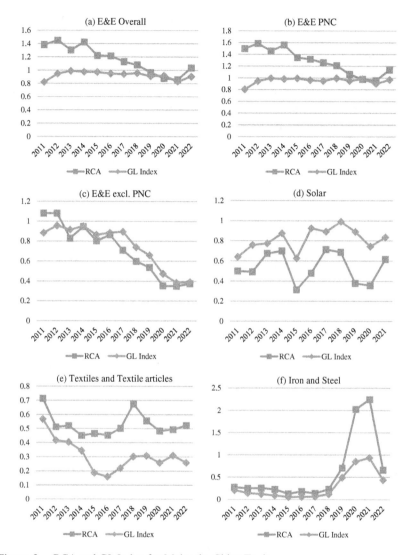

Figure 9. RCA and GL Index for Malaysia–China Trade.
Source: Calculated from UN Comtrade. See Appendix 2 for RCA and GL calculation.

comparative advantage threshold of 1 in 2020 and 2021, attributed to the disruptive impact of the COVID-19 pandemic on global trade dynamics, Malaysia's PNC E&E exports regained their comparative advantage (RCA > 1) in China by 2022. Notably, IIT within this sector remained consistently high, with the GL index hovering near one across the years under review. This resilience in IIT was particularly remarkable considering the challenging circumstances posed by both the trade war between the United States and China and the ongoing COVID-19 pandemic. It is worth highlighting that PNC E&E exports exhibited the highest GL index among all the products analyzed, indicating the robust and strong two-way trade between Malaysia and China within this crucial sector.

In contrast, exports of E&E final goods (referred to as E&E excluding PNC) to China exhibit a declining comparative advantage (RCA) and reduced intra-industry trade (IIT), as shown in Figure 9(c). This decline indicates a waning volume of Malaysian exports of E&E to China. The decrease in RCA started in 2012, suggesting that Malaysia's comparative advantage in these items has been gradually eroding over time. Furthermore, after 2017, there was a noticeable decline in the GL index, which gauges the intensity of trade within an industry. This suggests that throughout this time, Malaysia and China's level of trade integration within the E&E sector may have significantly decreased. One possible contributing element to this reduction could be the beginning of the US–China trade war. Due to the expected disruption of supply chains, rise in uncertainty, and reduction in bilateral trade flows, the trade tensions between the two largest economies in the world had an effect on the export dynamics of E&E final goods.

As shown in Figure 9(d), despite the relatively high GL index indicating significant trade integration between Malaysia and China in the solar product sector, Malaysia exhibits a comparative disadvantage in exporting solar products specifically to China. This paradox suggests that while Malaysia and China maintain a strong trade relationship in the solar sector, Malaysia struggles to compete effectively in supplying solar products to the Chinese market. It also implies that solar exports from Malaysia are meant for third countries, such as the US or other countries in the developed world.

Malaysia's textile exports to China lack a comparative advantage as the RCA is below 1 and its trend plateaued after 2017, indicating that Malaysia's competitive position in textile exports to China has reached a standstill or experienced minimal growth, as revealed in Figure 9(e). The declining GL index further reveals a diminishing degree of intra-industry trade between Malaysia and China in the textile sector during this period. Potential contributing factors to this decline may reflect increased competition from other trading partners or regions.

The iron and steel sector, on the other hand, has transitioned from a comparative "disadvantaged" position to an "advantaged" one in 2020.

However, it returned to a disadvantaged status in 2022, thus revealing a volatile landscape in the trade pattern of this sector. This fluctuation suggests a notable shift in the competitiveness of iron and steel exports between Malaysia and China over this period. The GL index displays an increase in intra-industry trade from 2018 to 2021, which is aligned with the enhancement of comparative advantage during the same period. This rise indicates a strengthening of trade ties between Malaysia and China in the iron and steel sector, potentially driven by factors such as increased demand, improved production efficiency, or favorable trade policies. However, the decline in 2022 can be attributed to the decrease in iron and steel exports from China.

Value-Added Trade

Changes in comparative advantage should also be analyzed along with the trade in value-added (TiVA) indicator to examine whether the sourcing of inputs from China has changed in the wake of an increase in Chinese investments in Malaysia. Table 3 shows an increase in the backward participation indicator, which suggests that China's contribution to Malaysia's total gross exports has increased to 6.6% in 2020. Even during the period of the trade war from 2017–2020, China's contribution to Malaysia's value-added content of gross export increased from 5.3% to 6.6% (a nearly 1.5% increase). The table also shows DVA in the exports of different industries of importance to the Malaysia–China trade. An increase in DVA content in exports implies an increase in local economic activities. If these local activities are of high quality or value, then they are competitive in the international arena. In other words, a high DVA and RCA imply that domestic producers have local advantages (such as labor, capital, and trade policy regimes) to specialize in the export of a particular product compared to other nations, industries, and/or companies (Kam, 2017).

Table 3 shows a significant shift in the Domestic Value-Added (DVA) share of iron and steel exports to China over the years, increasing from 41% to 56% from 1995 to 2020. Notably, during the trade war period from 2017 to 2020, this share experienced a further increment from 1.2% to 1.5% (using the *basic metals* and *basic metals and fabricated metal products* in TiVA classifications as proxy for iron and steel). This trend suggests a growing reliance on domestic value addition within the iron and

Table 3. Backward Linkages and Domestic Value-Added as Percent of Gross Exports in Malaysia–China Trade.

Backward Participation in GVC	China		
2015	5.3986		
2016	5.0894		
2017	5.2903		
2018	5.5122		
2019	5.6092		
2020	6.5799		
Domestic value-added as percentage of gross exports			
Industries	1995	2017	2020
Basic metals	40.9	54.9	56.4
Basic metals and fabricated metal products	44.5	55.1	56.4
Computer, electronic, and electrical equipment	38.1	48.2	49.2
Computer, electronic, and optical products	38.2	48.0	49.0
Electrical equipment	37.4	51.9	52.2
Machinery and equipment	50.5	56.2	57.1
Manufacturing	61.1	54.9	56.2
Textiles, wearing apparel, leather, and related products	53.7	67.0	70.4

Note: Backward linkage refers to the ratio of the "Foreign value-added content of exports" to the economy's total gross exports. This is the "Buyer" perspective or sourcing side of GVC, where Malaysia imports intermediates from China to produce its exports.
Source: OECD–TiVA database.

steel sector, indicating potential efforts to bolster domestic production capabilities or reduce dependence on foreign inputs amid trade uncertainties. This is similar to textiles and apparel which also exhibit a higher proportion of domestic content in exports compared to foreign content. The DVA share of exports in textiles, wearing apparel, leather, and related products to China increased from 67% to nearly 71% from 2017 to 2020. This suggests a strengthening of domestic value addition within the textiles and apparels sector, potentially driven by efforts to enhance domestic production capacities or improve value chain efficiencies.

In contrast, the DVA share of exports in the Electrical and Electronic (E&E) sector, encompassing computer, electronic, and electrical equipment, has remained below 50% from 1995 to 2020. However, within this category, the DVA share of electrical equipment exports surged from 37% to 52.2% in 2020. Interestingly, despite the trade war period, there are no indications of a decrease in DVA, implying a likely increase in foreign value-added (FVA) within the E&E sector from 2017 to 2020, potentially driven by supply chain diversification efforts or changes in production strategies. The high reliance on FVA implies that the industry is vulnerable to disruptions in global value chains. It also indicates that Malaysian SMEs operating within this sector are less competitive compared with China's SMEs that produce the inputs needed for this sector. Increasing geopolitical tensions can lead to delays, shortages, or increased costs for imported inputs, which can significantly impact the production and competitiveness of industries relying on those inputs.

Conclusion

The ongoing trade war between China and the US has brought some shifts in Malaysia's trade and investment links with China. China's investments in Malaysia remained buoyant in different key sectors. Investments in these sectors have further strengthened trade relations between Malaysia and China. The trade in E&E goods continues to dominate the bilateral trade between Malaysia and China. The E&E sector between China and Malaysia has demonstrated remarkable resilience in its value chains. This resilience stems from the deep integration of the E&E supply chain and the strong, well-established partnerships between Chinese and Malaysian firms.

Nevertheless, the impact on various manufacturing sectors, influenced by Chinese investments from 2013 to 2023, varies significantly. In the steel sector, contrary to expectations of exports to ASEAN countries, there has been a notable increase in exports to China, potentially due to anti-dumping duties on steel exports and the presence of large Chinese steel mills in Malaysia. Similarly, although textile exports to China remain weak, there has been an increase in DVA due to the growing number of textile factories established in Malaysia. Overall, Malaysia continues to depend on China for imported inputs used to produce Malaysian exports. This suggests that Malaysian SMEs are less competitive compared to Chinese SMEs, especially in terms of the scale of production since Malaysia is a much smaller economy compared to China. It is important for Malaysian SMEs to internationalize their operations to expand their scale of production rather than just produce for the small domestic economy if they are to compete successfully against the much bigger SMEs from China.

Regarding solar products, exports primarily target third countries, prompting further exploration into potential increases in exports to the US from 2013 to 2021. Therefore, it is important to identify third-country markets for these goods to gain a clearer understanding of their export destinations and optimize trade strategies accordingly. Emphasizing product differentiation and innovation can enhance the competitiveness of Malaysian solar products, thereby sustaining demand amid trade disruptions.

Appendix 1. Product Codes

Products	Classifications	Codes
Electronic final goods	SITC 3	751, 752, 761, 762, 763, 775
Electronic parts and components	SITC 3	759, 764, 772, 776,
Iron and steel	HS	72, 73
Textile and textile articles	HS	HS Section 11: Chapter 50 to 63
Solar	HS	854140, 850131, 850161, 850720, 850131

Appendix 2. Bilateral RCA and Intra-Industry Trade Index

Bilateral RCA

Bilateral RCA = (Exports of product Xi from Country A to Country B/ All exports of Country A to Country B) / (All exports of Xi from Country A to the World/All exports of Country A to the World). A value above one represents the comparative advantage of product Xi in Country B's sector.

A bilateral RCA > 1 suggests that the exporting country is efficient in producing and exporting the specific product to the destination market. This implies a strong trade potential and competitiveness in that particular product in the destination market. RCA < 1 suggests that Malaysia does not have a comparative advantage in producing and exporting that product to China.

IIT Index or GL Index

The GL index is a measure used to assess the extent of IIT between two countries. The formula for calculating the GL index is as follows:

$$GL\ index = 1 - (|X - M|) / (X + M),$$

where
X represents exports of similar goods from the exporting country to the importing country;
M represents imports of similar goods by the exporting country from the importing country.

The index ranges from 0 to 1, where
A value of 0 indicates no IIT (i.e., all trade is inter-industry);
A value of 1 indicates complete IIT (i.e., all trade is within the same industry).

References

Bond, David, Chunfu Yan, Matt Solomon, and Ian Saccomanno (2023). "US Department of Commerce Determines that Imports from Southeast Asia are Circumventing ADD/CVD Orders on Solar Cells and Modules from China." *White and Case LLP*, 22 August. https://www.whitecase.com/insight-alert/us-department-commerce-determines-imports-southeast-asia-are-circumventing-addcvd.

Cheng, Leonard K., and Ma Zhihui (2010). "China's Outward Foreign Direct Investment." In Robert C. Feenstra, and Shang-Jin Wei (eds.), *China's Growing Role in World Trade*, pp. 545–578. Chicago, IL: University of Chicago Press.

Gomez, Edmund Terence, Siew Yean Tham, Ran Li, and Kee Cheok Cheong (2020). *China in Malaysia: State-Business Relations and the New Order of Investment Flows*. Singapore: Palgrave Macmillan.

Kam, Andrew Jia Yi (2017). "Dynamics of Trade in Value-added in 'Factory Asia'." *Journal of Contemporary Asia*, Vol. 47, No. 5, pp. 704–727.

Malaysia (2011). *Malaysian Building Integrated Photovoltaic Project (MBIPV): Final Evaluation Report.* https://erc.undp.org/evaluation/documents/download/5207.

Nur Shahadah Jamil (2023). "Ten Years into the Belt and Road Initiative in Malaysia: Shift, Continuity and Way Forward." *East Asian Policy*, Vol. 15, No. 3, pp. 7–19.

Pike, Lili (2019). "Green Belt and Road in the Spotlight." *China Dialogue*. 24 April. https://chinadialogue.net/en/energy/11212-green-belt-and-road-in-the-spotlight/.

Tham, Siew Yean (2005). "Japan's Response to Globalization: Learning from Japanese Direct Investment." *Asia-Pacific Trade and Investment Review*, Vol. 1, No. 2, pp. 3–24.

Tham, Siew Yean (2019). "The Belt and Road Initiative: Case of Kuantan Port." *ISEAS Perspective*, No. 3, 15 January. https://www.iseas.edu.sg/articles-commentaries/iseas-perspective/20193-the-belt-and-road-initiative-in-malaysia-case-of-the-kuantan-port-by-tham-siew-yean/.

Tham, Siew Yean and Yeoh Wee Jin (2020). "Chinese Steel Investments in ASEAN," *ISEAS Perspective*, No. 50, 21 May. https://www.iseas.edu.sg/wp-content/uploads/2020/03/ISEAS_Perspective_2020_50.pdf.

The Edge (2024). "Long Steel Players Urge Close Scrutiny of Alliance Steel." 16 January. https://theedgemalaysia.com/node/696725.

Zhang, Miao (2021). "Beyond Infrastructure: Re-thinking China's Foreign Direct Investment in Malaysia." *The Pacific Review*, Vol. 34, No. 6, pp. 1054–1078.

© 2025 World Scientific Publishing Company
https://doi.org/10.1142/9789819801350_0008

Chapter 8

Analyzing the Middle-Income Trap in Malaysia: Of (Chinese) Investment and Industrial Upgrading

Guanie Lim and Yat Ming Ooi

Introduction

Following China's tighter economic integration with Southeast Asia, the former's investment flows are increasingly being courted by the region's economies, including but not limited to Malaysia, as a means to facilitate industrial upgrading. This viewpoint has been reinforced as industrial progress in most of these economies has stagnated in recent years, resulting in what is termed the middle-income trap (MIT) (Ohno, 2009). Researchers and policymakers alike have proposed that technological capabilities, learning, and innovation are the answers to freeing these developing economies from the MIT (Nayyar, 2021). Innovation and technology have been the main drivers of industrialization in developed economies. Developing economies, under the pretense of emulating the successes of industrialized nations, have attempted to build their technological and innovative capabilities through inward foreign direct investment (FDI). However, there is increasing evidence informing us that the supposedly positive effects of inward FDI on technology transfer and labor upgrading of developing economies are modest at best (Kaplinsky and Kraemer-Mbula, 2022).

This chapter provides insight into Malaysia's industrial upgrading efforts by examining the case of the Digital Free Trade Zone (DFTZ), a much-touted public–private partnership (PPP) involving Chinese FDI and anchor firms from both Malaysia and China. The DFTZ's purpose is to facilitate Malaysia's digital transformation journey through the purported transfer of technologies and innovative capabilities. Despite strong support from the Malaysian government and participation from Malaysia's state-owned firms and China's high-technology firms, the DFTZ has thus far not delivered on its technology transfer and labor upgrading promises.

One could draw on two perspectives to provide an initial explanation of the benefits of the DFTZ to the Malaysian economy. First, development studies indicate that upgrading from the MIT requires broad-based innovation that enables higher productivity and domestic innovation capability-building efforts through public–private interactions (Kang and Paus, 2020). Thus, the involvement of Malaysian state-owned firms as anchors in the DFTZ will facilitate innovation capability-building in domestic firms. Second, technology transfer studies posit that the transfer of technology, know-how, and capabilities requires favorable conditions, which include the availability of high-quality technologies, supportive and capable actors (e.g., firms), and the proximity of these firms to one another (Bozeman, 2000; Woodfield *et al.*, 2023). The DFTZ promises closer collaboration between Chinese high-technology firms and Malaysian state-owned firms and domestic firms, to facilitate the transfer of much-needed technologies and know-how. Theoretically, the DFTZ should be a huge success in upgrading Malaysia's technological and innovation capabilities. But is this really the case here or has reality painted a totally different picture? We explore this further in the following.

Background Information

Diplomatic relations between Malaysia and China began in May 1974 when the then Malaysian Prime Minister Abdul Razak Hussein (1970–1976) visited Beijing and established diplomatic ties with his Chinese counterparts. While cordial, the relationship did not blossom meaningfully until the 1990s. This period ushered in a new generation of Malaysian leaders who began to see China more as an economic partner following the conclusion of the Cold War and China's implementation of its 1978 "Reform and Opening-up" policies. Bilateral ties were also boosted during the 1997 Asian Financial Crisis, which damaged the economies of Malaysia

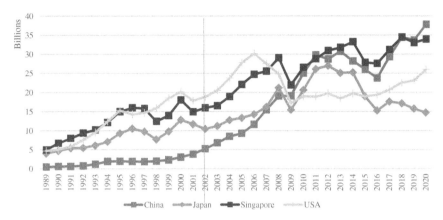

Figure 1. Malaysia's Key Export Markets (USD Billions).
Source: UN Comtrade Database.

and several Asian countries. One of the cornerstones undergirding China–Malaysia cooperation is the open pledge from Beijing that it will not devaluate the Chinese Yuan (CNY), thereby stabilizing the region's macroeconomic situation (Khor *et al.*, 2022).

Trade cooperation with China deepened as Malaysia and the other Asian economies picked themselves up after the 1997 Asian Financial Crisis. Further tailwinds undergirding such cooperation are China's ascension to the World Trade Organization in late 2001 as well as the tariff reduction brought about by the ASEAN–China Free Trade Agreement (ACFTA). Figure 1 illustrates how China has gradually become one of Malaysia's largest export markets. In 2019, it took the top spot from Singapore and has since extended its lead. When it comes to imports, Chinese dominance is felt more strongly (Figure 2). China became Malaysia's largest source of import as early as 2012, overtaking Singapore. A commanding lead has been built up from that point onward. The overarching picture is the steady trade integration between both economies, driven by the two-way exchange of electrical and electronics (E&E) goods, chemical products, optical and scientific equipment, and other resource-based products such as liquefied natural gas and rubber products (Tham and Kam, 2014).

Perhaps as a result of the increasingly dense bilateral trade ties, Chinese FDI in Malaysia has risen in recent times. Figure 3 outlines the

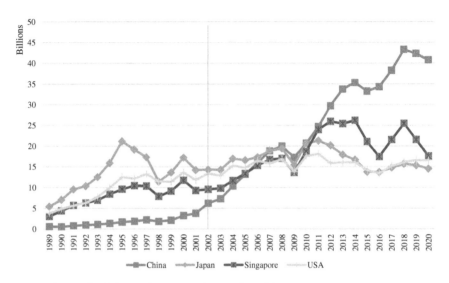

Figure 2. Malaysia's Key Import Markets (USD Billions).
Source: UN Comtrade Database.

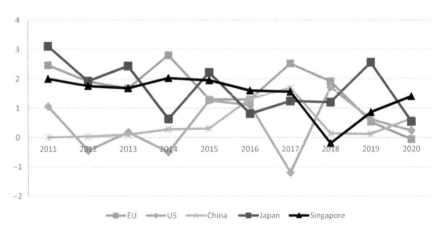

Figure 3. Net FDI Flows in Malaysia from 2011 to 2020 (USD Billions).
Note: *A negative value indicates an outflow or a decrease in investment.
Source: Statistics of FDI in Malaysia, Department of Statistics Malaysia (converted into USD).

net FDI inflow entering Malaysia from 2011 to 2020. It can be seen that the Chinese FDI inflow has been relatively modest compared to that of the other economies. It only began to gather momentum in 2013 (the year of the BRI's announcement). The year 2017 marked a turning point, however, as Beijing imposed capital controls to curb the outflow of money and stabilize the CNY (Liu and Lim, 2019). It was a calculated move to streamline Chinese firms' cross-border activities, especially those that were deemed speculative (e.g., real estate and entertainment). Since then, the inflow of Chinese FDI has suffered a dip before resurging in 2020.

Figure 4 illustrates that Chinese FDI stock in Malaysia remains behind most of the other economies. This is largely because of China's status as a latecomer investor *vis-à-vis* the other major economies. However, if one were to take a longer-term perspective, it would be easy to discern that the total stock of China's FDI has increased. The spike is especially obvious between 2015 and 2017. The overall picture inferred from Figures 3 and 4 is that Chinese FDI is slowly but surely jacking up its presence in Malaysia, even if we account for the head start enjoyed by the other "traditional" investors (i.e., industrialized Western countries, Singapore, and Japan).

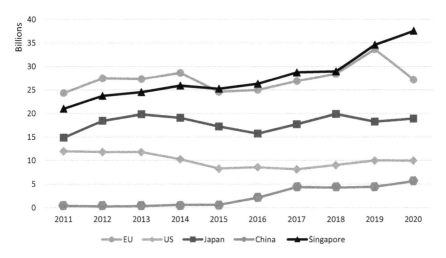

Figure 4. Stock of FDI in Malaysia, 2011 to 2020 (USD Billions).
Source: Statistics of FDI in Malaysia, Department of Statistics Malaysia (converted into USD).

Although a detailed industry-by-industry breakdown is not available publicly, it still is possible to make deductions regarding the whereabouts of Chinese FDI. The policy agenda of former Malaysian Prime Minister Najib Razak (in office from 2009 to May 2018) is particularly illuminating. Najib was especially keen to pull Malaysia out of the MIT, expending significant attention and effort to this end, at least in the early years of his tenure. One of his signature policies was to court Chinese TNCs. Indeed, his administration is viewed as one that grew increasingly reliant on Chinese firms to pursue ambitious projects with a longer-than-normal payback period (Gomez *et al.*, 2020). Some of the landmark undertakings include the East Coast Rail Link, Malaysia–China Kuantan Industrial Park, and Forest City (see Malgeri, 2019; He and Tritto, 2022; Camba *et al.*, 2022). In the development of the digital economy, of which substantial spillover is expected to be released, Najib courted the investment dollars of Alibaba, arguably the highest-profile Chinese TNC in recent years. Indeed, Alibaba's investment in Malaysia has primarily taken the form of the aforementioned DFTZ. Located in Sepang, Selangor, this project is envisioned as a catalyst to promote Malaysia's digital transformation. The technological and knowledge transfer is expected to move Malaysian firms away from activities that compete mainly on cheap labor toward more sophisticated ones that yield more value-added.

An On-the-Ground Perspective: Chinese Investment in the Digital Free Trade Zone

How has the DFTZ interacted with the development trajectory of the Malaysian ecosystem then? This project dates back to at least October 2016, when Najib announced the setting up of a DFTZ in his Budget 2017 speech. Within the space of a few weeks, Najib appointed Jack Ma, Alibaba's charismatic founder, as the government's digital economy advisor (Ho, 2016). Although Ma is expected to assist Malaysia in the packaging of e-economy in the implementation of, among others, e-payment, Alipay, online banking, and e-financing, one of the clearest manifestations to date is the DFTZ (*Bernama*, 2016). This project was launched in March 2017, with Alibaba swooping in merely months after the Malaysian government's overtures.

Alibaba's imprint is salient when one considers the business model of the DFTZ, in addition to the speed by which it has been implemented. It is

Analyzing the Middle-Income Trap in Malaysia 137

a dedicated zone whereby the whole range of services that are needed to ensure the speedy delivery of goods is scheduled to be made available over a staggered timeline. This zone is the first of Alibaba's Internet-based trading platforms, or electronic World Trade Platform (e-WTP). To this end, an eFulfilment hub, a satellite services hub, and an eServices Platform are being developed over two phases with the first phase undertaken by Pos Malaysia (a Malaysian SOE) at a cost of MYR60 million (Tham and Kam, 2019). The budget is being used to upgrade the former Low-Cost Carrier Terminal (LCCT) for the DFTZ's facilities, which have been operational since at least 2019. Little is known about the project's second phase. However, Alibaba is understood to continue playing a major role, taking on a 70% equity stake. The remaining 30% is held by Malaysia Airports Holdings Berhad (MAHB), another SOE (Gomez *et al.*, 2020).

The information revealed thus far indicates several interesting observations. Firstly, it is uncertain how much technology transfer the Malaysians have received from the DFTZ. Some inferences can, however, still be made. According to the Malaysian International Trade and Industry (MITI), small and medium enterprises (SMEs) have been encouraged to participate in the DFTZ to further galvanize e-commerce in Malaysia (Ee, 2018). As many as 13,000 local SMEs have also gained access to regional and global e-commerce markets as of the end of 2019, growing from 2,000 local SMEs at the end of 2017 (Chin *et al.*, 2021). Adopting a more critical perspective, Tham and Kam (2019) questioned the viability of these figures. There are two issues are pertinent here: The information does not distinguish SMEs that are new on e-commerce platforms from seasoned SMEs that have used e-commerce channels prior to the establishment of the DFTZ and there are no data on the attrition rate of the SMEs that have been listed on the e-commerce platforms in the DFTZ. Additionally, their study demonstrates that, while bilateral trade between China and Malaysia has expanded, the latter has been losing its bilateral revealed comparative advantage in its exports to China. At the same time, there is an increasing use of imports for exporting to China, which implies that Malaysian firms do not capture as large a value-added as conventionally imagined.

What is certain, however, is Malaysia's persistence in courting FDI to plug its technological shortcomings. More importantly, this partnership between a technologically sophisticated foreign TNC (i.e., Alibaba) and a select group of SOEs (i.e., Pos Malaysia and MAHB) is not alien to analysts who have been covering Malaysia's industrialization. This particular engagement model where seemingly high-technology industries are groomed in an almost enclave-like environment dates back to almost the late 1960s (Wong and Cheong, 2014). Facing a restive populace reeling from the 1969 sectarian violence, Malaysian policymakers were seeking a fix to address its mounting unemployment and income inequality.

Then, labor-intensive light industries which principally manufactured textiles, footwear, and electronic goods were aggressively courted from abroad. Various measures were introduced to facilitate and encourage export-oriented manufacturing, particularly the establishment of special economic zones (SEZs) and the disbursement of fiscal incentives (e.g., tax holidays) (Rasiah and Krishnan, 2020).

During the 1980s, when heavy industrialization growth was pursued aggressively, the government saw it fit to directly establish SOEs that plug their technological backwardness by establishing joint ventures with technology-intensive TNCs. This was most clearly exemplified by the (then) national carmaker Proton, which was the result of a 70/30 joint venture between the Heavy Industries Corporation of Malaysia Berhad (HICOM), itself an SOE, and the Mitsubishi Group of Japan (Hasan and Jomo, 2007). In exchange for a protected domestic market and generous royalty for the provision of technology, components, training, and other miscellaneous items, the government required the Japanese firm to transfer its expertise to HICOM and other local firms (Studwell, 2013). In spite of their financial outlay, the Malaysians did not enjoy much autonomy as inputs, factory design, and manufacturing workflow were primarily driven by the Western and Japanese investors. This prompted worries that the Southeast Asian nation was essentially pursuing "technology-less" development with the Malaysian SOEs discouraged (or in some cases, preempted by strict licensing requirements) from developing more sustainable forms of organic capabilities (such as striving for higher product standards in more advanced markets) (Yoshihara, 1988). True to form, most of these enterprises have since exited their respective industries. Malaysian presence (such as global market share) in these heavy industries has also been inconsequential.

Secondly, the strong reliance on FDI and domestic SOEs (in the DFTZ's case, they are Pos Malaysia and MAHB) to drive upgrading has coincided with the relative neglect of its private sector and other microeconomic factors (e.g., skill formation and a level playing field for all enterprises). According to Menon (2014), at least since the late 1990s, the number and influence of the SOEs have grown to such an extent that they now dominate various spheres of the Malaysian economy, which has created an uneven playing field deterring the entry of new (usually private) firms. Extending this perspective is Hill *et al.* (2012) and Lim (2014), who demonstrated that the SOEs have forged a niche for themselves largely in non-tradable industries primarily serving the domestic market. In recent years, following the emergence of a newer cohort of developing economies (e.g., Cambodia and Vietnam), Malaysian policymakers have found it increasingly difficult to attract FDI from its traditional sources (i.e., industrialized Western countries, Singapore, and Japan). Therefore, TNCs from alternative countries such as China and Saudi Arabia have become more appealing. Nevertheless, Lim (2014) showed that a significant portion of Chinese investors, when investing in Malaysia, have formed partnerships with the Malaysian SOEs in non-tradable industries such as construction. Some of the main reasons the SOEs are preferred is because of their ties to the state, especially their reliance on accessing state resources (e.g., awarding of projects) and their (usually) strong financial position. To a certain extent, one could claim that the ushering of Chinese TNCs, such as Alibaba, is enhancing the economic fortunes (and by extension, political longevity) of the ethnic Malay-dominated state institutions and state-owned enterprises. By the same token, this equilibrium has indirectly dimmed the urge to level the playing field for the country's (ethnic Chinese-dominated) SMEs.[1] This unevenness has been observed by Chin *et al.* (2021), who noted that a rather high proportion of SMEs are pessimistic about their prospects with the DFTZ. Apart from incompatible cost structures and infrastructure development, the lack of knowledge of technical support and the lack of digital talent in innovative marketing strategies are among the main grouses of the SMEs.

Thirdly, and related to the previous point, it appears that Malaysia's industrial policy formulation on the digital economy has broadly conformed to that observed in other more mature industries. Studies reveal

---

[1]Malaysia's relatively high growth rate in the post-independence decades was arguably sufficient to sway the opinions of a large enough portion of the citizenry (both Malays and non-Malays) to "go along" with this political architecture. However, the secular slowdown since the late 1990s meant that voters were no longer as docile as before. This can be seen in increasingly noticeable dissatisfaction with the UMNO-led government, which reached its peak in the general election of 2018. This election saw the widespread loss of UMNO and its allies, who lost power not only in the federal government, but also various state governments.

that Malaysia, at least under former Prime Minister Mahathir Mohamad's long tenure (1981–2003), has conceptualized industrial plans through overlapping (but not necessarily conflictual) mechanisms (Ohno, 2009).[2] Combined with Malaysia's rather highly centralized political system, it has meant that much planning power resides with the Prime Minister's Office (Hutchinson, 2015; Slater, 2003). The Economic Planning Unit (EPU), housed under the Prime Minister's Office, directs national efforts to coordinate policies and discussions across various interest groups through steering committees and technical resource groups. Although this policy structure may appear quite complex, Ohno (2009) noted that the Malaysian government managed it surprisingly well, without being bogged down in excessive bureaucracy. However, there is a considerable time lapse between this study and the current era. In the case of Alibaba's courting and the broader development of the digital economy, some worrying signs are appearing, which go against his rather sanguine prognosis.

Consider the Malaysia Digital Economy Blueprint 2021–2030 (Economic Planning Unit, 2021), unveiled on 19 February 2021. Prepared by the EPU, it is the latest plan to map out digital transformation in the Southeast Asian nation. Critics argue that it adopts arguably too all-encompassing an approach. Additionally, there are some doubts regarding the credibility of the targeted key performance indicators as well as the multiple layers of bureaucracy that govern the industrial progress (Tham, 2021). For the former, multiple ambitious key performance indicators are provided to signal the government's intention. However, it is close to impossible to gauge whether they are realistic or achievable because baseline numbers are not provided. For the latter, Malaysia Digital Economy Corporation (MDEC) and the Malaysian Global Innovation & Creativity Centre (MaGIC) are among two of the many implementing agencies that have been tasked with promoting the digital economy. While this overlapping governance network might have worked in the past, it is increasingly tricky to maintain or justify it in an industry where speed and flexibility is the essence for effective implementation. Complicating Malaysia's predicament is, as alluded to previously, the policy outreach of a newer generation of developing economies that have absorbed lessons from Malaysia and the other earlier industrializers, not least in attracting FDI to promote their digitalization.

---

[2]Mahathir returned as Prime Minister from May 2018 to March 2020.

Conclusion

This chapter's *raison d'être*, highlighted at the beginning, is to explore whether Chinese FDI in Malaysia is contributing to the technology transfer of the host country. Specifically, the case of DFTZ — an outcome of Chinese investment into building the technological and innovation capabilities needed to accelerate Malaysia's digital transformation journey — is unpacked. The DFTZ partnership extends the existing knowledge of the most prominent Chinese-financed infrastructure projects in Malaysia, such as the East Coast Rail Link and the Malaysia–China Kuantan Industrial Park (Gomez *et al.*, 2020). Additionally, the chapter seeks to contribute to the literature on development economics and innovation studies.

From the analysis outlined in the previous sections, three main conclusions are derived. First, Malaysia's reliance on FDI and domestic state-owned firms to drive industrial upgrading is witnessed in the fruition of the DFTZ. This observation underlines how actors and institutions are locked into the preexisting industrialization trajectory. Moreover, it indirectly ties Malaysian firms into a "technology-less" development model as it grants the lion's share of commercial autonomy to the foreign investors, including but not limited to facility design and process workflow. The history of development shows us that economic progress has almost entirely been driven by technological and innovation capabilities, but these capabilities need to trickle down to the domestic firms (Nayyar, 2021). The trickle-down process is in turn enabled by broader capitalist institutions crafted by the state. Within the context of this chapter, the inability of Malaysia's state-owned firms to disseminate the technologies and know-how they learnt from Chinese firms has proven to be a barrier for Malaysia to building sustainable innovation capabilities to upgrade its economy. Unless Malaysia is able to develop more robust technology transfer frameworks at the institutional level (Bozeman, 2000), no amount of Chinese FDI will be able to lift Malaysia up and out of the MIT.

Second, closer Chinese–Malaysian economic integration, especially in recent years, has provided an opening for Chinese TNCs to challenge the "traditional" Western and Japanese firms for a market share in Malaysia. From a development perspective, more FDIs, Chinese or otherwise, is good because they foster economic development and, to a certain extent, innovation and entrepreneurial activities (Kaplinsky and Kraemer-Mbula, 2022). However, the reality is closer to a "land grab," with each group of transnational firms competing among themselves and with domestic firms (usually SMEs) for consumer dollars. The unintended consequence of this is the crowding-out effect, where domestic SMEs exit the economy due to the lack of financial and technological capabilities to compete with well-funded, innovative TNCs (Malerba and Lee, 2021).

Third, Malaysia's digital economy policy formulation has not veered substantially from that observed in other more mature industries. Although industrial planning is conducted through overlapping mechanisms inter-linking various government bodies, much of the directive remains within the EPU (a unit under the Prime Minister's Office). This implies that market signals and other feedback might not be transmitted to the relevant policymakers in a timely manner. While this governance structure might have worked in the past, it is doubtful whether it can yield the desired results in the digital economy.

Some policy implications can be distilled from the above-stated findings. The DFTZ case study reveals that it is relatively straightforward to "transplant" an industry through orthodox measures such as the establishment of SEZs and the disbursement of fiscal incentives. Tie-ups involving "national champions" and technology-intensive TNCs are also attractive options. However, long-term progress and capability-building present a different proposition. An analysis of Malaysia's economic history and recent experimentation with the digital economy reveals that the preexisting capitalist development pathway is inadequate in moving the country toward the technological frontier and out of the MIT. It is perhaps time to break the mold and consider a newer generation of instruments and mechanisms that more sustainably foster the development of scientific institutions and innovative solutions.

References

Bernama (2016). "Jack Ma Can Help Spearhead Malaysia's Digital Economy — Pm Najib." *Astro Awani*, 4 November. https://www.astroawani.com/berita-malaysia/jack-ma-can-help-spearhead-malaysias-digital-economy-pm-najib-121545.

Bozeman, Barry (2000). "Technology Transfer and Public Policy: A Review of Research and Theory." *Research Policy*, Vol. 29, No. 4, pp. 627–655.

Camba, Alvin, Guanie Lim, and Kevin Gallagher (2022). "Leading Sector and Dual Economy: How Indonesia and Malaysia Mobilised Chinese Capital in Mineral Processing." *Third World Quarterly*, Vol. 43, No. 10, pp. 2375–2395.

Chin, Mui-Yin, Lee-Peng Foo, Mohammad Falahat, and Hon-Choong Chin (2021). "Digital Free Trade Zone in Facilitating Small Medium Enterprises for Globalization: A Perspective from Malaysia SMEs." Paper Presented at the *4th International Conference on Research in Management and Economics.*

Economic Planning Unit (2021). *Malaysia Digital Economy Blueprint.* https://www.epu.gov.my/sites/default/files/2021-02/malaysia-digital-economy-blueprint.pdf.

Ee, Ann Nee (2018). "Govt Wants More SMEs in Digital Free Trade Zone." *The Sun*, 3 December. https://www.thesundaily.my/business/digital-free-trade-zone-DY203566.

Gomez, Edmund Terence, Siew Yean Tham, Ran Li, and Kee Cheok Cheong (2020). *China in Malaysia: State-Business Relations and the New Order of Investment Flows.* Singapore: Palgrave Macmillan.

Hasan, Hasli and Kwame Sundaram Jomo (2007). "Rent-Seeking and Industrial Policy in Malaysia." In Kwame Sundaram Jomo (ed.), *Malaysian Industrial Policy*, pp. 157–178. Singapore: National University of Singapore Press.

He, Yujia and Angela Tritto (2022). "Urban Utopia or Pipe Dream? Examining Chinese-Invested Smart City Development in Southeast Asia." *Third World Quarterly*, Vol. 43, No. 9, pp. 2244–2268.

Hill, Hal, Siew Yean Tham, and Ragayah Haji Mat Zin (2012). "Malaysia: A Success Story Stuck in the Middle?" *The World Economy*, Vol. 35, No. 12, pp. 1687–1711.

Ho, Wah Foon (2016). "Najib: Alibaba Founder Jack Ma Agrees to Be Advisor to Malaysian Govt on Digital Economy." *The Star*, 4 November. https://www.thestar.com.my/news/nation/2016/11/04/alibaba-founder-jack-ma-agrees-to-be-advisor-to-malaysian-govt-on-digital-economy/.

Hutchinson, Francis (2015). *Mirror Images in Different Frames? Johor, the Riau Islands, and Competition for Investment from Singapore.* Singapore: ISEAS.

Kang, Nahee and Eva Paus (2020). "The Political Economy of the Middle Income Trap: The Challenges of Advancing Innovation Capabilities in Latin America, Asia and Beyond." *The Journal of Development Studies*, Vol. 56, No. 4, pp. 651–656.

Kaplinsky, Raphael and Erika Kraemer-Mbula (2022). "Innovation and Uneven Development: The Challenge for Low- and Middle-Income Economies." *Research Policy*, Vol. 51, No. 2, 104394.

Khor, Hoe Ee, Diwa C. Guinigundo, and Masahiro Kawai (eds.) (2022). *Trauma to Triumph: Rising from the Ashes of the Asian Financial Crisis.* Singapore: World Scientific.

Lim, Guanie (2014). "The Internationalisation of Mainland Chinese Firms into Malaysia: From Obligated Embeddedness to Active Embeddedness." *Journal of Current Southeast Asian Affairs*, Vol. 33, No. 2, pp. 59–90.

Liu, Hong and Guanie Lim (2019). "The Political Economy of a Rising China in Southeast Asia: Malaysia's Response to the Belt and Road Initiative." *Journal of Contemporary China*, Vol. 28, No. 116, pp. 216–231.

Malerba, Franco and Keun Lee (2021). "An Evolutionary Perspective on Economic Catch-up by Latecomers." *Industrial and Corporate Change*, Vol. 30, No. 4, pp. 986–1010.

Malgeri, Giuseppe (2019). *Malaysia and the Belt and Road Initiative: An Agency Perspective of the East Coast Rail Link (ECRL) Renegotiation Process*. Unpublished Master Thesis, University of Birmingham.

Menon, Jayant (2014). "Growth without Private Investment: What Happened in Malaysia and Can It Be Fixed?" *Journal of the Asia Pacific Economy*, Vol. 19, No. 2, pp. 247–271.

Nayyar, Deepak (2021). "Industrialization in Developing Asia Since 1970: Why Technology, Learning, and Innovation Matter." *Innovation and Development* Vol. 11, No. 2–3, pp. 365–385.

Ohno, Kenichi (2009). *The Middle Income Trap: Implications for Industrialization Strategies in East Asia and Africa*. Tokyo: National Graduate Institute of Policy Studies.

Rasiah, Rajah and Gopi Krishnan (2020). "Industrialization and Industrial Hubs in Malaysia." In Arkebe Oqubay and Justin Yifu Lin (eds.), *The Oxford Handbook of Industrial Hubs and Economic Development*, pp. 701–722. Oxford: Oxford University Press.

Slater, Dan (2003). "Iron Cage in an Iron Fist: Authoritarian Institutions and the Personalization of Power in Malaysia." *Comparative Politics*, Vol. 36, No. 1, pp. 81–101.

Studwell, Joe (2013). *How Asia Works: Success and Failure in the World's Most Dynamic Region*. New York, NY: Grove Press.

Tham, Siew Yean (2021). "Malaysia's Digital Economy Blueprint: More Is Not Better." *Fulcrum*, 2 March. https://fulcrum.sg/malaysias-digital-economy-blueprint-more-is-not-better/.

Tham, Siew Yean and Andrew Kam Jia Yi (2014). "Re-Examining the Impact of ACFTA on ASEAN's Exports of Manufactured Goods to China." *Asian Economic Papers*, Vol. 13, No. 3, pp. 63–82.

Tham, Siew Yean and Andrew Kam Jia Yi (2019). *Exploring the Trade Potential of the DFTZ for Malaysian SMEs*. Singapore: ISEAS.

Wong, Chan-Yuan and Kee-Cheok Cheong (2014). "Diffusion of Catching-up Industrialization Strategies: The Dynamics of East Asia's Policy Learning Process." *Journal of Comparative Asian Development*, Vol. 13, No. 3, pp. 369–404.

Woodfield, Paul J, Yat Ming Ooi, and Kenneth Husted (2023). "Commercialisation Patterns of Scientific Knowledge in Traditional Low- and Medium-Tech Industries." *Technological Forecasting and Social Change*, No. 189, 122349.

Yoshihara, Kunio (1988). *The Rise of Ersatz Capitalism in South-East Asia*. New York, NY: Oxford University Press.

© 2025 World Scientific Publishing Company
https://doi.org/10.1142/9789819801350_0009

Chapter 9

Malaysia's Digital Transformation: Navigating the Digital Silk Road

Ong Sheue-Li

Introduction: Digital Development Cooperation in the Digital Age

Digital development cooperation embodies collaborative efforts aimed at empowering developing countries and emerging economies to harness the transformative power of digital technologies effectively (Okano-Heijmans and Vosse, 2021). It encompasses a wide array of initiatives focused on enhancing telecommunications infrastructure, fostering conducive regulatory frameworks, and nurturing the growth of digital enterprises. At its core, digital development cooperation seeks to enable nations to address socioeconomic challenges, drive inclusive growth, and advance sustainable development agendas.

Infrastructure development stands as the foundation of digital development cooperation endeavors. Through strategic investments in telecommunications networks, broadband internet connectivity, and data centers, countries endeavor to enhance digital accessibility, reliability, and speed. By expanding digital infrastructure, especially in underserved or remote regions, governments can promote digital inclusion and unlock new opportunities for economic and social development.

Similarly, the establishment of robust regulatory frameworks is paramount for fostering an enabling environment conducive to digital innovation, investment, and consumer trust. Digital development cooperation initiatives focus on assisting countries in crafting and implementing policies and regulations tailored to the digital domain. This includes frameworks related to data protection, cybersecurity, e-commerce, digital privacy, and cross-border data flows. By providing clarity, transparency, and legal certainty, regulatory frameworks facilitate the growth of digital ecosystems and instill confidence among stakeholders.

Moreover, digital enterprises, start-ups, and entrepreneurs play a pivotal role in driving economic growth, job creation, and innovation. Thus, digital development cooperation extends support to these entities through various mechanisms. This encompasses capacity-building programs, technical assistance, mentorship, access to finance and investment, and market linkages. By empowering digital enterprises, countries can unlock new economic opportunities, enhance competitiveness, and foster inclusive growth.

In essence, digital development cooperation serves as a catalyst for navigating the complexities of the digital landscape, addressing challenges, and seizing opportunities in the digital domain. By bridging the digital divide, harmonizing regulatory frameworks, and nurturing digital entrepreneurship, countries can unlock the transformative potential of digital technologies and chart a path toward a more equitable and prosperous future.

Assessing Malaysia's Digital Landscape and Policy Frameworks

The COVID-19 pandemic brought about a significant shift in global dynamics, amplifying the reliance on digital connectivity for various aspects of daily life. In Malaysia, the implementation of the Movement Control Order (MCO) in March 2020 propelled internet usage to soar by 70%, driven by the widespread adoption of work-from-home arrangements and online learning platforms (Malaysian Communications and Multimedia Commission [MCMC] 2023). However, this surge highlighted existing gaps in Malaysia's digital infrastructure, including issues of network coverage and service quality, prompting the government to take action to address these challenges.

In response to the pressing need for improved digital connectivity, the Malaysian government initiated the Pelan Jalinan Digital Negara (JENDELA), a comprehensive national digital infrastructure plan aimed at strengthening the country's digital capabilities. By implementing long-term national policies and digital initiatives, Malaysia has positioned itself for success in the digital economy. These policies serve as frameworks to facilitate seamless digital adoption and foster a more robust digital economy. Table 1 lists several of these policies. In addition, it is crucial to ensure nationwide connectivity for their effective implementation. Therefore, JENDELA plays a pivotal role as an enabler of Malaysia's digital economy strategy, targeting the achievement of 100% Internet coverage in populated areas by 2025. This initiative represents a significant shift in prioritizing digital infrastructure, as communications have been officially recognized as a public utility, alongside water and electricity (Local Government Department, 2022). This recognition underscores Malaysia's commitment to accelerating nationwide digital infrastructure development, particularly in underserved rural areas (Hakimie Amrie Hisamudin, 2021).

The pivotal role of digital technology in Malaysia's socioeconomic landscape became increasingly evident as the pandemic unfolded. Projections indicate that Malaysia's digital economy is poised to significantly contribute to the national GDP by 2025, with ambitious targets set for productivity enhancement and the widespread adoption of e-commerce among micro, small, and medium-sized enterprises (MSMEs). Moreover, Malaysia's proactive approach to digital transformation is underscored by the establishment of long-term national policies and initiatives aimed at fostering a robust digital economy capable of driving sustained growth and innovation.

However, a critical priority at the forefront of the policy agenda should be the construction of robust high-speed broadband networks (Lund and Tyson, 2018). Internet access in Malaysia is delivered through wired connections (88.3% for fiber and 11.62% for copper) and wireless broadband. Users typically subscribe to services provided by companies such as Unifi and TIME for fiber connectivity and CelcomDigi, Maxis, and U Mobile for mobile connectivity.

MCMC recorded 64,020 network-related complaints during the period from January to December 2022 (MCMC, 2023). Most of these complaints were related to 4G coverage and the quality of service. Efforts by

Table 1.   Digital Connectivity in Support of National Policies in Malaysia.

Date	Policy	Responsible Ministry/ Agency	Description
November 22, 2019	National Entrepreneurship Policy (NEP) 2030	Ministry of Entrepreneur Development and Cooperatives	The NEP outlines a comprehensive, long-term strategy aimed at transforming Malaysia into a leading entrepreneurial hub by 2030. This initiative focuses on equipping entrepreneurs with essential 21st-century skills, fostering the digitalization of business operations, and encouraging collaboration among entrepreneurs to flourish in the digital era.
December 8, 2020	The 10–10 Malaysian Science, Technology, Innovation and Economic	Akademi Sains Malaysia, MOSTI	The framework integrates 10 core Malaysian socioeconomic drivers with 10 leading global science and technology drivers, aligning with Malaysia's strengths and requirements. It offers a systematic methodology to transition Malaysia into a knowledge-intensive economy and propel the nation up the global innovation value chain.
December 31, 2020	Licensing Framework for Digital Banks	Bank Negara Malaysia (BNM)	BNM has devised a framework for digital banks aimed at providing banking products and services to underprivileged or overlooked markets via digital or electronic channels. The licensing of new entities with inventive business models is anticipated to inject vitality into the banking sector, catering to the needs of the economy and the populace.

February 18, 2021	Malaysia Digital Economy Blueprint	Strategic Change Management Office (SCMO), EPU	The Malaysian Digital Economy Blueprint serves as a roadmap, delineating strategic endeavors and initiatives to foster a competitive and resilient digital economy. Its vision is for Malaysia to emerge as a regional frontrunner in the digital realm, driving inclusive, responsible, and sustainable socioeconomic development aligned with the 12th Malaysia Plan (12MP).
June 19, 2021	National Fourth Industrial Revolution (4IR) Policy	Ministry of Science, Technology and Innovation	The National 4IR policy serves as a comprehensive and overarching national directive aimed at fostering coherence in the country's socioeconomic transformation through the ethical deployment of 4IR technologies. It aligns with key national development strategies such as the Twelfth Malaysia Plan (RMKe-12), Wawasan Kemakmuran Bersama 2030 (WKB 2030), and the MyDigital Blueprint.
September 27, 2021	Rancangan Malaysia ke-12 (Twelfth Malaysia Plan)	Economic Planning Unit, Prime Minister's Department	As a policy facilitator, the Twelfth Malaysia Plan will expedite Malaysia's utilization of digital and advanced technologies to generate and capitalize on new opportunities. This approach aims to fully leverage the potential of the digital economy while ensuring inclusive, responsible, and sustainable socioeconomic growth for both the people and businesses.

MCMC and service providers to address these issues included enhancing 4G quality, monitoring traffic utilization, and consumer education. Unfortunately, challenges persist in deploying digital infrastructure and connectivity in areas with low population density, which are often deemed commercially unviable by service providers, leaving those in remote areas without access to the Internet (*The Malay Mail*, 2021). Key constraints to rural connectivity are driven by both technological and economic concerns. It remains MCMC's target that residents in rural areas will have access to 4G mobile networks and Internet connectivity by 2025, ensuring that no new development areas are left without digital connectivity.

In light of these challenges, Malaysia's participation in digital development cooperation becomes even more crucial. By leveraging partnerships and collaborations with international stakeholders, Malaysia aims to further enhance its digital infrastructure, regulatory frameworks, and support mechanisms for digital businesses. Initiatives such as the Digital Silk Road (DSR) present opportunities to catalyze Malaysia's digital transformation, driving innovation, connectivity, and economic prosperity for all stakeholders involved.

Exploring China's Digital Silk Road

The DSR initiative, a pivotal component of China's expansive Belt and Road Initiative (BRI), marks a significant shift in strategic focus from physical to virtual connectivity. Initially introduced by President Xi Jinping in 2013, the BRI has since expanded its scope to encompass a comprehensive framework spanning infrastructure development, economic collaboration, and cultural exchange across continents. The emergence of the DSR in 2015 introduced a new dimension to the BRI, prioritizing information and communications technology (ICT) exchanges and digital cooperation among participating nations.

Indeed, the DSR represents one of China's adaptations of the BRI, signaling a departure from the initiative's original design heavily focused on physical connectivity. As elucidated in a recent analysis, the DSR's conceptualization reflects China's recognition of the evolving dynamics of global trade and technological competition. Unlike the BRI's initial emphasis on traditional infrastructure such as railways, roads, and ports, the DSR underscores the importance of virtual connectivity and digital infrastructure in driving global connectivity and cooperation (Cheng and Zeng, 2023: 6).

Moreover, the DSR's emergence has catalyzed a shift in the role of key stakeholders within the BRI framework. While state-owned enterprises were initially at the forefront of BRI development, the rise of the digital sector has propelled private enterprises into prominence (Dossani, Bouey, and Zhu, 2020). Encouraged by government policies promoting private sector participation, private enterprises have emerged as key players in shaping the digital landscape of the BRI.

In essence, the DSR initiative represents a strategic response to the evolving landscape of global connectivity, positioning China as a leading advocate for digital cooperation and infrastructure development within the BRI framework. Key elements of the DSR initiative encompass the development of cross-border optical cable networks, transcontinental submarine optical cable projects, and satellite information passageways. These infrastructure projects align with China's broader objectives of enhancing connectivity, promoting economic development, and facilitating digital transformation across participating countries. Sectors such as telecommunications, artificial intelligence, cloud computing, e-commerce, mobile payment systems, and smart city development are integral to the initiative's scope.

China's engagement in the DSR spans diverse regions, demonstrating its commitment to fostering digital connectivity and cooperation on a global scale. Through partnerships and cooperation agreements, China aims to promote green, low-carbon, and digital transformation initiatives among partner countries, stimulating new avenues for growth and development.

Participation in the DSR offers recipient countries access to critical technology and infrastructure financing, addressing the urgent need for digital connectivity and modernization. Additionally, Chinese firms contribute to capacity-building and knowledge transfer through various initiatives, spanning smart cities, artificial intelligence, clean energy, and robotics. This exchange of technical expertise fosters innovation and sustainable development, empowering nations to navigate the complexities of the digital era.

The DSR intersects with the BRI's official agenda of promoting the five dimensions of connectivity (policy coordination, facilities' connectivity, trade facilitation, financial integration, people-to-people exchanges) and fostering the convergence of interests, destinies, and responsibilities. As a subset of the BRI, the DSR serves three primary purposes. Firstly, the DSR aims to enhance regional and international connectivity across

152   *Ong Sheue-Li*

Table 2. Key Aspects of China's Digital Silk Road.

Digital Connectivity Elements	Key Aspects	Details
Infrastructure	Infrastructure	• Telecommunications • AI infrastructure • For example, Huawei, Xiaomi, Beidou Navigation
Business	Trade	• All-channel online shopping • Shared economy • Supply chain/logistics • 3D printing • E-commerce • For example, Alibaba, JD.com
	Finance	• Online payment and financial services • P2P finance • Regional bond market • Regional financial institutions • For example, Antfinancial, Silkroad Fund, AIIB
	People's hearts	• Traditional media and social media • Video games • Online education platform • Online cultural exchange • For example, WeChat, NewsDog, Perfect World
Regulation	Policy	• Digital governance • Cybersecurity • Data sharing • For example, Digital Silkroad and China's cooperation with G7

Source: Fudan University Digital Belt and Road Center, 2018: 10.

the "five dimensions" (Dekker, Okano-Heijmans, and Zhang, 2020). These dimensions can be further categorized into three elements, infrastructure, business, and regulation, as can be seen in the analytical delineation done by the Digital Belt and Road Center of Fudan University (see Table 2). Secondly, the DSR aims to facilitate the upgrade and innovation of traditional industries and employment in BRI countries by opening up China's market with its digital assets. Lastly, the DSR, as articulated by various Chinese experts, aims to optimize the regional industrial layout and establish the foundation of a regional community with shared economic interests to create a global value chain where China assumes a central role. This indicates a greater integration between Chinese and overseas technological networks, particularly in China's neighboring region, such as Southeast Asia, and extending into Africa and beyond.

Malaysia's Engagement with the Digital Silk Road Initiative: Opportunities and Challenges

Malaysia has committed to enhancing digital connectivity and collaboration with China, aligning closely with the objectives of the DSR initiative. This alignment is exemplified through the signing of a memorandum of understanding (MoU) on digital cooperation, aimed at deepening bilateral relations and fostering mutual growth across various strategic sectors.

In 2022, Malaysia and China formalized their collaboration in digital telecommunications by signing an MoU at the *International Telecommunication Union Plenipotentiary Conference 2022* in Romania. This agreement, signed by Malaysia's Communications and Multimedia Minister, Tan Sri Annuar Musa, and China's Deputy Minister of Industry and Information Technology, Zhang Yunming, focuses on key areas, such as 5G technology, digital economy, and cybersecurity. The MoU outlines a comprehensive framework for cooperation, encompassing sectors such as 5G app technology, e-commerce, start-up innovations, cloud computing, big data, artificial intelligence, and the Internet of Things. Furthermore, both countries aim to collaborate on policy formulation, standards development, emergency response mechanisms, data security technologies, and cybersecurity training and awareness initiatives (*Bernama*, 2022). Prior to this official endorsement, various private sector ICT firms from China had already established a footprint in Malaysia. In 2020, China's Huawei signed an MoU with Malaysia Digital Economy Corporation to help Malaysia become a digital hub in Southeast Asia (*Bernama*, 2020).

Malaysia's proactive engagement and fostering bilateral cooperation with China in the digital sector reflects its recognition of the pivotal role of digital connectivity in driving economic growth and regional development. Through these collaborative efforts, Malaysia seeks to strengthen its digital economy, stimulate local digital economic growth, and contribute to the broader national economy. This aligns with Malaysia's vision of establishing itself as a hub for high-technology industries in the region, resonating with the overarching goals of the DSR initiative. Engaging with China's DSR initiative presents Malaysia with significant opportunities, particularly in addressing digital inclusion and enhancing digital resilience. These initiatives aim to provide crucial digital infrastructure, including telecommunications networks and broadband internet connectivity, which serve as foundational pillars for driving digitalization and fostering e-economies. In many African and Indo-Pacific countries, access to such digital infrastructure remains a basic necessity, and China's investments in this realm have been instrumental in meeting these pressing needs.

For Malaysia, harnessing China's expertise and resources in digital infrastructure development can expedite its own digital transformation journey. Through collaboration with China, Malaysia can effectively bridge the digital divide, ensuring that all segments of society have equitable access to the transformative benefits of the digital revolution. This commitment to inclusivity is not only pivotal for driving socioeconomic development but also resonates with Malaysia's overarching ambition to emerge as a leading digital hub within the region.

Moreover, China's investments in digital infrastructure open avenues for collaboration and knowledge sharing among Malaysia and neighboring countries. Through participation in joint projects and initiatives, Malaysia can bolster its technological capabilities while fostering stronger regional cooperation in the digital sphere. This collaborative approach not only enhances resilience but also facilitates the seamless integration of Malaysian e-economies into broader regional and global networks.

Conversely, there are also concerns surrounding the implementation of the DSR initiative in Malaysia. The first is the negative perception associated overall with the idea of the BRI itself. While Malaysia has been overall consistently supportive of the BRI, there are lingering doubts in Malaysia that the BRI projects fuel debt unsustainability and impose unnecessary financial burden (Gunasegaram, 2021). The notion of debt trap diplomacy that is popular in the West and in some developing countries suggests that countries engaging in large-scale infrastructure projects financed by China will find themselves entangled in unsustainable levels of debt, potentially compromising their sovereignty or strategic assets. Although many academic studies have refuted this notion and suggested a more multifaceted explanation of the phenomenon (Himmer and Rod, 2022; Nishizawa, 2023; Jones and Hameiri, 2020; Clark, 2023), such a perception has persisted and the BRI continues to be seen as associated with massive borrowing from China at the expense of the interest of the borrowing country. This discourse will be similarly applied to the DSR for those who are doubtful of China's intention in Malaysia and the region.

Another challenge surrounding the implementation of the DSR initiative in Malaysia revolves around the perception of China's expanding geopolitical influence, particularly in the context of the BRI as conceived as a grand strategy (Clarke, 2017). The cybersecurity dimension is especially of note here as digital cooperation with China will supposedly make countries vulnerable to China's ill-intentioned cyber operations. However, recent analysis suggests that these concerns may be exaggerated and that the BRI, including its DSR component, is not really a meticulously orchestrated geopolitical strategy but can more accurately be understood as a political slogan (Cheng and Zeng, 2023). This interpretation acknowledges the dynamic and evolving nature of Chinese foreign policy concepts, which are often shaped by a multitude of actors and interests. The DSR, in particular, has emerged as a rallying slogan for Chinese digital actors, especially private forms, which are eager to carve out a larger role within the BRI framework in going abroad. By adopting a slogan politics approach, the flexible and inclusive nature of the DSR concept will be better understood. Rather than representing a unified and coherent strategy, it serves as a broad umbrella term encompassing various initiatives driven by both state and private actors. This decentralized approach allows for greater flexibility and adaptability, but it also introduces complexities and challenges in terms of coordination and implementation.

Moving forward, it is important to recognize the evolving nature of the DSR and its implications. While it may not conform to a conventional geopolitical framework, it still has significant implications for global digital governance and competition. As China continues to assert its influence in the digital realm, Malaysian policymakers must remain vigilant and adapt their strategies accordingly. This may involve closer coordination between state and private actors as well as a more nuanced understanding of China's digital ambitions and capabilities to harness them for the benefit of Malaysia's own development without compromising on the necessary security.

Recommendations for Future Implementation

In light of the above-mentioned discussions, enhancing transparency and communication surrounding Malaysia's involvement in the DSR initiative is crucial. Clear articulation of the initiative's objectives, benefits, and potential risks to both the public and stakeholders is necessary. This will be critical to ensuring responsible and informed decision-making and governance, mitigating risks, and essentially creating a strong foundation for cooperation.

In addition, Malaysia also stands to benefit from diversifying its partnerships beyond China, engaging with a broader range of international stakeholders, including other countries, multilateral organizations, and private sector entities. As the old saying goes, "Do not put all your eggs in one basket." There are numerous digital development initiatives available, such as the World Bank's development partnership, the Global Forum on Cyber Expertise's (GFCE's) Cyber Capacity Building, and the Organization for Economic Co-operation and Development's (OECD's) Development Assistance. This diversification helps mitigate dependency on any single partner and enhances resilience against potential risks.

Moreover, investing in capacity-building initiatives is essential to bolster Malaysia's expertise in infrastructure development, digital technologies, and project governance. This involves fostering knowledge sharing and collaboration with international partners to leverage best practices and lessons learned from similar projects elsewhere.

Taking a pragmatic approach to assessing the risks and benefits of participating in DSR projects is vital for Malaysian policymakers. Maintaining open channels of dialogue with China and other stakeholders involved in the DSR initiative is also necessary. This facilitates addressing concerns and building mutual understanding through constructive engagement and negotiation. Finally, establishing mechanisms for monitoring and evaluating the impact of DSR projects on Malaysia's socioeconomic development, digital transformation, and strategic interests is crucial for ensuring effective implementation and maximizing the benefits of these projects. By systematically tracking the progress and outcomes of DSR initiatives, Malaysia can gain valuable insights into their impact on various aspects of its society and economy. This includes assessing how these projects contribute to job creation, GDP growth, technological innovation, and overall digital readiness. Monitoring and evaluation also enable policymakers to identify any potential challenges or shortcomings early on, allowing for timely interventions and adjustments to project implementation strategies. Ultimately, the data collected through monitoring and evaluation could serve as a valuable resource for evidence-based decision-making. By using this information to inform future policy decisions and project planning, Malaysia can adapt its approach to digital development cooperation, address emerging challenges, and capitalize on new opportunities in the evolving digital landscape.

Conclusion

Overall, this chapter provides an initial examination of Malaysia's involvement in digital development cooperation within the DSR initiative, offering some thoughts for further exploration and analysis in this area. Against the backdrop of rapid advancements in digital technologies and heightened tensions between the US and China, the importance of digital infrastructure and the digital economy has never been more pronounced. The COVID-19 pandemic further emphasized the indispensability of digital technology, fueling remote learning, e-commerce, and remote work arrangements, thereby enhancing the relevance of the DSR initiative.

Moreover, as the pandemic rendered major physical infrastructure projects less appealing and financially challenging, digital connectivity has emerged as a crucial alternative to sustain the momentum of the BRI. Given these circumstances, Malaysia's active participation in the DSR initiative becomes imperative to harness the transformative potential of digital connectivity for socioeconomic advancement.

This chapter has illuminated the concept of digital development cooperation, delved into Malaysia's digital landscape, and discussed its involvement in the DSR initiative, elucidating both opportunities and challenges. Malaysia stands to gain significantly from the initiative, particularly in terms of addressing digital inclusion, enhancing digital resilience, and fostering regional collaboration. Strategic partnerships and initiatives focused on improving digital infrastructure and fostering innovation play a pivotal role in realizing these benefits.

However, it is also important to acknowledge the challenges associated with Malaysia's participation in the DSR initiative, including concerns regarding transparency, cybersecurity, and China's geopolitical influence. Addressing these challenges demands proactive measures, such as enhancing transparency, strengthening governance, diversifying partnerships, investing in capacity-building, and adopting a pragmatic approach to risk assessment.

By considering the recommendations outlined in this chapter, Malaysian policymakers can potentially navigate the complexities of the digital landscape more effectively and maximize the benefits of digital connectivity facilitated by the DSR initiative. It is advisable for policymakers to maintain open channels of dialogue, monitor and evaluate the impact of DSR projects, and adapt strategies and policies accordingly, as these actions are crucial for sustainable economic growth and digital innovation in Malaysia.

In essence, Malaysia's engagement in digital development cooperation through the DSR initiative holds immense potential for driving socioeconomic development and shaping the future of the digital economy. With strategic foresight, collaborative efforts, and a commitment to responsible governance, Malaysia can seize the opportunities presented by the digital age and emerge as a regional leader in digital transformation.

References

Bernama (2020). "MDEC, Huawei Sign MoU to Spearhead Malaysia as ASEAN Digital Hub." *The Star*, 31 July. https://www.thestar.com.my/business/business-news/2020/07/31/mdec-huawei-sign-mou-to-spearhead-malaysia-as-asean-digital-hub.

Bernama (2022). "Malaysia, China Sign MOU on Digital Telecommunications Cooperation." *The Star*, 28 September. https://www.thestar.com.my/news/nation/2022/09/28/malaysia-china-sign-mou-on-digital-telecommunications-cooperation.

Cheng, Jing and Zeng, Jinghan (2023). "'Digital Silk Road' as a Slogan Instead of a Grand Strategy." *Journal of Contemporary China*, Online First Article, pp. 823–838. https://doi.org/10.1080/10670564.2023.2222269.

Clark, Nadia (2023). "The Rise and Fall of the BRI." *Council on Foreign Relations – Asia Unbound*, 6 April. https://www.cfr.org/blog/rise-and-fall-bri.

Clarke, Michael (2017). "The Belt and Road Initiative: China's New Grand Strategy?" *Asia Policy*, No. 24, pp.71–79.

Dekker, Brigitte, Okano-Heijmans, Maaike, and Zhang, Eric Siyi (2020). "Unpacking China's Digital Silk Road." *Clingendael Report*, July 2020. https://www.clingendael.org/sites/default/files/2020-07/Report_Digital_Silk_Road_July_2020.pdf.

Dossani, Rafiq, Bouey, Jennifer, and Zhu Keren (2020). *Demystifying the Belt and Road Initiative: A Clarification of Its Key Features, Objectives and*

Impacts. RAND Corporation, Working Paper WR-1338. https://www.rand. org/pubs/working_papers/WR1338.html.

Fudan University Digital Belt and Road Center (2018). *Shuzi yidayi yilu (2018 lanpishu)* (*Digital Silk Road [2018 Bluebook]*). https://brgg.fudan.edu.cn/ articleinfo_1049.html.

Gunasegaram, P. (2021). "China the Only Winner in ECRL Deal." *The Vibes*, 8 April. https://www.thevibes.com/articles/opinion/23170/china-the-only-winner-in-ecrl-deal.

Himmer, Michal and Rod, Zdeněk (2022). "Chinese Debt Trap Diplomacy: Reality or Myth?" *Journal of the Indian Ocean Region*, Vol. 18, No. 3, pp. 250–272.

Hakimie Amrie Hisamudin (2021). "After Water and Electricity, Internet now a Public Utility." *Free Malaysia Today*. 3 June. https://www.freemalaysiatoday.com/category/nation/2021/06/03/after-water-and-electricity-internet-now-a-public-utility/.

Jones, Lee and Hameiri, Shabar (2020). "Debunking the Myth of 'Debt-trap Diplomacy': How Recipient Countries Shape China's Belt and Road Initiative." *Chatham House Research Paper Asia-Pacific Programme*. https://www.chathamhouse.org/sites/default/files/2020-08-19-debunking-myth-debt-trap-diplomacy-jones-hameiri.pdf.

Local Government Department (2022). Perundangan Subsidiari Persekutuan: Uniform Building by-Laws 1984. https://jkt.kpkt.gov.my/sites/default/files/2022-10/UKBS%201984%201C.pdf.

Lund, Susan and Tyson, Laura (2018). "Globalization is Not in Retreat: Digital Technology and the Future of Trade." *Foreign Affairs*, Vol. 97, No. 3, pp. 130–140.

Malaysian Communications and Multimedia Commission (MCMC) (2023). "Digital Connectivity, Ensuring Everyone Gets Connected: A Glance at Malaysia's Digital Connectivity Journey." *Strategy Paper*, March 2023. https://www.mcmc.gov.my/skmmgovmy/media/General/pdf2/Insight-Digital-Connectivity.pdf.

Nishizawa, Toshiro (2023). "China's Double-edged Debt Trap." *East Asia Forum*, 19 September. https://eastasiaforum.org/2023/09/19/chinas-double-edged-debt-trap/.

Okano-Heijmans, Maaike and Wilhelm, Vosse (2021). "Promoting Open and Inclusive Connectivity: The Case for Digital Development Cooperation." *Research in Globalization*, Vol. 3, 100061.

The Malay Mail (2021). "More Rural Areas to Enjoy Internet Access once Jendela Implemented, Says MCMC Chairman." 4 February. https://www.malaymail.com/news/malaysia/2021/02/04/more-rural-areas-to-enjoy-internet-access-once-jendela-implemented-says-mcm/.

© 2025 World Scientific Publishing Company
https://doi.org/10.1142/9789819801350_0010

Chapter 10

Prospects of Malaysia–China Climate Cooperation

Lee Pei May

Introduction

Climate change presents an urgent environmental and social challenge that has drawn the attention of scholars, environmentalists, policymakers, international organizations, and ordinary citizens. It is already adversely affecting lives and livelihoods, and Malaysia is one of the many countries experiencing extreme changes in weather and climate. While floods on the east coast of Peninsular Malaysia have always been common, especially during the monsoon season, in recent years, the west coast has also experienced floods of unusual severity. Environmental experts have argued that increasingly extreme weather events were caused by climate change (Amir Yusof, 2021).

The Malaysian government established the Climate Change Action Council (MyCAC) in 2021 to address the adverse impacts of climate change while pursuing sustainable development. The council aims to facilitate green technology development and ensure low-carbon growth at all levels of society. The government's initiatives include promoting the use of electric vehicles (EVs) and establishing eco-friendly transportation systems and green cities (Ministry of Foreign Affairs of Malaya, 2021). Former Prime Minister Ismail Sabri's administration took the challenge of climate change seriously and developed a National Adaptation Plan (Chan, 2022). The current government led by Anwar Ibrahim has also demonstrated a serious commitment to promoting sustainable development. Anwar chaired the first National Climate Change Action Council Meeting for 2023 to discuss the carbon market mechanism, which will help reduce greenhouse gas levels (Prime Minister's Office of Malaysia, 2023).

The Chinese government has also been forthright about the need to address the impacts of climate change. China's top leadership believes climate change is the greatest threat to humanity, and only with a unified approach to addressing climate change can all countries create a stronger global community with a shared future. President Xi Jinping announced that protecting the environment has become a priority for China (*Reuters*, 2022). Though China's status as a developing country does not require it to directly contribute to the Green Climate Fund (GFC) established within the United Nations Framework Convention on Climate Change (UNFCCC), China has proactively reached out to other countries to work together in this area. China's progress, skills, and experience in addressing climate change challenges have enabled it to support other developing countries. Indeed, China has long been a pioneer in advocating for South–South cooperation in relation to climate issues. In 2016, China announced its intention to set up the China South–South Climate Cooperation Fund, pledging over USD3 billion to assist developing countries in combating the challenges of climate change (Weigel, 2016). China's policies aimed at assisting developing countries tackle climate change have continued to grow steadily over the years, ranging from providing technology, equipment, and goods to capacity-building.

Though Malaysia–China cooperation in coping with the challenge of climate change has been quite limited until now, this cooperation could certainly contribute to Malaysia's net-zero transition. This chapter aims to examine various aspects of climate engagement between China and Malaysia: first, the role played by China in global climate governance and, second, Malaysia–China climate collaboration both within the ASEAN framework and subsequently on a bilateral basis. Discussions, exchanges, and investments between Malaysia and China, along with other activities that accelerate green development, helped to set Malaysia on the path to becoming a low-carbon, climate-resilient country.

China's Role in Global Climate Governance

The Belt and Road Initiative (BRI), proposed by China in 2013, has dramatically expanded in recent years. As initially conceived, the BRI tended to give less consideration to the environmental impacts of the projects in host countries, leading some to question BRI projects' sustainability. As a result, the Chinese government reframed the BRI by adding environmental goals to portray the initiative as one that aims to protect the environment. In line with its ecological civilization philosophy, the Chinese government produced "Guidance on Promoting the Green Belt and Road" (Ministry of Ecology and Environment of the People's Republic of China, 2017) in 2017. This reframing of the BRI has led to the creation of a green financial system to finance green projects (Zhang *et al.*, 2022). The shift in the Chinese government's focus toward sustainability also indicates an important change in foreign policy. China increasingly emphasizes global cooperation on climate change and has since forged various partnerships with other countries, particularly in the Global South. Southeast Asia is one of the regions that has benefited immensely from the Green Silk Road; of the USD36.6 million in Chinese investment in solar power projects in BRI countries, USD10.4 billion was invested in Southeast Asian countries (Mukherji, 2024).

Some critics argue that China still emits immense quantities of carbon dioxide, accounting for approximately 30% of global emissions (Hale, 2023). However, one must also consider how globalization has led to the relocation of carbon-intensive manufacturing from Western countries to developing countries, including China. Therefore, a significant proportion of China's emissions is connected to Western rather than local consumption. Moreover, this kind of criticism overlooks the steady and persistent commitment by the Chinese government to develop and deploy renewable energy sources and technologies. In 2022, Bloomberg's NEF data reported that Beijing ranked number one globally in clean energy investments (Hale, 2023). The speed at which China has invested in green energy, technology, and infrastructure is incomparable. The Green BRI helped facilitate this growth through its push for sustainable projects.

China's role in global climate governance is indispensable. A well-known international relations scholar Barry Buzan has argued that China is in a much better position than the West to lead the world toward decarbonization as China has the capacity to do so — from drafting a long-term plan to mobilizing resources to fight climate change (Buzan, 2022). Apart from being the world's largest producer of renewable energy and equipment, China also has the money and skills to assist other developing countries in pursuing greener growth (Buzan, 2022; Chia, 2022). The world can learn from China in terms of renewable energy technologies. China has led other countries for at least five years in hydropower and related storage facilities. In terms of wind power, Chinese manufacturers have captured well over 50% of the world's wind turbine market share (Lueng, 2023).

Malaysia–China Collaboration on Climate Action within the ASEAN Framework

China and ASEAN have a long-established cooperative relationship that has continued to strengthen over time. In 2022, China and ASEAN elevated their relationship to a Comprehensive Strategic Partnership, showing the broad and deep engagements between the two sides. China and ASEAN have collaborated in several areas and have been actively looking to expand their cooperation to areas including climate change. As China has increasingly become the world's leading power in green technology innovation, it will benefit ASEAN to work with China to reduce its own carbon footprint. As a member of ASEAN, Malaysia stands to gain from these collaborations within the ASEAN framework.

In contrast to the US approach of rules-based climate governance, China's approach is strikingly goal-oriented (Seah, 2021). This has led China to emphasize practical cooperation. Over the years, under its own cooperative framework, China has been conducting various capacity-building climate-related workshops to transfer skills and knowledge related to climate change, particularly in mitigation and adaptation efforts. Cooperation between ASEAN and China on climate change extends beyond capacity-building to dialogue, information sharing, joint research, and more. In 2010, based on a proposal from China's top leadership, the ASEAN–China Environmental Cooperation Center (CAEC) was established (Ministry of Environmental Protection of China and Environmental Authorities of ASEAN Member States, 2016). The platform is crucial for ASEAN and China to jointly push forward green and sustainable development in the region. The CAEC's aims include conducting joint policy studies, providing technical support, and fostering cooperation with external parties. ASEAN and China also formulated an environmental cooperation strategy and associated action plans. The first ASEAN-China Strategy on Environmental Protection Cooperation was implemented from 2009–2015, followed by the second cooperation strategy adopted for 2016–2020 (*China Development Brief*, 2021). At the 24th ASEAN–China Summit, ASEAN and China welcomed the adoption of the Framework of the ASEAN–China Environmental Cooperation Strategy and Action Plan (2021–2025). Within the cooperative framework, ASEAN and China organized various forums that have allowed leaders from China and ASEAN countries to coordinate their environmental policies and promote sustainable development.

Cultivating public awareness and ensuring the public's participation are also critical to the success of a country's transition to a sustainable development model. Public education is therefore key to ensuring popular support for sustainable development initiatives (Lee, Yang, and Kwong, 2023). ASEAN members developed the ASEAN Environmental Education Action Plan (AEEAP), a regional framework, to educate the public about managing the environment sustainably (ASEAN Secretariat, 2007). Under the AEEAP framework, ASEAN members have cooperated with other partners, including China, to promote awareness about sustainability, including via the ASEAN Plus Three Youth Environment Forum (AYEF). The first forum was held in 2007 (ASEAN Environment Knowledge Hub, n.d.) and aimed to instill a sense of love for the environment among the youth attendees, expose them to environmental issues in the region, and facilitate an exchange of ideas on addressing the region's environmental issues (ASEAN Secretariat, 2010). Following the 2013 AYEF, delegates pledged to organize activities to promote environmental awareness in their respective countries (ASEAN Environmental Education Inventory Database, 2016).

Besides, there are also programs under the established cooperative framework between ASEAN and China to raise awareness and educate. The ASEAN–China Green Envoys Program, launched in 2011, was designed for policymakers, young people, and enterprises. Within the program, there are three initiatives: Green Innovation, which aims to impart knowledge and skills to policymakers; Green Pioneer, which aims to educate young people; and lastly, Green Enterpreneur, which seeks to encourage partnerships between companies to pursue green development (Ministry of Environmental Protection of China & Environmental Authorities of ASEAN Member States, 2016).

Malaysia–China Cooperation in Renewable Energy

Chinese firms have been the leading producers of solar panels globally. According to a solar sector analyst at BloombergNEF, "China holds a dominant position in the global PV supply chain. Benefiting from a complete life-cycle supply chain and rapid advancements in PV power generation technology, China has emerged as a leader, achieving significant cost reductions and shaping the landscape of solar energy on a global scale" (Liu, 2024). For instance, Chinese company LONGi Green Energy has made several breakthroughs in the conversion efficiency of solar power. As of December 2023, LONGi Green Energy attained the highest efficiency record for silicon-based solar cells, breaking its own previous record (Liu, 2024).

With numerous Southeast Asian countries vying to attract green investment, LONGi Green Energy has chosen Malaysia as a key investment destination. The company explains that there are three reasons for investing in Malaysia: (1) accessibility of talent, (2) availability of natural resources, and (3) supportive government policies (Hayatun Razak, 2023). LONGi Green Energy established its presence in East Malaysia in 2016. The company set up manufacturing plants in Sarawak with cumulative investments of RM5.4 billion (*China Daily*, 2023). As of 2023, the company had hired more than 8,000 workers, 99.9% of whom are Malaysians. In 2023, the company announced that it is allocating RM1.8 billion for the construction of the Serendah Module Plant in Selangor, which will be completed in two phases. The first phase is now complete, and construction is underway for phase two. Besides the large amount of capital invested in the construction of the manufacturing plant, LONGi Green Energy will also establish its Asia-Pacific headquarters in Kuala Lumpur in 2023. The investment is expected to generate more than 2,000 jobs (Hayatun Razak, 2023).

LONGi is far from the only Chinese company collaborating with Malaysian firms to build solar farms (*Nikkei Asia*, 2023). Trina Solar signed a memorandum of understanding (MoU) with Cypark Resources, Malaysia's leading integrated renewable energy provider. The collaboration will see both parties jointly promoting renewable energy usage and also supplying electricity to Singapore (*The Star*, 2023a). A Chinese firm, Jinko Solar, has chosen Malaysia to build its overseas production facility. To date, it is the only overseas Jinko Solar plant that is fully powered by renewable energy (*Jinko Solar*, 2022). These investments and developments are crucial in helping Malaysia reduce its carbon footprint.

Collaboration between Chinese and Malaysian firms extends beyond manufacturing to energy generation itself. Malaysia's Majuperak Holdings signed a MoU with a Chinese company to promote initiatives in renewable energy (*The Star*, 2023b). During a forum organized by Shanghai Energy Technology Development (SETD), research on Malaysia's Integrated Intelligent Impactless Power Plant (3iPP) was unveiled. The adoption of the smart, zero-carbon power plant is vital to aid Malaysia in achieving carbon neutrality by 2050 (*The Star*, 2023b). The Science, Technology and Innovation Minister of the Government of Malaysia, Chang Lih Kang, applauded joint efforts between Malaysian and Chinese firms. According to Chang, 3iPP can be a flagship project under Malaysia's National Energy Transition Roadmap (NETR), and through international collaboration, Southeast Asian countries can achieve their climate goals (*Xinhua*, 2023).

Malaysia stands to reap greater benefits from green investment than from other forms of investment. According to a report by the World Resources Institute, green investment would create more jobs compared to unsustainable investments such as in fossil fuels (Jaeger *et al.*, 2021). Green investment, therefore, makes sound long-term economic sense to promote a more resilient economy. It is estimated that by 2030, 38 million people will be employed in the renewable energy sector and Malaysia should jump at the opportunities (Augustin and Pathmanathan, 2023). The creation of green jobs would enable Malaysia to gradually phase out jobs that are detrimental to the environment. Besides, through collaboration, Malaysian firms could also leverage the technical skills of the world's leading companies to provide renewable energy solutions to Malaysian households. Cooperation between Malaysia and China in renewable energy could help Malaysia achieve the target of a 20% renewable energy mix by 2025 (Sustainable Energy Development Authority, 2009).

Malaysia–China Collaboration in the Electric Vehicle Industry

Vehicles powered by fossil fuels release substantial amounts of greenhouse gases into the atmosphere, contributing to global warming. As such, EVs are seen as a more sustainable alternative. Governments worldwide are pushing for the adoption of EVs, and EVs have become an emerging sector that could provide quality growth to the global economy. Western companies such as Tesla may have been the early manufacturers of EVs, but Chinese electric car companies are claiming a dominant market share. Chinese companies now manufacture the largest number of EVs, accounting for 60% of total sales of EVs globally (Oxford, 2024). The Chinese government has played a fundamental role in accelerating the public's adoption of EVs within the Chinese market. Various incentives are given to the public, including subsidies, cost-free license plates, and exemptions from consumption tax (Ren, 2023). As a result, EVs accounted for 36% of total cars sold in China in 2023 (Terasawa and Tiberghien, 2024). It is also expected that "60% of all new vehicles will be electric by 2030" (Ren, 2023).

While China is one of the fastest adopters of electric cars, Malaysia is clearly lagging behind. Fitch estimated that in 2023, less than 5,000 units would be sold in Malaysia (Huong, 2022). Yet there are abundant opportunities to increase the penetration rate of EVs in the local market with Chinese companies' assistance. For instance, Zhejiang Geely Holding Group has partnered with Proton Holdings to roll out EVs in Southeast Asia. Proton signed a MoU with Smart Automobile, a joint venture between Geely and Mercedez-Benz, to assemble EVs at Proton facilities (Malaysian Investment Development Authority, 2023). Such partnerships would facilitate the transfer of knowledge and skills to Malaysian workers at the assembly facilities.

Moreover, Proton, which is jointly owned by Malaysia's DRB-Hicom and Geely, will launch its own EV in 2025. Proton's decision to expedite the launch of its first EV under its brand will aid the government's aspiration to develop the domestic EV sector (Mohd Zaky Zainuddin, 2023). As part of its hopes to take a leading position in the Southeast Asia auto market, specifically in EVs, Geely plans to make Proton one of the top three automobile brands in the region. To this end, Geely is planning to invest USD10 million to develop Malaysia's Automotive High-Technology Valley (AHTV). AHTV is expected to be a global automotive center for new energy vehicles. Indeed, the Malaysian government plans not only to attract automobile manufacturing plants but also invest in related components and parts of new energy vehicles (*Bernama*, 2023).

This ambitious plan is already taking shape, driven partly by existing investments from Chinese companies to produce components related to EVs. Eve Energy Co., Ltd. invested RM1.9 billion to build a new manufacturing plant for cylindrical lithium-ion batteries which can be used in electric two-wheel vehicles (Asila Jalil, 2023). Additionally, INV New

Material Technology will invest RM6.4 billion to build a lithium-ion battery separator factory in Penang — the first separator factory in Southeast Asia (*The Star*, 2023c). Although these investments are not a form of partnership with Malaysian firms, they will nevertheless substantially boost local skills and contribute to helping Malaysia develop an EV ecosystem.

Other Green Initiatives

Malaysia's Ministry of Investment, Trade and Industry (MITI) has urged Malaysia and China to work more closely together to develop the green economy, particularly in renewable energy, support services for EVs, and other areas (Beatty, 2023). One positive development in this direction was the signing of Memorandums of Agreements (MoAs) and Memorandums of Understanding (MoUs) in February 2024 that paved the way for Malaysian and Chinese institutions to cooperate in the areas of renewable energy and carbon neutrality. The joint research collaboration between University of Malaya and Tsinghua University's Architectural Design and Research Institute in these areas will provide new impetus to local green BRI projects (*The Star*, 2024). Other partners include China Smart Energy Industry Alliance, China Power International Development, and Guoann Dot Com Bhd. Besides research, the construction of a renewable energy power station is to be jointly undertaken by Malaysian firm Guoann Dot Com Bhd and China Smart Energy Industry Alliance. The cooperation is to include the construction of a zero-carbon park. According to the Vice Chairman of China Smart Energy Industry Alliance, it is projected that these two projects would attract approximately RM14 billion worth of investment (Syafiq Mazalan, 2024).

Malaysia and China are also collaborating on sustainable architecture. China Mobile International Malaysia and i-City Properties are planning to jointly build the first smart green corporate tower in i-City. The tower will also incorporate artificial intelligence (AI) technology, which will allow building management to anticipate peak hours and make appropriate work arrangements for staff (Kaur, 2022). The Malaysian government intends to utilize the skills and expertise of Chinese firms to help Malaysia build smart cities. In a recent trip to Beijing, Housing and Local Government Minister Nga Kor Ming obtained a deal with China to enhance smart homes and smart cities. According to Nga, Malaysia is looking to benefit from the technology transfer from China, which has many cutting-edge technologies in this sector (*The Sun*, 2024). As early as 2012, China introduced the smart city pilot policy to build cities that are sustainable, innovative, and smart (Yu, Yu, and Gao, 2024). China has made great strides in this area with investment reaching trillion dollars. It is reported that there are more than 500 cities attempting to be smart cities with Shanghai, Beijing, Guangzhou, Shenzhen, and Hangzhou a step ahead of others in terms of adoption of advanced technologies and innovative methods in city planning (Sun, 2023). Malaysia too launched the Malaysia Smart City Framework in 2019 to guide local authorities in the development of smart cities (Ministry of Housing and Local Government of Malaysia, 2021). The formulation of the framework reflects the government's serious commitment to developing sustainable cities, viewed as a key initiative in helping Malaysia achieve net-zero emissions.

Malaysia–China Prospective Collaboration on Climate

Despite good intentions and some promising early initiatives, Malaysia and China's cooperation on climate is still limited. Tham Siew Yean, a Malaysian senior economist and trade expert, pointed out that China's green investment predates BRI. Even after the BRI went "green", the ratio of green investment within the total of Chinese FDI into Malaysia does not show any significant increase. There is much rhetoric about the "Green BRI" but the pace of materialization in Malaysia has not noticeably picked up yet (Tham, 2024). Moving forward, both sides should prioritize forging cooperation in climate protection, aligned with the global agenda of sustainable development.

As Malaysia strives to meet a key target set by the NETR — that by 2030, EVs should account for 20% of new cars sold annually (*New Straits Times*, 2023) — Chinese automakers could be of vital assistance. Chinese automakers can accelerate the expansion of EV charging stations in various locations across the country, which will encourage EV adoption. Moreover, as sales of EVs grow, repair and maintenance will increasingly become an issue. In this instance, China could provide vocational training to Malaysian workers to ensure that there are enough skilled mechanics to meet the surging demand. Skills transfers such as this are fundamental to Malaysia's human development.

For Malaysia to be able to meet its target of 45% reduction in carbon intensity emissions by 2030, Malaysia also requires support and funding from the international community (Susskind *et al.*, 2020). Malaysia has signed the Paris Agreement, which would allow it to access funds from the GFC. At present, only four national projects and one regional project have been funded by the GFC. Malaysia has also received funding from the Global Environment Facility (GEF) to fight climate change. The total amount received is close to USD77 million since Malaysia joined the GEF in 1994 (Nor Ain Mohamed Radhi and Qistina Sallehuddin, 2023). Still, overall Malaysia lacks sufficient international funding to fight climate change. This is also where China could play a role. While there is no obligation for China to donate funds to developing countries to fight climate change, China has done so voluntarily in the past. Apart from directly contributing funds to Malaysia to fight climate change, China could also choose to make in-kind contributions such as providing technical assistance and advice to Malaysia in implementing mitigation and adaptation plans. For example, in the field of AI, where China is one of the leading countries, AI technology can be utilized to address climate challenges.

As China has been leveraging AI technologies in environmental management, Malaysia could benefit from China's advice, technical assistance, and technologies. One area in which China has been developing and applying AI technologies is meteorology. Chinese scientists developed forecast weather models that use AI technology to predict extreme weather more accurately and much earlier (Zhao, 2024). Some of its AI prediction weather models are as good as those developed by European companies, if not better, demonstrating China's leading edge in utilizing AI in meteorological forecasting. As such, Malaysia and China could cooperate on using AI to intelligently predict the weather, enabling timely responses to potential disasters. In fact, there are enormous prospects for China and Malaysia to collaboratively engage in developing climate plans for prevention, mitigation, and adaptation using AI technologies.

Conclusion

China has been portraying itself as a global climate leader in helping developing countries tackle climate change. China's serious commitment to accelerating low-carbon development extends from its understanding that if the world continues to follow a business-as-usual trajectory, it will certainly lead to climate catastrophe. Solidarity in climate action is indispensable to building a community with a shared future. As Malaysia works to transform itself into a low-carbon economy, cooperation with China is certainly essential, as is cooperation with other countries, especially within the ASEAN region.

Malaysia has benefitted from climate engagement with China within the ASEAN framework and also bilaterally. ASEAN and China jointly established the ASEAN–China Environmental Cooperation Centre (CAEC) and formulated environmental cooperation strategies and action plans. Under the cooperative framework, ASEAN and China jointly organized various activities, including fora and capacity-building workshops, along with public education efforts.

Though, until recently, China had been relatively slow to promote green development through BRI projects, Malaysian and Chinese counterparts have undertaken various partnerships including in renewable energy, EVs, research and development for carbon neutrality, and green construction. Though cooperation between the two countries in climate remains limited, these initiatives remain important to propel Malaysia toward becoming a climate-resilient economy. Moving forward, huge opportunities exist for these two countries to further their engagement in terms of climate cooperation.

References

Amir Yusof (2021). "Malaysia's 'Once in 100 Years' Flood Exposes Reality of Climate Change, Better Disaster Planning Needed: Experts." *Channel News Asia*, 21 December. https://www.channelnewsasia.com/asia/malaysia-once-100-years-flooding-climate-change-disaster-planning-2391316.

Augustin, Sean and Krishaant Pathmanathan (2023). "Malaysia Should Jump on the Green Jobs Bandwagon, Says Expert." *Free Malaysia Today*, 9 June. https://www.freemalaysiatoday.com/category/highlight/2023/06/09/malaysia-should-jump-on-the-green-jobs-bandwagon-says-expert/.

ASEAN Environment Knowledge Hub (n.d.) "Environmental Education and Sustainable Consumption and Production." https://environment.asean.org/environment-education-and-sustainable-consumption-and-production/about.

ASEAN Environmental Education Inventory Database (2016). "ASEAN Plus Three Youth Environment Forum: Youth and Sustainability." 1 February. https://aeeid.asean.org/asean-plus-three-youth-environment-forum-youth-and-sustainability/.

ASEAN Secretariat (2007). *ASEAN Environmental Education Action Plan (AEEAP) 2008-2012: Environmental Education for Sustainable Development.*

ASEAN Secretariat (2010). "Statement on ASEAN PLUS Three Youth Actions on Environment." 25 April. https://asean.org/statement-on-asean-plus-three-youth-actions-on-environment-25-april-2010/.

Asila Jalil (2023). "Eve Energy Breaks Ground for RM1.9 Billion Factory in Kedah." *New Straits Times*, 6 September. https://www.nst.com.my/business/esg/2023/08/939838/eve-energy-breaks-ground-rm19-billion-factory-kedah%C2%A0.

Beatty, Gloria Harry (2023). "Miti: Malaysia, China Should Deepen Cooperation in Green Economy." *The Sun*, 6 December. https://thesun.my/business/miti-malaysia-china-should-deepen-cooperation-in-green-economy-KI11087058.

Bernama (2023). "DRB-Hicom Inks Agreement With Geely On Auto Hub Development." 10 November. https://www.bernama.com/en/business/news.php?id=2233842.

Buzan, Barry (2021). "China and Climate Change Governance: A Golden Opportunity." *China Quarterly of International Strategic Studies*, Vol. 7, No. 1, pp. 1–12.

Chan, Dawn (2022). "Ismail Sabri: Govt Has Identified Three Actions to Prepare for Climate Change, Boost Public Health." *New Straits Times*, 21 June. https://www.nst.com.my/news/nation/2022/06/806976/ismail-sabri-govt-has-identified-three-actions-prepare-climate-change.

Chia, Theodore (2022). "How China Is Winning the Race for Clean Energy Technology." *Fairbank Center for Chinese Studies*, 26 October. https://fairbank.fas.harvard.edu/research/blog/how-china-is-winning-the-race-for-clean-energy-technology%EF%BF%BC/.

China Daily (2023). "LONGi's PV Module Factory in Selangor Commences Production." 18 October. https://regional.chinadaily.com.cn/en/2023-10/18/c_931765.htm.

China Development Brief (2024). "China-ASEAN Environmental Cooperation Center." https://chinadevelopmentbrief.org/ngos/1779684/.

Hale, Erin (2023). "China Promised Climate Action. Its Emissions Topped US, EU, India Combined." *Al Jazeera*, 1 September. https://www.aljazeera.com/economy/2023/8/30/chinas-coal-habit-clouds-climate-fight-as-emissions-top-us-eu-combined.

Hayatun Razak (2023). "China Solar Panel Maker LONGi Invests RM1.8b to Build Plant in Serendah." *The Sun*, 18 October. https://thesun.my/business-news/china-solar-panel-maker-longi-invests-rm18b-to-build-plant-in-serendah-JF11639275.

Huong, Thomas (2022). "EV Demand seen to Soar in 2023." *The Star*, 2 December. https://www.thestar.com.my/business/business-news/2022/12/22/ev-demand-seen-to-soar-in-2023.

Jaeger, Joel, Ginette Walls, Ella Clarke, Juan-Carlos Altamirano, Arya Harsono, Helen Mountford, Sharan Burrow, Samantha Smith, and Alison Tate (2021).

The Green Jobs Advantage: How Climate-friendly Investments Are Better Job Creators. World Resources Institute Work Paper, 18 October. https://www.wri.org/research/green-jobs-advantage-how-climate-friendly-investments-are-better-job-creators.

Jinko Solar (2022). "JinkoSolar Announces its First Overseas 'RE100 Factory' Completely Powered by Renewables." 15 June. https://www.jinkosolar.com/en/site/newsdetail/1748.

Kaur, Sharen (2022). "I-City and China Mobile International Malaysia to Build the Country's First Smart Green Corporate Tower." *New Straits Times*, 22 February. https://www.nst.com.my/property/2022/01/766275/i-city-and-china-mobile-international-malaysia-build-countrys-first-smart.

Leung, Andrew (2023). "Climate Action: How China Is Accelerating the Drive Towards a Net Zero World." *South China Morning Post*, 31 December. https://www.scmp.com/comment/opinion/article/3246696/climate-action-how-china-accelerating-drive-towards-net-zero-world.

Lee, Pei May, Chuan Choong Yang, and Wei Choong Kwong (2023). "An Exploratory Study on Students' Electricity Consumption in RCE Gombak for Sustainable Communities." *Malaysian Journal of Social Sciences and Humanities* Vol. 8, No. 3, e002170.

Liu, Yukun (2024). "China's Solar Sector Readying for New Challenges." *China Daily HK*, 3 January. https://www.chinadailyhk.com/hk/article/369568.

Syafiq Mazalan (2024). "RM 14 Bil China Investment for Malaysia Carbon Neutral R&D Center and Smart Renewable Energy Power Plant." *Asia News Channels*, 31 January. https://www.asianewschannels.com/latest/malaysia-china-carbon-neutrality-collaboration.

Malaysian Investment Development Authority (2023). "Geely Eyes EV Foothold in Southeast Asia With US$10bn Malaysia Hub." 5 December. https://www.mida.gov.my/mida-news/geely-eyes-ev-foothold-in-southeast-asia-with-us10bn-malaysia-hub/.

Ministry of Ecology and Environment of the People's Republic of China (2017). "Guidance on Promoting Green Belt and Road." https://english.mee.gov.cn/Resources/Policies/policies/Frameworkp1/201706/t20170628_416864.shtml.

Ministry of Environmental Protection of China and Environmental Authorities of ASEAN Member States (2016). "ASEAN-China Strategy on Environmental Cooperation 2016-2020."

Ministry of Foreign Affairs of Malaysia (2021). "Statement by Mr. Azril Abd Aziz, Deputy Permanent Representative of Malaysia to The United Nations Agenda Item 20: Sustainable Development." 11 October. https://www.kln.gov.my/web/usa_un-new-york/news-from-mission/-/blogs/statement-2c-sustainable-development-agenda-item-20-11-october-2021#:~:text=In%20confronting%20the%20climate%20crisis,carbon%20growth%20at%20all%20levels.

Ministry of Housing and Local Government of Malaysia (2021). *Smart City Handbook Malaysia*. https://www.kpkt.gov.my/index.php/pages/view/675?mid=405.

Mohd Zaky Zainuddin (2023). "Proton Hastens EV Launch to 2025 From 2027: Deputy CEO." *New Straits Times*, 12 April. https://www.nst.com.my/business/2023/04/898962/proton-hastens-ev-launch-2025-2027-deputy-ceo.

Mukherji, Biman (2024). "ASEAN Renewable Energy Sector Gets Boost from China's Solar Projects, Faces Hurdle of Fossil Fuels Reliance." *South China Morning Post*, 2 February. https://www.scmp.com/week-asia/economics/article/3250686/asean-renewable-energy-sector-gets-boost-chinas-solar-projects-faces-hurdle-fossil-fuels-reliance.

New Straits Times (2023). "Electric Bus Adoption Still Low Due to High Costs — Experts." 27 December. https://www.nst.com.my/news-cars-bikes-trucks/2023/12/994807/electric-bus-adoption-still-low-due-high-costs-experts.

Nikkei Asia (2023). "China's Biggest Green Tech Projects in Southeast Asia." 3 October. https://asia.nikkei.com/Spotlight/The-Big-Story/China-s-biggest-green-tech-projects-in-Southeast-Asia.

Oxford, Dwayne (2024). "Are Chinese Electric Vehicles Taking Over the World?" *Al Jazeera*, 20 April. https://www.aljazeera.com/economy/2024/4/20/are-chinese-evs-taking-over-the-car-market.

Prime Minister's Office of Malaysia (2023). "Climate Change: M'sia Steadfast In Stance For Developed Countries To Fulfill Commitment — Pm Anwar." 31 October. https://www.pmo.gov.my/2023/10/climate-change-msia-steadfast-in-stance-for-developed-countries-to-fulfill-commitment-pm-anwar/.

Nor Ain Mohamed Radhi and Qistina Sallehuddin (2023). "Malaysia to Receive RM364.8 Mil in International Funds to Fight Climate Change." *New Straits Times*, 16 October. https://www.nst.com.my/news/nation/2023/10/967640/malaysia-receive-rm3648-mil-international-funds-fight-climate-change.

Ren, Daniel (2023). "China's EV War: Only the Strongest Will Survive as BYD, Xpeng's Dominance Knock Out 15 Pretenders Amid Supply Glut." *South China Morning Post*, 7 October. https://www.scmp.com/business/china-business/article/3237078/chinas-ev-war-only-strongest-will-survive-byd-xpengs-dominance-knock-out-15-pretenders-amid-supply.

Reuters (2022). "Xi Vows to Prioritise Environment, Protect Nature and Promote Green Lifestyles." 16 October. https://www.reuters.com/world/china/xi-vows-prioritise-environment-protect-nature-promote-green-lifestyles-2022-10-16/.

Seah, Sharon (2021). "ASEAN's Climate Cooperation with China and the US: Challenges and Prospects." *ISEAS Perspective*, No. 77, 9 June. https://www.iseas.edu.sg/articles-commentaries/iseas-perspective/2021-77-aseans-climate-cooperation-with-china-and-the-us-challenges-and-prospects-by-sharon-seah/.

Sun, Luna (2023). "China's Smart Cities: 4 Areas Where AI, the IoT, Big Data and Cloud Computing Are Making a Difference." *South China Morning Post*, 2 May. https://www.scmp.com/economy/china-economy/article/3218514/chinas-smart-cities-4-areas-where-ai-iot-big-data-and-cloud-computing-are-making-difference.

Susskind, Leonard, Chun Jungwoo, Goldberg Selmah, Gordon Jessica, Smith Griffin, and Zaerpoor Yasmin (2020). "Breaking Out of Carbon Lock-In: Malaysia's Path to Decarbonization." *Frontiers in Built Environment*, Vol. 6. https://doi.org/10.3389/fbuil.2020.00021.

Sustainable Energy Development Authority (2009). *National Renewable Energy Policy*. https://www.seda.gov.my/policies/national-renewable-energy-policy-and-action-plan-2009/.

Terasawa, Mei and Yves Tiberghien (2024). "Asia Ground Zero in the Revolution of Electric Vehicle Markets." *East Asia Forum*, 23 March. https://eastasiaforum.org/2024/03/19/asia-ground-zero-in-the-revolution-of-electric-vehicle-markets/.

Tham, Siew Yean. 2024. "Greening China's Belt and Road Initiative in Malaysia: Rhetoric versus Reality." *Journal of Southeast Asian Economies*, Vol. 41, No. 1, pp. 13–27.

The Star (2023a). "Cypark, Trina Solar in Clean Energy Tie-up." *The Star*, 5 October. https://www.thestar.com.my/business/business-news/2023/10/06/cypark-trina-solar-in-clean-energy-tie-up.

The Star (2023b). "Renewable Energy Pact." 12 September. https://www.thestar.com.my/business/business-news/2023/09/12/renewable-energy-pact.

The Star (2023c). "RM6bil Battery Factory Coming Up." 12 December. https://www.thestar.com.my/metro/metro-news/2023/12/12/rm6bil-battery-factory-coming-up.

The Star (2024). "Malaysia-China Carbon Neutrality Collaboration." 2 February. https://www.thestar.com.my/news/nation/2024/02/02/malaysia-china-carbon-neutrality-collaboration.

The Sun (2024). "Malaysia, China to Sign Pact on Enhancing Smart City, Smart Home Capabilities." 17 January. https://thesun.my/business-news/malaysia-china-to-sign-pact-on-enhancing-smart-city-smart-home-capabilities-HA11994267.

Weigel, Moritz (2016). *More Money, More Impact? China's Climate Change South-South Cooperation to Date and Future Trends.* Beijing: UNDP China. https://www.undp.org/china/publications/more-money-more-impact-chinas-climate-change-south-south-cooperation-date-and-future-trends.

Xinhua (2023). "Malaysia Welcomes China's Innovative Power Plant Tech to Facilitate Energy Transition: Minister." 11 September. https://english.news.cn/20230911/c9e4e22e41e94696a389f2aa35b8b8ed/c.html.

Yu, Chengfeng, Jiyu Yu, and Da Gao (2024). "Smart Cities and Greener Futures: Evidence from a Quasi-Natural Experiment in China's Smart City Construction," *Sustainability*, Vol. 16. No. 2, pp. 1–28.

Zhang, Meihui, Zhang, Chi, Li, Fenghua, and Liu, Ziyu (2022). "Green Finance as an Institutional Mechanism to Direct the Belt and Road Initiative towards Sustainability: The Case of China." *Sustainability*, Vol. 14, No. 10. https://doi.org/10.3390/su14106164.

Zhao, Yusha (2024). "China's AI Weather Forecasting Model Front-runner Worldwide." *Global Times*, 11 January. https://www.globaltimes.cn/page/202401/1305205.shtml.

© 2025 World Scientific Publishing Company
https://doi.org/10.1142/9789819801350_0011

Chapter 11

Thirty Years of Islamic–Confucian Dialogue in Malaysia and China

Tee Boon Chuan

Introduction: Islamic–Confucian Dialogue as a Commitment to Avoid the Clash of Civilizations

The theory of the "clash of civilizations" was first proposed in 1993 by American political scientist Samuel Huntington. Huntington argued that as ideologies (communism versus liberal democracy) faded after the end of the Cold War, cultural identities would be the next sources of conflict between societies and peoples, and "civilizations" as the highest units of cultural entities would become coherent forces contending with each other. Both Confucianism and Islam were identified by Huntington as "civilizations" that would clash with the Western world.

This "clash of civilizations" theory created many discussions, debates, and disagreements in both the Western and non-Western worlds. It painted Islam and Confucianism as adversaries of the Western Judeo-Christian civilization. Prominent scholars and philosophers within the Islamic and Confucian intellectual communities felt that it was necessary to respond to this theory. While responding, there was also a reckoning that there was a great need for dialogue and mutual understanding between Islamic and Confucian traditions, not just between Islamic and Western civilizations or between Confucian and Western civilizations. These scholars included well-known Iranian Islamic philosopher (exile in the United States after the 1979 Iranian Revolution) Professor Seyyed Hossein Nasr, his students Professors William Chittick and Sachiko Murata, and the famed Confucian scholar Professor Tu Wei-Ming. Together, they organized the first Islamic–Confucian dialogue conference in the United States in 1994.

In the following year (1995), another Islamic–Confucian dialogue conference followed in Kuala Lumpur. Professor Osman Bakar, a doctoral student of Seyyed Hossein Nasr, played a leading role in organizing this second Islamic–Confucian dialogue conference, in which Tu Wei-Ming also participated. Osman Bakar organized the conference with encouragement from Nasr, who felt strongly about the fact that Malay Muslims and Chinese in Malaysia live in peace and harmony (and also in a country with many Western influences and influences from other civilizational heritages such as Hinduism and Buddhism), which is the best refutation of the theory of clash of civilizations (Ren, 2013: 24). The conference received strong support from the then Deputy Prime Minister of Malaysia Dato' Seri Anwar Ibrahim, who has consistently been an eloquent advocate for more inter-civilizational dialogues and mutual understanding.

Efforts to continue this dialogue persisted. Nasr, Chittick, Murata, and Tu organized another collaborative effort in the Unites States in 2000. Tu also brought this intellectual endeavor to China. He collaborated with Nanjing University to organize several Islamic–Confucian dialogue conferences in Nanjing (2002, 2010), Yinchuan (2005), Kunming (2006), and other places (Hua, 2016: 135). In Malaysia, Osman Bakar continued to promote Islamic–Confucian dialogue, although it was not until 2019 that another conference on Islamic–Confucian dialogue (titled *Islam-Confucianism Civilizational Dialogue: Empowering Common Values*) was held (in Penang). In 2023, with the support of Anwar Ibrahim again, having become the Tenth Prime Minister of Malaysia since November 2022, another Islamic–Confucian dialogue conference (titled *Islam-Confucianism Leadership Dialogue*) was held. Similar endeavors have also taken place in the Middle East and Indonesia, carried out by scholars with similar commitments. In other words, the Islamic–Confucian dialogue held in Malaysia is not an isolated phenomenon, but a link to similar dialogues around the world.

Osman Bakar and Tu Wei-Ming: Engaging Islamic–Confucian Dialogue in Malaysia and China

Without a doubt, Osman Bakar and Tu Wei-Ming are the two intellectuals/scholars who have done the most in promoting Islamic–Confucian dialogue in Malaysia and China, respectively. Osman Bakar obtained a doctorate degree from Temple University and served at Universiti Malaya, Universiti Brunei Darussalam, and Universiti Islam Antarabangsa Malaysia (International Islamic University of Malaysia [IIUM]) throughout his scholarly career. He is currently Holder of the Al-Ghazali Chair of Epistemology and Civilizational Studies and Renewal at the International Institute of Islamic Thought and Civilization (ISTAC), IIUM. Tu Wei-Ming obtained a doctorate degree from Harvard University. For many years, he was affiliated with Harvard University and served as the director of the Harvard-Yenching Institute. In 2010, he became a faculty member at Peking University.

Osman Bakar and Islamic–Confucian Dialogue in Malaysia

In the context of Islamic revivalism in Malaysia, and from the perspective of the Islamic–Confucian dialogue, Angkatan Belia Islam Malaysia (ABIM) or the Muslim Youth Movement of Malaysia deserves special attention. Founded in 1972, ABIM has been one of the most enduring, influential, intellectually sophisticated, and resilient movements in Malaysia (ABIM, 2021). ABIM has maintained an open attitude toward other religious communities and encouraged interreligious dialogue. In the collection of writings and speeches of the first three presidents of ABIM between 1972 and 1991 (Razali Nawawi, Anwar Ibrahim, and Siddiq Fadzil), for example, one can see their articles or speeches on "Dialogue between Islam and other Civilizations" (Siddiq Fadzil, 2009, 2022). Hence, ABIM's open attitude toward dialogue between civilizations laid a solid foundation for Islamic–Confucian dialogue in Malaysia. In addition, aside from ABIM, other important Muslim scholars such as Uthman El-Muhammady and Chandra Muzaffar also often encourage interreligious dialogue in Malaysia and in the world, although they often focus more on Buddhism or Christianity in the dialogue (Muhamad Razak Idris, 2021).

Osman Bakar is one of the founding members of ABIM and served as its secretary when Anwar Ibrahim served as its leader (1974–1983).

Osman Bakar also founded Akademi Sains Islam Malaysia (ASASI) or the Malaysian Academy of Islamic Sciences in 1977, with colleagues from mathematics, engineering, and other backgrounds, and served as ASASI president from 1987–1992. Similar to ABIM, ASASI is not exclusively concerned with Islamic or Islam-related knowledge. Its active members (such as Shaharir Mohamad Zain and Mohammad Alinor Abdul Kadir) pay a lot of attention to Malay science studies from the pre-Islamic period (Shaharir Mohamad Zain, 2015, 2021, 2023).

Since his involvement in Islamic–Confucian dialogue from the mid-1990s onward, Osman Bakar has been the main torchbearer within Malay/Malaysian academia for such an endeavor. From an Islamic perspective, Osman Bakar argues that Confucius could be considered as one of the prophets before Prophet Muhammad and the *Analects* can be given the same status as the Christian Bible or the hadith of the Prophet (Osman Bakar, 1997a). This is an inclusive perspective that encourages Islam–Confucianism dialogue (Tee, 2014). Since Islam arrived in China centuries ago, Islamic–Confucian dialogues in fact took place in the past centuries "within the religious and philosophical universe of Chinese civilization," which can especially be seen in the cases of those "Muslim Confucian" scholars (discussed later) who made efforts to reconcile the teachings of Islam and Confucianism. Fundamentally, Osman Bakar argues "for the complementariness and acceptability of Confucian ideals within Islamic philosophy" and further argues that the works of "Muslim Confucian" scholars be considered foundational to Islamic–Confucian dialogue as these scholars "lived with both cultures and saw no conflict between them" (Kahteran, 2022: 168).

Osman Bakar advocates not only for Islamic–Confucian Dialogue but also dialogues between Islam and other faiths and civilizations including the Western Judeo-Christian civilization and Buddhism (Osmam Bakar, 1997b, 2008). However, the Islamic–Confucian dialogue was especially relevant in the context of the multicultural pluralism within Malaysia (Chang, 2022). His edited volume on the 1995 conference on Islamic–Confucian dialogue, published in 1997, has remained the standard text on this subject (Osman Bakar and Cheng, 1997, 2019).

Osman Bakar is not the only scholar to have promoted Islamic–Confucian dialogue. Prior to Osman Bakar, two notable Muslim scholars stood out: Ibrahim T. Y. Ma and Obaidellah Mohamad (Tee, 2014; Ngeow and Ling, 2019). Ma was a diplomat of the Republic of China government stationed in Ipoh, Malaya, before he eventually adopted Malaya/Malaysia as his homeland. A Chinese Muslim of the Hui ethnicity, he produced many works both in the Chinese language and Malay language, introducing Islam to Chinese readers and Chinese history and culture (including Islam in China) to Malay readers. Obaidellah Mohammad taught for many years at Universiti Malaya and was the first Malay scholar to translate *The Analects* and *Mencius* into the Malay language (Obaidellah Mohamad, 1994, 1995).

Tu Wei-Ming and Islamic–Confucian Dialogue in China

In China, after 1978, Confucianism gradually ceased to be a political taboo. Scholars were given the space to initiate a process of re-understanding and learning about Confucianism, which gradually contributed to the revival of Confucianism. The Chinese government itself also became gradually more supportive and established the China Confucius Foundation (1984) and the International Confucian Association (1995) to supervise and regulate activities related to the promotion of Confucianism. Confucianism has enjoyed a revival since the 1980s, and many Confucian groups and academic institutions emerged in the course of the reform years. Prominent scholars such as Feng Youlan, Zhang Dainian, Zhu Bokun, and Tang Yijie advocated a re-understanding of traditional culture and ideas. Tang established the Chinese Culture Academy in Beijing in October 1984, uniting academic institutions such as Peking University, Tsinghua University, Renmin University of China, and the Chinese Academy of Social Sciences to organize the promotion of Confucianism through lectures, conferences, and publications (Xu, 2012a: 232). In the 1990s, the trend of "Chinese Studies" (*guoxue*) became widespread in Chinese society, as indicated by the voluminous publications and high sales of traditional classics, the emerging phenomenon of recitation of Chinese classics among ordinary people, and the growing number of academic conferences in the name of Chinese Studies and Confucianism, with an average of seven or eight conferences held every year (Xu, 2012b: 239–240).

The traditional Marxist–Leninist ideology of the Chinese communist leadership was profoundly anti-traditional and anti-Confucian. The reemergence of Confucianism created some unease among those who adhered to the official canon of Marxism (Fang, 1996). Nonetheless, instead of rejecting Confucianism as "feudal" and backward, as it had done in the past, in more recent years, the Chinese government came to embrace Confucianism, albeit with the understanding that the elements that are incompatible with the government's approved values will be removed. Today, the Chinese government under Xi Jinping has made it clear that it will embrace the combining of "the basic principles of Marxism with China's excellent traditional culture," which includes Confucianism. Confucianism is no longer a tradition that the Chinese government denies or denounces, but rather a heritage that must be actively integrated with Marxism.

With the blessing of the leadership, Confucianism in China nowadays flourishes in academia and has entered the era of "the sky full of stars" (*fanxing mantian*), a metaphor indicating the emergence of many Confucian scholars who have made original theoretical achievements. However, among these many scholars, only Tu Wei-Ming appears to have a sustained interest in Islamic–Confucian dialogue. The mainstream Confucian circle in China has yet to participate in this dialogical activity.

This of course does not mean that Chinese Confucian scholars do not pay attention to civilizational dialogue, but generally, they pay more attention to the West and less attention to Islam. We can understand the scope of civilizational dialogue among Confucian scholars through the Nishan Forum on World Civilizations. Nishan (in Qufu, Shandong province) is the birthplace of Confucius, and the Nishan Forum is an important platform in China with a focus on dialogues between world civilizations. From 2010 to 2023, the Nishan Forum held nine conferences. Many Confucian scholars have attended the Nishan Forum. From the perspective of dialogue between Confucianism and Abrahamic religious civilizations, including the third conference with the specific theme of "Common Ethics of Humanity under Different Faiths," Chinese and foreign scholars mostly focused on dialogues with Christianity. Chinese Confucian scholars' dialogue with Islam is not even as strong as their dialogue with Judaism. From this, we can see how valuable the work of Tu Wei-Ming is in promoting Islamic–Confucian dialogue in China, Malaysia, and around the world.

Like many other scholars engaged in civilizational dialogue, Tu Wei-Minig also became more concerned about peace and harmony between different civilizations in the wake of the "clash of civilizations" theory proposed by Samuel Huntington, his colleague at Harvard University. In fact, Tu and Huntington had many private discussions and debates on this topic as scholarly colleagues (Tu, 2001: 18). Tu believed that there were also many critical self-reflections within the west, and many western scholars also looked into non-western civilizations in search of common values for the humanity. Confucian heritage and ethics, especially the essential humanistic concern for fellow human beings, provide ample resources to engage in dialogue with Western and Islamic traditions (Tu, 2001: 14–15). Moreover, Confucianism is also adaptable and can combine with other civilizational traditions or religions. For example, just as there are Confucian Muslim scholars (discussed below) in Chinese history, today there are also Confucian Christians or Confucian Buddhists. In this sense, Tu believes Confucianism can also play a role as an intermediary in the dialogue between different civilizations (Tu, 2001: 19).

Tu Wei-Ming visited China in 1978. As a Chinese American scholar, Tu Wei-Ming is also an important participant in the revival of Confucianism since the 1980s and is not an outsider in China. Tu had attempted to promote Islamic–Confucian dialogue in China like in Malaysia, but the response was not as forthcoming as he wished. Only after the 9/11 incident in the United States in 2001 did China realize the need to encourage a "dialogue among civilizations." As the director of the Harvard-Yenching Institute, Tu worked with Nanjing University in China to organize civilizational dialogue conferences between the Chinese civilization and the Islamic civilization (Hua, 2016: 135). Participants in these conferences included Confucian scholars and mostly ethnic Hui scholars. A 2012 conference on *Confucian-Muslim Worldview and the Contemporary Value of Chinese Islamic Studies* at Peking University, organized by Tu, emphasized dialogue with Uighur Muslim scholars in China as well (Alimu Tuoheti, 2013: 191–192). The Institute for Advanced Humanities at Peking University, where Tu Wei-Ming served as the director, and other Chinese academic institutions still held Islamic–Confucian dialogue conferences in subsequent years, although they became more like academic platforms for Islamic Studies scholars in China. Many important Islamic Studies scholars (including ethnic Hui scholars) have emerged in Chinese academia in recent years, such as Yang Huaizhong, Hua Tao, Ji Fangtong, Yang Guiping, Yao Jide, Sha Zongping, Ding Shiren, and Liu Yihong. These scholars often engage in arguing for the acceptance and integration of Confucianism in Chinese Muslim writings. Even today, leading scholars of Confucian Studies in China are still mostly absent from these Islamic–Confucian dialogue conferences. Most Confucian scholars still rarely touch upon Islamic elements or traditions in their writings and studies.

Thirty Years of Islamic–Confucian Dialogue: Reflective Observations

Reflecting on the effects of these dialogue conferences over the past 30 years, one of the biggest and most important positive outcomes has been the rediscovery and increased attention on Chinese "Hui-Ru" or "Confucian-Muslim" scholars throughout Chinese history (Ma, 2015: 76; Hua, 2016: 135–137), especially during the Ming–Qing period, such as Wang Daiyu (1584–1670), Ma Zhu (1640–1711), Liu Zhi (1669–1711), Jin Tianzhu (1690–1765), and Ma Dexin (1794–1874). These scholars were Chinese Muslims well versed in both Islamic and Confucian teachings. They used the concepts and terminologies of the Neo-Confucianism of the Song and Ming Dynasties to express Islamic thought, which is why many modern and contemporary scholars regard their work as Confucianized Islamic works. As Seyyed Hossein Nasr said in 2000, there were no experts and scholars in Confucian–Islamic comparative studies, so studying these historic Confucian–Muslim scholars has become the main task in the present era (Ma, 2001: 16). Both Sachiko Murata and William Chittick first learned of the existence of Confucian–Muslim scholars at the 1995 Kuala Lumpur conference. Subsequently, they collaborated (also with Tu Wei-Ming) and translated the works of these scholars into modern English (Sachiko, 2000; Sachiko, Chittick, and Tu, 2009), allowing wider and contemporary access to the intellectual world of Confucian–Muslim scholars. Renowned scholar James D. Frankel has also translated and researched Liu Zhi's works since 2011. Therefore, these Islamic–Confucian dialogue conferences have been crucial in making China's historical Confucian–Muslim scholars known to the world, resulting in appreciation of these Confucian-Muslim scholars in the modern era (Frankel, 2011; Lipman, 2017).

However, there are no contributors from Malaysia in these books, meaning that the local effect of Islamic–Confucian dialogue has not yet reached this level. Within Malaysia, the effect of Islamic–Confucian dialogue is rather mixed. In the beginning, the Chinese people in Malaysia generally did not have the same sentiment toward Confucianism as the Malays had toward Islam. While under the supervision of Osman Bakar and Zailan Morris (another well-known Islamic scholar and student of Seyyed Hossein Nasr), some doctoral dissertations related to the Islamic–Confucian dialogue were completed (Ma, 2009; Abdul Salam Yusoff, 2015; Yang, 2017), the responses to "Confucianism" in Malaysia are rather limited since there are no real Confucian scholars in Malaysia. In the absence of Confucian scholars, the Islamic–Confucian dialogue cannot be promoted as expected.

At a more popular level, the Islamic–Confucian dialogue played a role in the effort to introduce a more general understanding of different cultures and civilizations to students and the public within Malaysia. The Ministry of Education decided to launch a compulsory course called Tamadun Islam dan Tamadun Asia (TITAS, meaning "Islamic Civilization and Asian Civilizations") in public universities in 1998. Students were expected to understand the composition of Malaysian society from various civilizational heritages, namely, Malay civilization, Islamic civilization, Indian civilization, Chinese civilization, and modern (Western) civilization. Osman Bakar and the Center for Civilization Dialogue (founded in 1996 at the University of Malaya) prepared the TITAS module, the final version of which was officially published in 2009 (Osman Bakar, Azizan Baharuddin, and Zaid Ahmad, 2009). TITAS finally became a compulsory course in all public and private colleges and universities across the country in 2002, until the Ministry of Higher Education canceled it (along with another compulsory course, *Ethnic Relations*) in 2019 and replaced it with two other courses, *Philosophy and Current Issues* and *Appreciation of Ethics and Civilization*. Some studies about the TITAS course were done in Malaysia to find out why it was discontinued. From the learner's perspective, a survey conducted in 2000 pointed out that 47% of the respondents thought it was not necessary to take the TITAS course, 43% did not agree that this course should be made mandatory, and 65% responded that the TITAS course was not relevant to their life (Noor Aza Mansor *et al.*, 2001). From the teacher's perspective, there were basically no lecturers who could truly understand and appreciate all the topics covered under TITAS, including Malay, Islamic, Chinese, Indian, and modern civilizations in the context of Malaysia's nation-building (Yaacob Yusoff, 2000). It is a challenging task to make both learners and teachers understand that civilizational dialogue is important.

From the perspective of Malaysia and China, the two countries obviously do not agree with the theory of the clash of civilizations but emphasize a dialogue of civilizations. However, the Islamic–Confucian dialogue has not received a robust response from the Chinese society in Malaysia (since there is no community of Confucian scholars so far), while the dialogue among civilizations as a college course was officially withdrawn in 2019. Similarly, Chinese Confucian scholars, other than Tu Wei-Ming,

188   *Tee Boon Chuan*

have generally been absent from the Islamic–Confucian dialogue, although the Chinese government has vigorously advocated global dialogues among civilizations in recent years.

Conclusion

A common misunderstanding among the advocates of civilizational dialogues is the overestimation of the significance and role of Confucianism in modern Chinese society, whether in China, Malaysia, or other East Asian regions. The revival of Confucianism in China has indeed produced a more visible community of Confucian scholars, but fundamentally, the sociological trend of de-Confucianization in contemporary Chinese societies (not just in China but also in other Chinese societies in East Asia) has not changed. Yu Ying-Shih, a well-known historian and Sinologist, and also a colleague of Tu Wei-Ming, once used the term "wandering soul" to describe the role of Confucianism in modern Chinese societies, meaning that except for a few Confucian scholars and people, Confucianism is not in the "soul" of ordinary people and social institutions in modern Chinese societies (Yu, 1996: 159–164).

Xu Jialu, a prominent Confucian scholar and the promoter of the Nishan Forum, contends that civilizational dialogue has always been limited to a small circle of scholars, theologians, and political figures of some countries (Xu, 2013: 1). What Seyyed Hossein Nasr said in 2000, about the lack of experts in the comparative studies of Confucianism and Islam, has only marginally improved since then. Nonetheless, Islamic–Confucian dialogue is still a very meaningful endeavor despite the limited effects so far. Officially, Malaysia and China have expressed their distaste for the clash of civilizations theory, and both prefer civilizational dialogue. Samuel Huntington mentioned in his preface to the Chinese translation of his book *The Clash of Civilizations and the Remaking of World Order* that the theory of the clash of civilizations is a prediction, indicating that there is such a possibility among civilizations (just like the prediction in the 1950s and 1960s that a nuclear war between the Soviet Union and the United States could occur); so, civilizational dialogue must be promoted to prevent it from happening (such as making sure that nuclear war does not happen) (Huntington, 1998: 3). From this perspective, the various Islamic–Confucian dialogue activities symbolize a commitment to mutual understanding, friendship, peace, and harmony between the two civilizations and also between Malaysia and China where Islam and Confucianism form the core of the civilizational heritages. In this sense, the two countries will continue to promote dialogue among civilizations in the coming decades. Whether the Islamic–Confucian dialogue will have a better, more intellectually substantive development will depend on the commitment of the intellectuals and scholars on both sides who need to increase their efforts in addressing the highlighted shortcomings.

References

ABIM (2021). *Legasi Perjuangan: Perkisahan Separuh Abad ABIM – Shaykh Dr Razali Nawawi & Prof. Dato' Dr. Siddiq Fadzil*. Kuala Lumpur: ABIM.

Abdul Salam Yusoff (2015). *Idea-Idea Pendidikan Berkesan Al-Ghazali dan Konfusius*. Bangi: Penerbit Universiti Kebangsaan Malaysia.

Alimu Tuoheti (2013). "Report of the Conference on 'Confucian-Muslim Worldview and the Contemporary Value of Islamic Studies in China'." *Shijie zongjiao yanjiu* (*Studies in World Religions*), No. 5, pp. 191–192.

Chang, Peter T. C. (2022). "Bridging Civilizational Divides: Osman Bakar's Life-Long Quest for the Middle Ground." In Khairudin Aljunied (ed.), *Knowledge, Tradition and Civilization: Essays in Honour of Professor Osman Bakar*, pp. 361–374. Oldham: Beacon Books.

Fang, Keli (1996). "Ping dalu xinrujia tuichu de liangbenshu (A Comment on Two Books published by Mainland New Confucianists)." *Jinyang xuekan* (*Academic Journal of Jinyang*), No. 3, pp. 31–38.

Frankel, James D. (2011). *Rectifying God's Name: Liu Zhi's Confucian Translation of Monotheism and Islamic Law*. Honolulu, HI: University of Hawaii Press.

Hua, Tao (2016). "Zhongguo Huiru wenming duihua shiwunian huigu (A Review of Fifteen Years of Confucian-Islam Dialogue in China)." *Xibei minzu yanjiu* (*Northwestern Journal of Ethnology*), No. 4, pp. 132–137.

Huntington, Samuel (ed.) (1998). "Preface to Chinese Translation." In *Wenming the chongtu yu shijie zhixu de chongjian* (*The Clash of Civilizations and the Remaking of World Order*), pp. 1–3. Beijing: Xinhua chubanshe.

Kahteran, Nevad (2022). "Osman Bakar and the Dialogue with the Chinese Civilization and Philosophies." In Khairudin Aljunied (ed.), *Knowledge, Tradition and Civilization: Essays in Honour of Professor Osman Bakar*, pp. 163–174. Oldham: Beacon Books.

Lipman, Jonathan M. (ed.) (2017). *Islamic Thought in China: Sino-Muslim Intellectual Evolution from the 17th to the 21st Century*. Edinburgh: Edinburgh University Press.

Ma, Xiaohe (2001). "Hafuo daxe 'huiru duihua guoji xueshu huiyi' zongshu (A Report on the 'International Conference on Islam-Confucian Dialogue' at Harvard University)." *Huizu yanjiu* (*Journal of Hui Studies*), No. 1, pp. 16–19.

Ma, Zhanming (2009). *Jin Tianzhu's Qingzhen Shiyi: An Eighteenth Century Comparative Study between Islam and Confucianism and Other Religions in China.* Unpublished Doctoral Thesis, International Islamic University of Malaysia.

Ma, Xiaoqin (2015). "Huiru: Cong 'Qingzhen xianzheng' dao 'wenming duihua' de shijian, guiyun Huiru de yanjiu jianshi (Confucian-Muslim Scholars: From 'Pure Truth' to the Practice of 'Civilizational Dialogue' and a Brief History of Research on Confucian-Muslim Scholars)." *Beifang minzu daxue xuebao* (*Journal of Beifang University of Nationalities*), No. 4, pp. 76–79.

Muhamad Razak Idris (2021). "Malaysian Scholars' Perspectives on the Role of Dialogue of Civilizations as An Approach in Promoting World Peace." *Malaysian Journal of Islamic Movements and Muslim Societies.* Vol. 1, No. 1, pp. 59–73.

Ngeow, Chow-Bing and Ling Tek Soon (2019). "China Knowledge in the Malay-Language Intellectual World: A Bibliographic Essay." In Ngeow Chow-Bing (ed.), *Researching China in Southeast Asia*, pp. 67–90. New York, NY: Routledge.

Nishan Forum (ed.). (2014). *The Proceedings of the Second Nishan Forum on World Civilizations*, in Three Volumes. Jinan: Shandong University Press.

Noor Aza Mansor, Ermita Amir, Mohd Rashid Kassim, Noor Shuhada Ibrahim, S. Normalis Abd. Samad, and Yuskimi Mohd Yusof (2001). *The Implementation of Islamic and Asia Civilization (TITAS) Course to Students in Universiti Teknologi MARA, Shah Alam.* Shah Alam: Penerbit Universiti Teknologi MARA.

Obaidellah Mohamad (1994). *Lun Yu: Perbicaraan Confucius.* Kuala Lumpur: Dewan Bahasa dan Pustaka.

Obaidellah Mohamad (1995). *Meng Zi.* Kuala Lumpur: Dewan Bahasa dan Pustaka.

Osman Bakar (1997a). "Confucius and the *Analects* in the Light of Islam." In Osman Bakar and Cheng Gek Nai (eds.), *Islam and Confucianism: A Civilizational Dialogue*, pp. 61–74. Kuala Lumpur: Centre for Civilizational Dialogue, University of Malaya.

Osman Bakar (1997b). *Islam and Civilizational Dialogue: The Quest for a Truly Universal Civilization.* Centre for Civilizational Dialogue, University of Malaya.

Osman Bakar (2008). "Challenges to Dialogues of Civilizations and Ways of Overcoming Them." In Thomas W. Simon and Azizan Baharuddin (eds.),

Dialogue of Civilisations and the Construction of Peace, pp. 23–39. Kuala Lumpur: Centre for Civilizational Dialogue, University of Malaya.

Osman Bakar and Cheng Gek Nai (eds.) (1997). *Islam and Confucianism: A Civilizational Dialogue*. Kuala Lumpur: Centre for Civilizational Dialogue, University of Malaya.

Osman Bakar and Cheng Gek Nai (eds.) (2019). *Islam and Confucianism: A Civilizational Dialogue*, New Edition. Kuala Lumpur: International Institute of Islamic Thought and Civilisation, International Islamic University of Malaysia.

Osman Bakar, Azizan Baharuddin, and Zaid Ahmad (eds.) (2009). *Modul Pengajian Tamadun Islam dan Tamadun Asia*. Kuala Lumpur: University of Malaya Press.

Ren, Jun (2013). *Nasaier zhexue sixiang zhaji (Research Notes on the Philosophical Thoughts of Seyyed Hossein Nasr)*. Yinchuan: Ningxia renmin chubanshe.

Sachiko, Murata (2000). *Chinese Gleams of Sufi Light: Wang Tai-yu's Great Learning of the Pure and Real and Liu Chih's Displaying the Concealment of the Real Realm*. New York, NY: SUNY Press.

Sachiko, Murata, William C. Chittick, and Tu Wei-ming (2009). *The Sage Learning of Liu Zhi: Islamic Thought in Confucian Terms*. Cambridge, MA: Harvard University Asia Center.

Shaharir Mohamad Zain (2015). *Unsur Etnosains Malayonesia dalam Bahasa Melayu Sejak Abad ke-5 Masihi*. Kuala Lumpur: Dewan Bahasa dan Pustaka.

Shaharir Mohamad Zain (2021). *Unsur Etnosains Matematik Malayonesia: Jilid II & III*. Kuala Lumpur: Dewan Bahasa dan Pustaka.

Shaharir Mohamad Zain (2023). *Tujuh Ilmu Pilihan dalam Bahasa Melayu yang mendahului Bahasa Inggeris*, Jilid 1 & 2. Kuala Lumpur: Dewan Bahasa dan Pustaka.

Siddiq Fadzil (2009). *Pendidikan Al-Hikmah dan Misi Pencerahan: Himpunan Pidato Kependidikan*. Kuala Lumpur: Aras Mega.

Siddiq Fadzil (2022). *Fikrah Siddiq Fadzil*. Kajang: Akademi Kajian Ketamadunan, Kolej Dar Al-Hikmah.

Tee, Boon Chuan (2014). "Is Confucius Still a Prophet in Islam?" In Haiyun Ma, Chai Shaojin, and Ngeow Chow Bing (eds.), *Zhenghe Forum: Connecting China and the Muslim World*, pp. 87–96. Kuala Lumpur: Institute of China Studies, University of Malaya.

Tu, Wei-Ming (2001). *Du Weiming: Wenming de chongtu yu duihua (Tu Wei-Ming: Conflict and Dialogue between Civilizations)* (Compiled by Zhu Hanmin and Xiao Yongming). Changsha: Hunan University Press.

Xu, Jialu (2013). "Preface." In Nishan Forum Organizing Committee (ed.), *Research Report on Dialogue of World Civilizations*, pp. 1–3. Beijing: Renmin chubanshe.

192　*Tee Boon Chuan*

Xu, Qingwen (2012a). "Confucianism in the 'Cultural Craze' of the 1980s." In Pang Pu (ed.), *20 shiji ruxue tongzhi (jishi yuan)* (*General Chronicle of Confucianism in the 20th Century* [Volume on Events]), pp. 230–235. Hangzhou, China: Zhejiang University Press.

Xu, Qingwen (2012b). "'Chinese Studies Craze' in the 1990s." In Pang Pu (ed.), *20 shiji ruxue tongzhi (jishi yuan)* (*General Chronicle of Confucianism in the 20th Century* [Volume on Events]), pp. 236–242. Hangzhou, China: Zhejiang University Press.

Yaacob Yusoff (2000). "Aspek Pedagogi Dalam Pengajaran TITAS – Pengalaman di UiTM." *Prosiding Seminar TITAS Peringkat Kebangsaan*. Shah Alam: Pusat Pendidikan Islam, Universiti Teknologi MARA.

Yang, Jie (2017). *A Comparative Study of the Teachings of the Quran and the Analects on Man and Nature*. Unpublished Doctoral Thesis, Universiti Sains Malaysia.

Yu, Ying-Shih (1996). *Xiandai Ruxue Lun* (*On Modern Confucianism*). New Jersey, MA: Bafang wenhua.

© 2025 World Scientific Publishing Company
https://doi.org/10.1142/9789819801350_0012

Chapter 12

The Development of Malay Language Teaching and Malay Studies in China: A Historical Review from the Perspective of Knowledge Autonomy

Fu Congcong and Li Gengrun

Introduction

The national language of Malaysia is Malay. According to Article 152 of the *Federal Constitution*, "The national language shall be the Malay language and shall be in such script as Parliament may by law provide." Successive Malaysian governments have placed significant emphasis on Malay language education and the use of Malay, as well as the development of Malay Studies. In recent years, policies have been implemented to mandate the use of Malay in all government documents. Moreover, given the widespread use of Malay in ASEAN countries — it is the official language in Indonesia, Brunei, Singapore, and Malaysia, and is also commonly spoken in parts of southern Thailand, southern Philippines, and in some regions of Myanmar and Cambodia — the Malaysian government proposed in 2017 and 2022 to make Malay the second language of ASEAN as part of its effort to elevate the national language of Malaysia to the international level.

In the promotion and internationalization of the Malay language, the Malaysian government has established numerous professorial chairs focused on Malay Studies across the world. These include positions at

Leiden University in the Netherlands (Europe), Ohio University's Tun Abdul Razak Chair in the United States (North America), Victoria University of Wellington in New Zealand (Oceania), Beijing Foreign Studies University (BFSU) in China (Asia), and Hankuk University of Foreign Studies in Seoul, South Korea (Asia). Additionally, over 140 higher education institutions in more than 40 countries worldwide, including China, Japan, South Korea, the United States, the United Kingdom, Russia, the Netherlands, Germany, Egypt, Iran, and Pakistan, offer Malay language courses. Among these, prominent universities such as the School of Oriental and African Studies at the University of London, Lomonosov Moscow State University and St. Peterburg University in Russia, Goethe University Frankfurt in Germany, Deakin University in Australia, Tokyo University of Foreign Studies, and Hankuk University of Foreign Studies in Korea have established Malay language programs (Azizul Haji Ismail and Subramaniam, 2017).

China also has a long history of learning the Malay language, dating back to the dynastic era. Since the establishment of the People's Republic of China in 1949, Malay and Indonesian were among the first Southeast Asian languages for which programs were offered in China's universities. Since 2013, with the launch of the Belt and Road Initiative (BRI), the construction of Malay language teaching programs in China has flourished. As of 2024, a total of 12 universities and 3 colleges have been approved by China's Ministry of Education to offer Malay language programs, while two more institutions also offer Malay language as an elective course.

In 2024, on the occasion of the 50th anniversary of diplomatic relations and the "China–Malaysia Friendship Year," cultural exchanges and mutual learning between civilizations have become integral components of the bilateral relationship. The interactions between the leaders of the two countries focus not only on strategic and economic issues but also encompass philosophy, culture, and exchanges between Chinese and Islamic civilizations. President Xi Jinping's emphasis on a people-centered governance philosophy aligns closely with Prime Minister Anwar Ibrahim's vision of Malaysia Madani. China is committed to the joint construction of a China–Malaysia community of shared future that will cover many aspects of bilateral relations, including education, culture, and language.

This chapter examines the history of the development of Malay language programs in China, their educational and research achievements, and the paths to produce autonomous and indigenous knowledge in the

Malay language and in Malay Studies in China. The first two sections of the chapter outline the construction of Malay language programs and the development of Malay Studies in China, reviewing the academic achievements in Malay language teaching and research. The first section describes Malay language teaching and research prior to 1949, while the second section discusses the history of Malay language education programs and the development of Malay Studies from 1949 to the present. The second section will focus in particular on the Malay language program at BFSU as a case study to illustrate the evolution of Malay language teaching and Malay Studies in China. The third section discusses the directions for developing an autonomous knowledge system in China's Malay Studies. The final section concludes with a summary and outlook.

The History of Early Malay Language Education in China: Before 1949

Since the Qin and Han Dynasties, the Malay Peninsula has served as a maritime bridge between China and India. Ancient Chinese classics and travelogues provide rich, detailed, and reliable information about the politics, economy, trade, and local customs of the Malay world centered on what is today known as the Malay Peninsula. As the need for closer ties with the Malay world grew, interest in the Malay language and culture gradually increased among Chinese officials, diplomats, and merchants, who began to engage with the people living in the Malay world and learn the language. In ancient times, Malay language education lacked an organized teaching/learning system and professional institutions. It was during the Republican era that modern, professionalized, and systematic Malay language education and Malay Studies emerged, with overseas Chinese citizens and scholars laying a solid foundation for Sino-Malay cultural exchange and language learning.

Ancient Chinese Accounts, Learning, and Translation of the Malay Language

Throughout ancient times, China maintained close ties with maritime Southeast Asia, including the Malay world. The *Han Shu Di Li Zhi* (*The Geographical Records of the Han History*) documents the maritime route used during the reign of Emperor Wu of the Han Dynasty, which passed

196   Fu Congcong & Li Gengrun

through the Strait of Malacca to Burma and Sri Lanka. Fan Ye's *Hou Han Shu* (*Late Han History*) first recorded the formal establishment of relations between China and the kingdom of Ye Diao (*Javadvipa*) on the island of Java (Liang, 1996: 15). Extensive contact and exchanges between China and Southeast Asia intensified during the Tang and Song Dynasties. In the 7th century, the Tang Dynasty saw frequent trade and cultural exchanges with Srivijaya, pioneered by the renowned Tang monk Yijing (635–713). Yijing considered Srivijaya an ideal place for Buddhist studies, where he lived for over a decade, engaging in Buddhist research and translation of scriptures. Yijing believed that before seeking Dharma in India, one should first study in Srivijaya. Yijing was the first historical figure to mention the Chinese people learning the Malay language. In his book, *Biographies of Eminent Monks Who Sought the Dharma in the Western Regions*, Yijing named monks such as Yunqi, Dajin, and Menggu as being proficient in "Kunlun sounds" and "understanding the Kunlun language." Here, the "Kunlun language" refers to the historical "Ancient Malay" language used in Srivijaya, which Chinese monks studied to learn Sanskrit grammar in preparation for their journeys to India (Liang, 1996: 33–34, 2005: 26–27; Kong, 1990).

During the early Ming Dynasty, the Ming government actively pursued a policy of good neighborliness and dispatched Admiral Zheng He (Cheng Ho) on voyages to the Western Seas, significantly boosting interactions between China and the Southeast Asian countries, including what is now Malaysia. The *Ming Shi* (*Ming History*) contains records about the Malacca Sultanate. Accordingly, the first sultan of Malacca, Parameswara, led possibly the largest delegation in Ming history (consisting of 540 people including wives and officials) to Nanjing in 1411, where he was received with the highest honors by Emperor Zhu Di. The Malay chronicle, *Sejarah Melayu* (*The Malay Annals*), recounts the story of Sultan Mansur Shah of Malacca marrying the Chinese princess Hang Li Po (Liang, 1996: 57, 2005: 32–33).

It was during the Ming Dynasty that there were specialized institutions dedicated to organizing or compiling ancient Malay vocabulary or dictionaries to facilitate the learning of the language. In 1405, the Ming government founded the first foreign language academy in Chinese history, the Siyi Guan, in Nanjing. This institution focused on the development and teaching of foreign languages and scripts and was responsible for translating tributary documents and drafting foreign decrees. Under the supervision of the Hanlin Academy, the Siyi Guan emphasized the importance of foreign language education, as indicated by the inscription on the academy's stele: "The study of translation may be intermittently unnecessary, but preparations must never cease." The Siyi Guan comprised eight different language departments, including those for Malay, Siamese, and Burmese, among which the Malay language was taught in the "Huihui Guan" (Muslim department) (Liang, 2005: 37).

In addition to the Siyi Guan, the Ming Dynasty also established the Huitong Guan, under the jurisdiction of the Ministry of War, which primarily handled the reception, escort, and accommodation of tributary missions from various countries. It included thirteen departments for countries such as Korea, Japan, Annam (Vietnam), Champa, Malacca, and Siam, staffed by interpreters fluent in the languages of these nations. In the early Qing Dynasty, the system from the Ming period was continued, maintaining the Huitong Guan and Siyi Guan for interactions with various missions. In 1748, Emperor Qianlong ordered the merger of the Huitong Guan and Siyi Guan, into a single entity, the Huitong Siyi Guan, which was then incorporated into the Ministry of Rites (Liu and Sun, 2008).

For reference in everyday translation and the training of interpreters, a series of Sino-foreign dictionaries were compiled by the Siyi Guan, among which the *Man La Jia Guo Yi Yu* (*The Foreign Language of the Malacca State*) is the earliest known Chinese–Malay dictionary. In 1549, the Chinese interpreter Yang Lin completed the revision of this dictionary. It is a categorized collection of Malay–Chinese vocabulary, containing a total of 482 words divided into 17 categories: astronomy, geography, seasons, flora and fauna, palaces, objects, characters, personal affairs, body parts, clothing, food and drink, treasures, literature and history, colors, numbers, and general vocabulary. Many of the words included are related to maritime navigation and tributary activities, compiled to meet the diplomatic needs of the Zheng He expeditions (Liang, 1996: 82–90; Kong, 1992).

The Beginning of Modern Malay Language Teaching and Malay Studies in China

Despite this long history of Malay language learning in China, before the modern period, such learning efforts were very much only limited and restricted to an small number of officials assigned to deal with external affairs. The real initiation of Malay language teaching, Malay language programs, and Malay Studies, as an academic endeavor, can be traced back to 1942 when the Ministry of Education of the Republic of China established the National School of Oriental Languages.

198   *Fu Congcong & Li Gengrun*

In the early 1940s, during wartime, attention given to and research concerning Southeast Asia and overseas Chinese issues expanded significantly. Many institutions and organizations related to Southeast Asian studies and overseas Chinese, such as the Institute of Nanyang Studies, Nanyang Overseas Chinese Association, Overseas Affairs Research Office, and Nanyang Bulletin Society, were successively established. Simultaneously, academic and educational sectors showed increasing interest in the region through initiatives like the publication of the *Nanyang Studies* journal by Jinan University's Nanyang Hall, the establishment of a Nanyang group at Zhejiang University's Institute of Literature and History, and the introduction of Nanyang history courses at Fudan University and Northeastern University. In the autumn of 1941, the Ministry of Education of the Republic of China planned to establish a specialized school for language studies, which was delayed due to the war and financial constraints (Yun, 2016).

In the spring of 1942, as China actively prepared for counteroffensive operations in places like Myanmar and Vietnam, trained translators were needed. This led to the establishment of military-oriented language training classes to cultivate interpreters to meet military needs. Initially located in Dali (Yunnan province) at the former site of the Institute of Ethnic Culture, the classes recruited individuals who had "completed high school or possessed equivalent educational qualifications, were proficient in one of the languages of Thailand, Vietnam, Myanmar, or Malay, and were competent in Mandarin," with the goal of "training translators and interpreters for Thai, Vietnamese, Burmese, and Malay languages." This military-purposed language training program was later relocated to Chenggong County. Although not a precursor to the National College of Oriental Languages, the training classes laid the organizational and locational groundwork for its establishment (National College of Oriental Languages, 1946: 3–4).

Compared to many other oriental studies institutions established around the world at that time, China's discipline in oriental languages was not yet mature. Yao Nan, one of the pioneers of modern Chinese scholarship in Malay Studies, stated the following:

> The study of foreign languages in China has a long history. During the Han dynasty, translators were part of the Shaofu, and the Sui dynasty established the Sifang Guan. The Ming dynasty had the Siyi Guan, and the early Qing dynasty continued the Ming practices with institutions like the Huitong Siyi Guan. However, the role of translators at that time

was limited to accompanying state emissaries abroad or guiding foreign envoys to the imperial court, with a narrow focus and little academic contribution. By the late Qing dynasty, although Li Hongzhang established the Guangfangyan Guan in Shanghai, it was solely focused on the study of Western languages and did not cover Eastern languages. However, in Europe and America, these countries cultivated specialists and conducted research beyond their colonial and commercial activities in the East. They had scientific inventions and historical and geographical studies, providing data for government policy and facilitating East-West cultural exchange. Institutions such as the Far Eastern Africa Institute in Britain, the Paris University Oriental Institute in France, Leiden University's Sinology Institute in the Netherlands, the Oriental University in the Soviet Union, and the Tongwen College in Japan, though their objectives varied, were all impressive in scale and achievement. By comparison, China's efforts seemed relatively modest (cited in National College of Oriental Languages, 1946: 1).

Yao Nan's argument reflected the urgent need at that time to advance Eastern cultural studies and establish China's own authoritative institutions for Eastern studies. On 1 November 1942, after nearly a year of preparations, the National College of Oriental Languages officially opened in Dou Nan Village, Chenggong, Kunming. Initially, it offered courses in Indian, Vietnamese, Burmese, and Thai languages with a two-year program. After Japan's defeat in August 1945, when Yao Nan became the third president of the college, it added a Malay language department and implemented several reforms. The college was also revitalized. To facilitate close contact between the college and various cultural groups, it was relocated to Chongqing (Sichuan province), operating out of the former site of the Institute of Nanyang Studies. Several renowned professors were hired, course content was enriched, and the two-year programs were extended to three years to enhance the quality of education. In 1946, by order, the college was moved to Zizhulin in Nanjing (then the national capital). By January 1946, the first batch of Malay language students enrolled in the college, totaling 32 — 25 males and 7 females. By 1947, there were 39 students enrolled, predominantly from Yunnan, Hunan, Guangdong, and Sichuan. At that time, many leaders from the Malayan overseas Chinese community independently donated scholarships to encourage outstanding students in the college (National College of Oriental Languages, 1946: 6, 45–46).

200   *Fu Congcong & Li Gengrun*

Whether judged from the standards of the curriculum, faculty qualifications, or research outputs, the Malay language program at the National College of Oriental Languages could, during its time, be characterized as outstanding. Academic training in the program included four main components: language disciplines, general disciplines, specialized subjects concerning various Southeast Asian regions, and special training (see Table 1). The language discipline placed equal emphasis on both Chinese and Malay education, aiming to enhance Chinese literacy and introduce Chinese culture while progressively training students in the four

Table 1.   Malay Language Curriculum at the National College of Oriental Languages in September 1947.

Curriculum Overview (1947)

Common Required Subjects (Malay Language):
Malay Language (34 credit hours) Second Foreign Language (Choose one between English and Dutch) (26 credit hours) General Chinese History (4 credit hours) Chinese Geography (4 credit hours) Political Science (6 credit hours) Ethnology (4 credit hours) Sociology (4 credit hours) Economics (4 credit hours) General Law (Choose one among three) (4 credit hours) Phonetics (4 credit hours) Civics (2 credit hours) Physical Education (12 credit hours) Chinese National Language (4 credit hours) History of India (6 credit hours) Geography of Southeast Asia (6 credit hours) History of the Indochina Peninsula (4 credit hours) Comparative Phonetics and Comparative Grammar (Choose one, credits not listed)

Overseas Chinese Affairs Group:
Introduction to Overseas Chinese Issues (2 credit hours) History of Western Expansion Eastwards (4 credit hours) Current International Affairs (4 credit hours) International Relations (2 credit hours) History of Chinese Diplomacy (4 credit hours) History of Overseas Chinese Resettlement (4 credit hours) Immigration Policies of Various Countries (4 credit hours) Political History of China in Asia (2 credit hours) Western Diplomatic History (4 credit hours) Social Surveys (2 credit hours) Administration of Overseas Chinese Affairs (2 credit hours) International Public Law (3 credit hours) International Private Law (3 credit hours) Special Topic Studies (credits not listed)

Education Group:
Introduction to Education (6 credit hours) Introduction to Philosophy (4 credit hours) History of Education (4 credit hours) Selected Readings in Historical Prose and Poetry (4 credit hours) Research and Practice in Various Writing Styles (4 credit hours) Elementary Education (3 credit hours) Secondary Education (3 credit hours) Education Administration (4 credit hours) Overseas Chinese Education (2 credit hours) Special Topic Studies

Curriculum Overview (1947)
Journalism Group: News Editing (4 credit hours) Introduction to Journalism (6 credit hours) News Reporting (4 credit hours) Current International Affairs (4 credit hours) Editorial Writing (4 credit hours) Journalistic Literature (4 credit hours) Newspaper Management (4 credit hours) Social Surveys (2 credit hours) International Public Law (3 credit hours) International Private Law (3 credit hours) Special Topic Studies
International Trade Group: Accounting (6 credit hours) Statistics (6 credit hours) Money and Banking (4 credit hours) Commercial Law (4 credit hours) Business Administration (4 credit hours) International Trade (3 credit hours) International Currency Exchange (3 credit hours) Economic Overview of Asian Countries (4 credit hours) Economic Geography (4 credit hours) Special Topic Studies

Source: Compiled by the Authors (National College of Oriental Languages, 1947: 15–17).

skills of listening, speaking, reading, and writing in Malay. By the third year, students were expected to be able to "select and study classical works from various regions." The textbooks used were the Surabaya edition of *New Malay Language* (*Melajoe System Baroe*). Students who excelled in the program were capable of "reading Malay newspapers or writing letters" (National College of Oriental Languages, 1946: 9–10).

Yao Nan, the college's president, was an outstanding scholar in Southeast Asian history and Malay history in China. A native of Shanghai and a graduate of the National Jinan University, Yao had served as a member of the Royal Asiatic Society of Great Britain, a member of the Overseas Chinese Affairs Committee, chief editor of the publishing department at *Sin Chew Daily*, head of the Economic Research Group at the Ministry of Education's Institute of Southeast Asian Studies, a special researcher at Central Bank, and a founding member of the Central Institute for Southeast Asian Studies. Among the Malay-teaching faculty at the college was Ling Ruigong. He joined the faculty in August 1945, teaching Malay and working on the compilation of a Malay–Chinese dictionary. By 1947, Ling, though advanced in years, was described as being "more vigorous in old age" and had spent many years engaged in international trade. He was also a special correspondent for several Dutch East Indies embassies. The textbooks, monographs, and dictionaries developed by the early faculty members of the National College of Oriental Languages laid a solid foundation for future academic endeavors and trained the first generation of scholars dedicated to Malay Studies in China (National College of Oriental Languages, 1944: 7, 44, 54; National College of Oriental Languages, 1947: 9).

Additionally, scholars at that time were already intending to conduct research on the Malay world and had plans to establish a Department of Oriental Cultural Studies. In a proposal in December 1944 for the addition of research departments to the National College of Oriental Languages, it was noted that the existing academic setup was "hardly sufficient for the study of Oriental languages." The limited focus on Malay in the "Malay Language Department" was seen as insufficient because important languages from the region such as Javanese, Acehnese, Batak, Dyak, Buginese, Tagalog, and Moluccan were all significantly underrepresented, and there was a need for a more comprehensive humanistic-based curriculum (National College of Oriental Languages, 1946: 49). Moreover, scholars of the college also harbored a grander vision of transforming the college into a *University of the Orient*, where students would undergo enhanced four-year degree programs with detailed departmental divisions, adjusted curriculums to ensure specialized expertise, and rigorous research programs (National College of Oriental Languages, 1947: 11–12). The idea never materialized, but this vision and ambition would come to fruition in China over the following 80 years.

The History of Early Malay Language Education in China: 1949 to the Present

In 1949, following the directives of the Central Committee of the Chinese Communist Party, the National College of Oriental Languages was relocated to Beijing and eventually integrated into the Department of Oriental Languages at Peking University. Consequently, over 230 students from the college also transferred to Peking University. It was from this integration that the modern discipline of Malay language studies and education began to be systematically and professionally developed as part of the Asian-African languages and less commonly taught languages (LCTLs).

The Origin of the Less Commonly Taught Foreign Languages in China

In June 1949, the Department of Oriental Languages was established at Peking University, inheriting from the language programs of the former

National College of Oriental Languages. This new department also incorporated the faculty from the Frontier College and Frontier Normal School during the Republic of China era, as well as some staff from the Department of Border Affairs at the National Central University. As waves of national independence movements surged across Asia and Africa in the late 1950s and early 1960s, China sought to strengthen friendship and exchange with these newly independent countries. In 1961, BFSU founded the Department of Asian and African Languages, introducing new programs in Cambodian, Laotian, Sinhalese, Swahili, and Arabic languages (Wu, 2021: 40).

In 1954, the Russian Department at Peking University launched Polish and Czech language programs, and in 1956, Beijing Foreign Studies College (predecessor of BFSU) started a Romanian language program, marking the beginning of the training of specialists in less commonly taught European languages. In February 1959, the Beijing Russian Institute was incorporated into BFSU. China's academic system henceforth began the tradition for both comprehensive universities and specialized foreign language universities to offer foreign language programs. Institutions such as Peking University, BFSU, PLA Foreign Languages Institute, University of International Relations, Beijing Broadcasting Institute (the precursor to Communication University of China), University of International Business and Economics, and Guangxi University for Nationalities subsequently launched foreign languages departments or programs. Numerous dedicated teachers contributed to the establishment and development of these new programs, fostering a generation of scholars excelling in the teaching and research of those less mainstream languages. These programs were aimed at training urgently needed foreign affairs officials and translators for the purposes of diplomacy, cultural exchanges, and economic cooperation (Wu, 2021: 40).

In 1962, the Ministry of Foreign Affairs of China included a report on the curriculum planning of BFSU, in which all foreign languages other than English, Russian, French, Spanish, and Arabic were referred to as "minor languages." During his review of the report, Premier Zhou Enlai changed every reference from "minor languages" to "LCTLs." In December 1997, the Committee for the Teaching of LCTLs, under the National Higher Education Foreign Language Teaching Steering Committee of the Ministry of Education, was established, officially introducing the concept of "LCTLs" into the realm of foreign language education in Chinese higher education. Broadly, LCTLs refer to all foreign languages other than English, while narrowly, they refer to languages other than the six official working languages of the United Nations (Chinese, English, French, Russian, Arabic, and Spanish). This term is a classification concept unique to China, adopted for convenience in language education in the country. By 2008, 45 LCTLs were offered across 71 universities in China. By 2021, the number of LCTLs in China had grown to 81, with BFSU hosting the broadest array of language programs (Wu, 2021: 41).

The Establishment and Initial Development of the Malay Language Program in the People's Republic of China

In 1950, the "Malay Language Department" at Peking University was renamed the "Indonesian Language and Literature Program," with the research focus shifted toward Indonesia. At that time, returnees and scholars such as Tang Jiahan, Wu Shihuang, Tu Bingli, Li Yusen, and Liang Liji taught in the Indonesian language program at Peking University. In 1956, Professor Wu Zongyu, the founder of the Malay language program in New China, began studying Indonesian at Peking University. In September 1961, Wu Zongyu graduated from the Indonesian language program at Peking University and was assigned to work in the Department of Asian and African Languages (now expanded and renamed as the School of Asian and African Studies) at BFSU. In November 1961, the Ministry of Foreign Affairs decided to establish a Malay language program in China. The leaders of BFSU assigned Wu Zongyu to switch to Malay language studies, and recruitment for the program began the following year. In 1962, the first batch of 16 students in New China's Malay language program commenced their studies at the Department of Asian and African Languages at BFSU (Wu, 2011: 279).

During the early years when Wu Zongyu was responsible for setting up the Malay language program and curriculum, China was facing a difficult period, lacking foreign experts and reference materials. He wrote a letter to Vice Premier and Foreign Minister Chen Yi in 1965 detailing the difficulties faced by the program, which received understanding and support from the Ministry of Foreign Affairs. Wu authored the first Malay language textbook in New China. He continued to learn the language, wrote textbooks, and taught students, delivering 16 lessons per week. To address the lack of listening materials, Wu Zongyu used a military radio at 2 am every day to listen to broadcasts from Malaysia, using them as materials for language imitation and learning (Wu, 2011: 279).

From 1962 to the early 1990s, BFSU was the only institution in China that offered a Malay language program. During the Cultural Revolution from 1966 to 1976, Malay language teaching and research in China were significantly impacted. The main teachers responsible for Malay language instruction during this period included Wang Qing, Gu Qiling, Gu Fenghua, Li Wenzhong, and Qin Xuetian. Wang Qing recalled that she joined BFSU in October 1973 to teach the first cohort of worker, peasant, and soldier students. Initially, she had to develop teaching materials while teaching classes, and it was not until this cohort was about to graduate that the teaching materials were somewhat finalized. During the 70s and 80s, BFSU also helped in the training of several Malay language specialists for North Korea. However, for a long period, the LCTLs program at BFSU was marginalized, and teachers such as Li Wenzhong, Gu Qiling, and Gu Fenghua left their positions due to various reasons, leading to significant shortages and turnover of the faculty.

The Cultural Revolution had a very negative influence on the Malay language program, and it took a long time for the program to regain its strength and vitality, even after the Cultural Revolution had ended. Hence, research based on Malay language teaching and translation became stagnant, with outcomes mostly consisting of textbook development and literary translations. For instance, Wang Qing compiled *Basic Malaysian Language* (Volumes I and II), Sun Baoping participated in the translation of the Malay literary classic *Salina* (1985), and Ai Ma and others translated *Bunga Mawar di dalam Pasu* (1991), while Bai Can, Zheng Shuxuan, and others translated *Antologi Cerpen Penulis Wanita Malaysia* (1993) (Goh, 2015).

After China established diplomatic relations with Malaysia in 1974, Wu Zongyu wrote to the Malaysian Embassy in Beijing, hoping to get support for the Malay language program at BFSU, but received no response. In 1988, a Malaysian writers' delegation visited China and Wu learned that the delegation head was a secretary to Prime Minister Mahathir Mohammad; Wu met with him to seek assistance in contacting the Malaysian Embassy to support Malay language teaching. This meeting finally established a connection between the Malaysian Embassy and BFSU. Since then, both sides have maintained a friendly relationship, with the Malaysian Embassy regularly donating books and materials to the Malay language program and inviting faculty and students to participate in the Embassy's events (Wu, 2011: 281).

The Two Decades of Rapid Evolution in Malay Language Programs in China

The 1990s and the first decade of the 21st century marked a period of rapid development of the Malay language programs in China. The number of institutions offering Malay language programs increased from one to five, with better and stronger faculties, higher student enrollment numbers, expanded and improved curricula, and new pedagogy models. In addition, through international exchanges with Malaysia, particularly in teaching and research, the Malay language programs gradually moved from solely focusing on language translation training to incorporating scientific research related to the Malay language and the Malay world. The concept of Malay Studies and the related knowledge fields began to enter China during this period.

As the relationship between China and ASEAN countries, especially with Malaysia, grew closer, under active planning and promotion by Wu Zongyu, the Malay language program at BFSU began to see increased enrollment of students (Figure 1). From the mid-1990s onward, both faculty members and students would also have opportunities to undergo long-term or short-term training internationally through connections with universities in Malaysia and Brunei. Meanwhile, excellent undergraduates were selected and encouraged to pursue postgraduate degrees in Malay language and literature, which also helped form the reserve of future

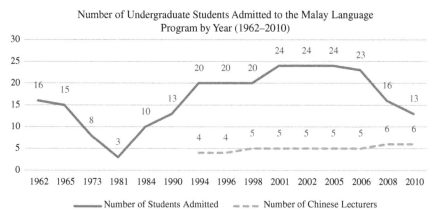

Figure 1. Enrollment in the Malay Language Program at BFSU (1962–2010).

teaching staff. Hence, many current leading academic specialists in the Malay language in China's universities today are former graduates of the Malay language program at BFSU, such as Su Yingying (Class of 1994), Shao Ying (Class of 1998), and Zhang Suhua (Class of 1998). Notably, they also went to study at the Department of Malay Language and Literature at Universiti Kebangsaan Malaysia. Additionally, with the support of Dewan Bahasa dan Pustaka, Malaysia's national body in promoting the national language, Malaysian experts were invited to teach Malay at BFSU. Since 1998, the university's faculty of the Malay language program has been among the best nationally, consistently maintaining a team of four to five Chinese lecturers and one visiting lecturer from Malaysia.

In addition to the strengthening of both undergraduate and postgraduate training at BFSU, and again under Wu Zongyu's planning and organization, the university's Malay language program hosted its first International Malay Language Seminar in Beijing in June 1996, the very first such seminar in China. The seminar invited nearly 200 scholars from 13 countries, including over 100 from Malaysia. Wu Zongyu wrote to invite the then Minister of Education of Malaysia, Najib Abdul Razak, to open the seminar. Impressed by the vigorous development of the teaching of the Malay language in China, Najib immediately invited teachers and students of BFSU to visit Malaysia. With Wu's determined efforts, in 1997, the Chinese State Education Commission and the Malaysian Ministry of Education jointly established a Center for Malay Language Teaching at BFSU, the first research center dedicated to going beyond purely teaching and focusing on in-depth research relating to the Malay language in China.

The establishment of the research center thus further propelled the achievements of BFSU's Malay language program in terms of both its teaching and research. Subsequently, BFSU hosted international seminars in 1999, 2001, 2004, and 2005, focusing on academic exchanges on Malay language teaching and research, Malay literature, and the history of the Malay world, which were supported and welcomed by scholars from Malaysia, Brunei, Indonesia, and other countries. Additionally, the Malay language program signed memorandums of understanding with Universiti Teknologi Mara, Universiti Pertahanan Nasional Malaysia, and Dewan Bahasa dan Pustaka, among other institutions, to promote systematic cooperation in teaching and research.

Malay Studies Enters China

Malay Studies, as an academic concept, was introduced to China in the first decade of the 21st century. In 2004, to commemorate the 30th anniversary of diplomatic relations between China and Malaysia, the BFSU Malay language program and the Center for Malay Language Teaching held an International Seminar on China–Malaysia Relations, which was inaugurated by the then Prime Minister Abdullah Ahmad Badawi. Prime Minister Abdullah also awarded Chinese scholars Liang Liji and Wu Zongyu the *China–Malaysia Friendship Contribution Award* and announced the establishment of a Malay Studies Chair at BFSU. This pointed to a new and expanded conception of the BFSU Malay language program. In 2005, a delegation from Universiti Malaya visited BFSU, including leaders from its Academy of Malay Studies. This visit not only fostered a systematic student exchange program between the two institutions but also introduced BFSU's Malay language program to the larger academic concept of Malay Studies. In September 2005, with Najib, who was then Deputy Prime Minister of Malaysia, as the witness, BFSU's Center for Malay Language Teaching was upgraded to the China Malay Studies Center, with Najib serving as the honorary director. The concept of Malay Studies officially took root in China.

In 2007, BFSU sent 20 students for the first time to study at the Academy of Malay Studies at Universiti Malaya, where they learned about the Malay language, Malaysian society and culture, Malay arts, and Malay linguistics. Fu Congcong, one of the authors of this chapter, was one of the students fortunate to participate in all these courses and encountered the indigenous knowledge of the scholarly Malay community, which expanded my knowledge and understanding significantly. Language skills and related knowledge are only part of Malay Studies. Increasingly also, the BFSU Malay language program has gone beyond the pure focus on language, and it should be broadened to become a more comprehensive Malay Studies.

In late 2008, after being selected by the Malaysian Ministry of Higher Education, Professor Awang Sariyan became the inaugural Malay Chair (China) at BFSU, which came with an appointment of three to four years. His responsibilities included assisting in the training of undergraduate and graduate students in Malay language at BFSU, participating in curriculum design and teaching, and promoting the Malay language in China. Through the collaborative efforts of Wu Zongyu, Awang Sariyan, and the professional teaching and research office, BFSU developed a new "7+1" model for Malay language talent cultivation. This model entails that within the four-year undergraduate program (eight semesters), one semester is spent at Universiti Malaya's Academy of Malay Studies to study modules related to Malay Studies, including language skills, linguistics, social culture, arts, and field research. During the second decade, the frequency and number of enrollments at BFSU continued to increase, with nearly all students experiencing extended stays in Malaysia for their studies. Additionally, apart from China Communication University, which established its own Malay language program independently in 2001, Wu Zongyu and Awang Sariyan actively assisted in establishing Malay language programs at Guangxi University for Nationalities, Yunnan University for Nationalities, and Guangdong University of Foreign Studies. By 2010, the number of Chinese institutions offering Malay language programs had increased from one in the previous century to five.

Although the Malay language program at BFSU developed distinctive features in talent training over 15–20 years and began to construct the discipline of Malay Studies in collaboration with Malaysia, the academic output of this period was still primarily focused on textbooks and translations. For instance, Wu Zongyu led the compilation and translation of a series of works including *Collection of Malaysian Folktales* (2001), *Collection of Mahathir's Speeches* (1999), and *Chen Haosu-Usman Awang Poetry Anthology* (2004). Huang Yuanhuan translated and published the first Chinese version of *Sejarah Melayu* (1999). Additionally, another Malay language expert at BFSU, Zhao Yuejin, and her student Su Yingying compiled the textbook *Basic Malay Language for Chinese Students* (Volumes 1–2) (2005, 2006). Meanwhile, during their visit to the Institute of Malay World and Civilization at Universiti Kebangasaan Malaysia, Peking University professors Liang Liji and Kong Yuanzhi each published the monographs *Relations between the Melakan Empire and the Ming Dynasty in the Fifteenth Century* (1996) and *The Voyage of Zheng He and the Malay World* (2000), respectively, representing significant achievements in the field of Malay Studies in China at that time.

Rapid Development of Chinese Malay Language Programs after the Initiation of the Belt and Road Initiative in 2013

During the second decade of the 21st century, especially following the introduction of the BRI in 2013 by President Xi Jinping, China's Malay language programs have undergone rapid development. This period has

210 *Fu Congcong & Li Gengrun*

also seen the emergence of a new generation of scholars in Malay Studies, contributing a significant and growing body of knowledge from China to the field. Since 2013, the number of Malay language programs has surged dramatically. Universities across China, particularly those specializing in foreign languages, have been adding Southeast Asian language programs, including Malay. As of June 2024, 14 universities in China have established Malay language programs (Table 2). Additionally, three institutions

Table 2. List of Chinese Universities Offering Malay Language Programs.

No.	University	Category	Year
1	Beijing Foreign Studies University	Degree	1962
2	National University of Defense Technology (Information Engineering University)	Degree	1998
3	Communication University of China	Degree	2001
4	Guangxi University of Nationalities	Degree	2008
5	Yunnan Minzu University	Degree	2009
6	Guangxi Normal University Lijiang College (now Guilin University)	Degree	2012 (currently not enrolling students)
7	Guangdong University of Foreign Studies	Degree	2013
8	Tianjin Foreign Studies University	Degree	2014
9	Xi'an International Studies University	Degree	2017
10	Sichuan International Studies University	Degree	2020
11	Chengdu International Studies University	Degree	2020
12	Yunnan University	Degree	2020
13	Jilin International University	Degree	2022
14	Dalian University of Foreign Studies	Degree	2024
14	Minjiang Teachers College	Diploma	2016
15	Hainan College of Foreign Studies	Diploma	2017
16	Guangxi International Business Vocational College	Diploma	2008 (Program has been discontinued)
17	Hebei International Studies University	Elective Subject	2018
18	Hainan Normal University	Elective Subject	Tbc

Source: Authors' Compilation.

have introduced associate degree programs in the Malay language, and two universities have started offering Malay language elective courses.

In terms of faculty and student numbers, as of May 2022, there were 41 Chinese lecturers and seven Malaysian visiting lecturers teaching at 13 universities in China. There are 457 undergraduate students and six master's students enrolled. In the sixty years since the first establishment of the Malay language program in China, a total of 965 undergraduates and 10 postgraduates have successfully completed their studies (Abdul Aziz How Abdullah *et al.*, 2022).

The BFSU Malay language program has continuously sought to innovate its teaching and training methods, and over the years, it has achieved significant results in cultivating new talents, faculty recruitment, and research output, maintaining its status as the most established and strongest overall Malay language program in China. The educational philosophy of "Internationalization, Specialization, Excellence, Inclusiveness" guides the program in developing highly qualified Malay language talents with a deep understanding of China, an international outlook, proficiency in other languages (English), and capability of conducting research on Malaysia and its regional context. The goal is to evolve into a leading domestic and world-class Malay language program.

Since the 2010s, the total number of students at BFSU's Malay language program has grown slightly compared to the previous decade, maintaining stability in enrollment numbers and frequency (See Figure 2). Additionally, in terms of graduate recruitment, the program has enrolled a total of 6 graduate students and plans to continue recruiting 2–3 graduate students annually.

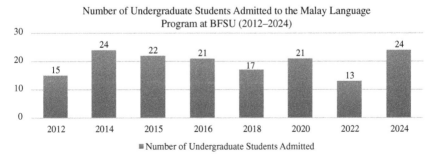

Figure 2. Enrollment in the Malay Language Program at BFSU (2012–2024).

In terms of talent cultivation, while continuing to uphold the original "7 + 1" model, the program has expanded its collaboration to include not only Universiti Malaya but also Universiti Sains Malaysia. Moreover, in response to the previous excessive focus on the five major language skills (listening, speaking, reading, writing, translating), the latest (2021) curriculum has undergone significant updates and adjustments (see Table 3). There is an increased emphasis on courses related to Malay and Malaysian Studies, supplemented by various Southeast Asian regional studies

Table 3. Curriculum Setup for Malay Language Major (2021 Version).

Core Courses for Malay Language Major	Required Courses	Elementary Malay Language (1–2), Intermediate Malay Language (1–2), Advanced Malay Language (1–2)
		Elementary Oral Skills, Intermediate Oral Skills, Advanced Oral Skills
		Elementary Listening and Speaking, Intermediate Listening and Speaking, Advanced Listening and Speaking
		Reading, Basic Writing, Advanced Writing, Grammar, History of Malay Literature
		Malaysian Society and Culture (1–2)
		Translation (1–2), Interpretation (1–2)
Directional Courses	Required	Traditional Malay Customs and Changes, Newspaper Reading, Malay Language Presentation on Chinese Culture, Contemporary Malay Literature: Readings and Critique, History of China–Malaysia Relations
	Electives	Brunei Studies, History of Malay Language Development, Malaysian History, Translation of Malay Political Essays, Ethnic Relations in Malaysia, Indonesian Folk Literature: Readings, Research Topics on Chinese–Indonesian Cultural Exchange
	Electives within the School	Introduction to Oriental Culture, Comparative Politics, Introduction to Regional Studies, Special Topics in Southeast Asian Regional Studies, History of China's Relations with Asia and Africa, Introduction to Cultural Anthropology, Classic Readings in Southeast Asian Studies, Anthropology of Southeast Asia, Introduction to Linguistics, Contemporary Society and Culture in Southeast Asia, Introduction to Comparative Literature, Classic Readings in Comparative Literature

Source: Curriculum for Malay Language Program 2021.

courses offered by the faculty. The aim is to cultivate versatile talents proficient in the language, who are knowledgeable about Malaysia and capable of conducting research and studies on Malaysia and Southeast Asia. Additionally, Malay language programs across universities nationwide in China are attempting to develop a composite and multilingual talent cultivation model, exemplified in this formula of "LCTLs plus Discipline plus English." BFSU's Malay language program has also been exploring undergraduate education models in Malay (Journalism) and Malay (Legal Studies) in recent years.

In terms of the faculty, the foundational generation of teachers in the Malay language major has by now retired. A new generation of young teachers has taken over, creating new initiatives in teaching, research, international cooperation, and cultural exchange. For example, at BFSU, in 2010, there were 6 Chinese lecturers, 1 Malaysian visiting expert, and 1 Malay Chair professor. By 2024, the faculty has evolved to include 1 professor, 3 associate professors, 1 lecturer, and 1 Malaysian expert, with a new Malay Chair professor set to commence duties at the university in 2024.

Over the course of 60 years, BFSU's Malay language program has made significant contributions to the field of Malay language education in China. It supplies a substantial number of faculty members to various universities across the country. Currently, heads of Malay language programs at eight universities in China are graduates of BFSU. The program is well recognized for its quality of education, its level of professional teaching and research, and its achievements in cultural exchange with Malaysia. It has received accolades from the Malaysian Ministry of Education and Ministry of Higher Education, as well as from professional peers in the field. Professor Wu Zongyu, the founder of the program, was honored by the Malaysian government in 2011 with the title of *Pejuang Bahasa Melayu Antarabangsa*. In 2014, the then Deputy Prime Minister and Minister of Education, Muhyiddin Yassin, awarded BFSU's Malay language program the designation of *Development Base for Malay Language in China*. In January 2019, with support from the Malaysian Embassy's education section, the China Malay Studies Secretariat was established to facilitate international cooperation in the globalization of the Malay language and Malay Studies in China (Su and Han, 2022).

As for the production of knowledge in Malay Studies, textbooks and translations remain the main scholarly output of China's Malay language programs. Nevertheless, Chinese scholars with professional or academic backgrounds in the Malay language have conducted fieldwork and research in Malaysia and Brunei, producing a series of original scholarly works in Malay Studies. Regarding textbooks, since the establishment of the Malay language program in China, a total of 32 different textbooks have been published, covering various language skills such as intensive reading, speaking, listening, reading, literature, social culture, grammar, and translation (see Table 4). The repetition in textbook titles and categories is primarily due to each university's efforts to develop its own textbooks tailored to its educational system and curriculum plans, thereby reducing dependence on textbooks from other domestic and foreign institutions.

Among the significant translation achievements is the collaboration between Luo Jie from Peking University's Indonesian Language Program and Fu Congcong from BFSU. They co-edited *Sulalat al-Salatin: Translation and Research*, which is the first Chinese translation of the Raffles MS No. 18 version of the *Malay Annals*. This work includes five research papers on the *Malay Annals* appended to the translation. Another notable translation led by Professor Zhang Yuan from Peking University was *The History of Classical Malay Literature* by Professor Liaw Yock Fang from Singapore. Additionally, Liu Zhiqiang and Xu Mingyue jointly translated another important classical text from the Malay world, *Nagarakretagama*, also known as *Desawarnana*. At Guangdong University of Foreign Studies, Tan Xiao and Li Wanjun selected and translated several ancient Chinese classics into Malay, including *The Analects, The Art of War, The Great Learning, The Doctrine of the Mean, Xunzi, The Book of Songs*, and *The Book of Changes*. However, these publications are not considered achievements in the field of Malay Studies.

In the 21st century, independent knowledge production in Malay Studies in China began to appear. These are the work of scholars proficient in Malay and Indonesian languages, who specialize in literature, linguistics, sociology, anthropology, and history. Kang Min, an anthropology PhD from Peking University, conducted ethnographic research in Kelantan, Malaysia, in 2004. Her doctoral dissertation, *The Blindness of 'Common Sense': An Ethnography of Everyday Life in a Malay Village*, is considered a representative work in the field of contemporary Malay Studies done by scholars in China. Another representative scholar combining expertise in Malay Studies and social sciences is Han Xiao from the School of Asian and African Studies at BFSU. Han Xiao obtained both her master's and doctoral degrees from the Academy of Malay Studies at Universiti Malaya.

Table 4. List of Malay Language Textbooks Published in Mainland China, As of June 2023.

No.	Textbook title	Publication year
1	*Grammar Reader for Malay Language*	1959
2	*Malay Grammar: For Beginners and Researchers*	1980
3	*Basic Malaysian Language (Vol. 1)*	1993
4	*Basic Malaysian Language (Vol. 2)*	1993
5	*300 Sentences in Malaysian Language*	2000
6	*300 Sentences in Malaysian Language*	2003
7	*Basic Malay Language (Vol. 1)*	2005
8	*Basic Malay Language (Vol. 2)*	2006
9	*Malay Language Course (Vol. 1)*	2006
10	*Malay Language Course (Vol. 2)*	2006
11	*Advanced Malay Language Course (Vol. 1)*	2007
12	*Advanced Malay Language Course (Vol. 2)*	2008
13	*Basic Malay Language (Vol. 3)*	2010
14	*Malay Oral Course*	2011
15	*Easy Speaking Malay from Zero*	2012
16	*Cultural Context of Malaysia*	2013
17	*Malay Reading Course 1*	2013
18	*Malay Reading Course 2*	2013
19	*Introduction to Malay Language*	2014
20	*Malay-Chinese Translation Course*	2015
21	*Morning Reading: Beautiful Essays in Malay*	2019
22	*Selected Contemporary Malaysian Literary Works*	2019
23	*New Classic Malay Oral Course 1*	2019
24	*New Classic Malay Oral Course 2*	2019
25	*New Silk Road Foreign Languages 101: Malay*	2020
26	*Malay Situational Conversation*	2020
27	*Theory and Practice of Malay-Chinese Translation*	2020
28	*Introducing Chinese Culture in Malay*	2021
29	*Selected Readings from Malay Newspapers*	2021
30	*Beginner Malay Reading*	2022
31	*Travel Malay Language Course*	2023
32	*New Classic Course — History of Malay Literary*	2023

Source: Authors' compilation.

216   *Fu Congcong & Li Gengrun*

Her research focuses on the impact of urbanization on the Malays. Her master's thesis, *Melayu Bandar: Menongkah Cabaran Merubah Penghidupan* (*Urban Malays: Facing Challenges and Transforming Lives*), was published by the Malaysian Ministry of Information in 2010.

In the field of history, Professor Wu Zongyu dedicated his life to compiling the book *Boni: Brunei dalam Sejarah China* (2010), which collects and translates into Malay the records and documents about Brunei found in ancient Chinese texts. This book was highly valued and funded for publication by the Brunei History Centre. Liu Zhiqiang from Peking University focuses on the history of ancient states in the Malay world. His doctoral dissertation, *The Cultural Exchange between Champa and the Malay World* (2013), is a representative work of Champa studies in China. Li Wanjun from Guangdong University of Foreign Studies and Professor Fan Ruolan from Sun Yat-sen University co-authored *An Outline of Malaysian History* (2018), and Luo Yongkun compiled *A General History of Malaysia* (2024). These are the latest national histories of Malaysia written by Chinese scholars proficient in Malay. Liao Bowen, a PhD candidate at the National University of Singapore who completed his undergraduate studies in Malay at BFSU, wrote a master's thesis titled *Bujang Valley: Heritage, Archeology and National Identity*. This thesis discusses the Malaysian government's cultural heritage policies concerning the Bujang Valley in Kedah and was published by SIRD in Malaysia in 2024.

Prominent figures in the field of literature include Professor Zhang Yuan from Peking University and Professor Tan Xiao from Guangdong University of Foreign Studies. Zhang Yuan mainly engages in the study of Southeast Asian folklore. He and Chen Ganglong co-authored the four-volume *Introduction to Oriental Folklore* (2006), with one volume dedicated to Southeast Asian folklore, including Malaysia and Indonesia. Zhang Yuan and Pei Xiaorui collaborated on *The Story of Rama in India and Southeast Asian Literature* (2005), which includes several chapters discussing the dissemination and evolution of the Rama story in Malaysia. Additionally, Tan Xiao's doctoral dissertation, *Pantun and Xintianyou: A Comparison*, focuses on comparing traditional Malay poetry Pantun with the Chinese folk song style Xintianyou. This dissertation was published in Malaysia in 2018.

Wu Jiang, a graduate of BFSU's Malay language program and currently a postdoctoral researcher at Leiden University specializing in linguistics, published his doctoral dissertation in 2023, titled *Malayic*

Varieties of Kelantan and Terengganu. This dissertation examines the Malayic varieties spoken in the states of Kelantan and Terengganu. It focuses on three varieties, namely, Kelantan Malay, Coastal Terengganu Malay, and Inland Terengganu Malay, all belonging to the Malayic subgroup within the Austronesian language family. Based on data gathered through linguistic fieldwork undertaken by Wu Jiang, the dissertation provides the most comprehensive description of these languages to date and offers an analysis of their historical developments.

In the field of regional and country studies, Professor Su Yingying from BFSU published her doctoral dissertation titled *A Study of Malaysia's South China Sea Policy* in 2019. This dissertation specifically examines the changes in the South China Sea policies of successive Malaysian governments, using a lot of original sources in the Malay language. Additionally, since 2019, Wu Zongyu and Su Yingying, along with Professor Zhai Kun from Peking University and others, have been co-editing the annual *Malaysia Development Report*, a bluebook series published by one of the most prestigious academic publishers in China. This *Report* series comprehensively analyzes the latest political, economic, and social developments in Malaysia. Most of the scholars involved in the report are university academics based in China who are proficient in Malay and capable of conducting policy-related studies.

Future Directions: Constructing an Autonomous Knowledge System

Currently, the world order is changing in unprecedented ways. China needs to gain a more comprehensive understanding of the external world, and its varied relationships with the world, and delve deeper into the study of various countries and regions. With China's deepening of reform and opening up, and extensive engagements with foreign countries, especially those countries involving in the BRI, it is increasingly felt that that China does not possess sufficient knowledge and expertise about these foreign countries. The traditional model of LTCL language experts, who are trained to be proficient in foreign languages and familiar with local cultures, is no longer adequate to produce area studies experts. In 2013, the Academic Degrees Committee of the State Council of China included "Country and Regional Studies" as one of the five major directions in the first-level discipline (*yiji xueke*) of "Foreign Languages and Literature."

First-level discipline is the highest categorization of the knowledge system in China, which is entitled to issue a doctoral degree in China's higher education system. In 2022, the Ministry of Education elevated Country and Regional Studies (Area Studies) into the 14th discipline category of "Interdisciplinary Studies," making it an official first-level discipline. These upgrades entail significant changes in the connotation and extension of China's foreign language talent cultivation.

Taking the Malay language program as an example, it has become clear that merely mastering Malay — but without comprehensive and in-depth knowledge of the country or countries concerned (Malaysia and Brunei) as well as of the region (Southeast Asia), and without sufficient understanding and expertise in particular disciplines (such as economics, political science, international relations, sociology, law, finance, etc.) — is no longer considered sufficient to meet the demands of both the state and society in this era.

Simultaneously, the lack of proficiency in critical languages, especially non-common languages in key countries along the BRI, has constrained China's efforts to advance in-depth area studies. For instance, research in world history demands high foreign language skills, yet doctoral candidates in world history often lack proficiency in non-common foreign languages, significantly limiting the quality of their research and innovation. The fields of comparative politics and international relations in China also face similar challenges. For a long time, China's area studies scholars largely remained in a traditional mode of relying on secondary materials. Researchers often engage in isolated scholarly work without extensive fieldwork or long-term study, research, or investigation in the concerned countries. There is a notable lack of systematic accumulation of primary materials, resulting in heavy reliance on borrowed sources — primarily from Western academic literature, data, and databases. Consequently, Chinese scholars frequently mimic Western research themes, concepts, and issues, hindering their own original and innovative contributions to area studies (Liu, 2023).

Malay Studies and Area Studies

Amid the rising prominence of area studies in China, a reflection on the knowledge produced by scholars with a Malay language background reveals several key insights. Firstly, the knowledge produced by Chinese scholars in Malay Studies still tends to be narrowly focused on specific disciplines, predominantly in comparative literature or linguistics. Consequently, there remains a scarcity of knowledge produced by Chinese scholars in sociology, anthropology, and political science within the field of Malay Studies.

Secondly, the geographical scope and subject matter of research are quite limited. Many researchers with a Malay language background have obtained their master's or doctoral degrees in Malaysia. This educational background influences them to focus primarily on Peninsular Malaysia, often neglecting broader regions such as Borneo, Indonesia, and Singapore — the wider "Malay World." Furthermore, their research subjects are usually confined to the Malay ethnic group on the peninsula, examining their language, literature, and society. This narrow focus equates Malay Studies predominantly with Peninsular Malaysia Studies.

Thirdly, the foundational and theoretical aspects of knowledge production in this field are relatively weak. The lack of systematic disciplinary training and scientific methods means that the knowledge produced often lacks deep theoretical exploration and understanding of underlying factors or mechanisms. Some scholars, influenced by the trend of think tank studies, have shifted toward policy-oriented research. While policy-related research has its merit, excessive focus on policy-driven research will further diminish the scientific and theoretical rigor of Malay Studies in China.

Fourthly, the field of Malay Studies in China has not yet integrated well with related research fields, and sometimes competition exists among them. Knowledge production about Malaysia in China can be categorized into Malaysian Studies, Malaysian Chinese Studies, and Malay Studies. Malaysian Studies generally encompasses political, economic, and international relations perspectives and often receives attention among foreign policy circles, while Malaysian Chinese Studies focuses on the social, historical, cultural, literary, and religious aspects of the Chinese diaspora in Malaysia. The subject of Malaysian Chinese Studies particularly has been quite strong and well established in a number of universities in southern China. Ideally, all three knowledge fields should reinforce each other and enhance China's understanding of Malaysia in a more coherent and systematic way, but this is still not yet the case. Due to the small research community and weaker scientific foundation, Malay Studies often receives less attention and recognition, in the face of competition from these more established fields.

220   *Fu Congcong & Li Gengrun*

After nearly two decades of development, China's Malay language education and Malay Studies have entered a new phase. It is now crucial to integrate various disciplinary perspectives within Malay Studies, with comprehensive explorations of the region's history and contemporary issues. Strengthening the foundational and theoretical aspects of research to enhance scientific rigor is essential. This will enable knowledge production to reveal patterns and provide reliable insights. Building a systematic and coherent knowledge framework is imperative to offer academic guidance for a profound understanding of the Malay world. This entails addressing several critical questions: How can we bridge the knowledge domains of different disciplines within Malay Studies? How can we enhance the scientific nature of research to ensure it reveals underlying factors and mechanisms and provides sound judgments? And how can we form a comprehensive knowledge system that offers scholarly direction for understanding the complexities of the Malay world? Addressing these questions is vital for advancing Malay Studies in China.

Constructing China's Autonomous Knowledge System for Malay Studies

China's regional and country studies are distinct from the colonial-driven research of Europe and the Cold War-era area studies of the United States. China's new imperative of advancing regional and country studies (in short, China's own development of area studies) is characterized by both developmental and moral dimensions, aiming not only to deepen the understanding of global regions but also to demonstrate the responsibilities of a major power by contributing to world peace and development and by providing public goods, new research paradigms, and theories for the global governance system, progress, and development. Fundamentally, it is about constructing an independent knowledge system for China. Looking ahead, China's Malay Studies must be cautious of imperial perspectives, avoid China-centrism, and resist the influence of Western post-colonialism. Instead, it should establish an equal and respectful academic dialogue between China and the Malay World. This involves the following:

1. *Strengthening macro planning*: It is essential to design and coordinate academic planning, policy support, talent cultivation, curriculum development, and research conditions. This comprehensive approach

will pool various resources and efforts to drive talent development and scientific research in Malay Studies, encouraging more students to engage in innovative activities within the field.

2. *Addressing major and practical issues*: China's Malay Studies should not be limited to explaining local issues. It should aspire to have inter-actions with more universal and global theories that transcend speci-ficities and regional characteristics, hence achieving more general relevance. Furthermore, it is crucial to delve into fundamental ques-tions about the development of the countries in the Malay world, regional challenges, and governance issues, thus continuously pro-ducing valuable and influential academic outcomes.

3. *Promoting innovation in paradigm, theory, and methodology*: Researchers in China should focus more on investigating facts and underlying principles and conducting theoretical research rather than purely policy studies. It is of course also important for China's schol-ars to learn Western perspectives, but it is important for China's schol-ars to avoid simply replicating Western perspectives and theories. Emphasis should be placed on conducting fieldwork in the Malay world to identify problems, construct concepts and theories, and use scientific methods for research. The rapid development of artificial intelligence and other scientific technologies has fundamentally impacted knowledge production, and it is necessary to explore the use of advanced technological tools to empower Malay Studies.

4. *Enhancing collaboration with local academics in the Malay world*: It is crucial for China's scholars to avoid arrogance and isolation. Researchers should establish systematic connections with universities and research institutions in Malaysia, Indonesia, Brunei, and Singapore (or even southern Thailand and the Philippines). Through online and offline academic exchanges, research workshops, and conferences, these collaborations can advance joint research, share findings, and build an academic community between China and the Malay world.

Conclusion

The ideas of Malaysian sociologist Syed Hussein Alatas on breaking free from the captive mind and resisting intellectual imperialism to build an independent social science basis align closely with the current objectives of China's regional and country studies (Syed Hussein Alatas, 1974). Those objectives include constructing China's indigenous, independent, and autonomous knowledge system; continuously innovating in knowledge, theory, and methodology; and promoting the development of academic, scholarly, and discourse systems. China urgently needs to fill gaps in its understanding of global knowledge, especially regarding countries in the Global South, with a mindset of mutual respect and inclusiveness. High-quality initiatives such as the BRI, the Global Development Initiative, the Global Security Initiative, and the Global Civilization Initiative cannot be successfully implemented without deep, comprehensive, equal, and independent research on different countries and regions.

This chapter has reviewed and reflected on the sixty years of development of the Malay language program in China, particularly using the model of BFSU as an example. It showcases the evolution of China's Malay Studies. It is important to note that, unlike Malay Studies, Malaysian Studies in China has a different developmental path, with more complex knowledge production networks and outcomes, which also merit careful examination, though this is beyond the scope of this chapter. Despite the achievements in knowledge production within China's Malay Studies, covering disciplines such as sociology, anthropology, history, literature, and linguistics, there is still a need for further introspection and reflection on existing paths, knowledge, and outcomes to build an independent knowledge system that "promotes the true essence of scholarship on Eastern world and integrates various cultures." The Chinese academic community must strengthen its planning for disciplines and talent cultivation, seek and address real and significant issues through fieldwork, promote theoretical and methodological innovation, and continue to enhance academic exchanges and cooperation with the Malay world.

Acknowledgments

The authors gratefully acknowledge support from Beijing Foreign Studies University's Major (Key) Landmark Project of "Double First-Class" Construction (Grant No. 2023SYLA001), *Research on the Construction of Modern Linguistics in World-Class Asian and African Less Commonly Taught Languages and Talent Cultivation: Focusing on Asian Universities*.

References

Abdul Aziz How Abdullah, Awang Sariyan, Su Yingying, and Han Xiao (2022). "Perkembangan Bahasa Melayu di Negara China Memberi Kesan kepada Hubungan Diplomasi Malaysia-China." In Ramiaida Darmi, Ramiaida and Mohd Musling (eds.), *E-Prosiding Seminar Pengantarabangsaan Pengajian Tinggi 2022*, pp. 155–169. Nilai: Universiti Sains Islam Malaysia.

Azizul Haji Ismail and Vijayaletchumy A/P Subramaniam (2017). "Pengajian Bahasa Melayu di Luar Negara." *Dewan Bahasa*, Bil. 7, pp. 4–7.

Curriculum for Malay Language Program (2021). "In Office of Academic Affairs." In *2021 Undergraduate Program Talent Cultivation Plan*, pp. 406–413. Beijing: Beijing Foreign Studies University.

Goh, Sang Seong (2015). "Sejarah Terjemahan Karya Melayu di China." *Melayu: Jurnal Antarabangsa Dunia Melayu*, Jilid 8, Bil. 1, pp. 121–136.

Kong, Yuanzhi (1990). "Malaiyu fazhanshi shang de zhongyao wenxian: Zhongguo gaoseng Yijing jizai de Kunlunyu (An Important Document in the History of Malay Language Development: Yijing's Records of Kunlun Language)." *Dongnanya yanjiu (Southeast Asian Studies)*, No. 2, pp. 20–23.

Kong Yuanzhi (1992) "'Manlaga Guo Yiyu': Huaren bianzhuan de diyibu Malaiyu Hanyu cidian (The Language of Melaka: The First Malay-Chinese Dictionary Compiled by the Chinese)." *Dongnanya yanjiu (Southeast Asian Studies)*, No. 1, pp. 55–56.

Liang, Liji (1996). *Lembaran Sejarah Gemilang: Hubungan Empayar Melak-Dinasti Ming abad ke-15*. Bangi: Penerbit Universiti Kebangsaan Malaysia.

Liang, Liji (2005). "Zheng He's Expeditions and the Ming Policy of Good Neighbourly Relations with Southeast Asia." *Journal of Malaysian Chinese Studies*, Vol. 8, pp. 25–41.

Liu, Zhiqiang (2023). "Zhongguo Dongnanya yuyan zhuanye yu Dongnanyaxue de jiangou yu fazhan: cong yuyan zhichi dao xueke zhichi (The Construction and Development of Southeast Asian Language Programs and Southeast Asian Studies in China: From Language Support to Disciplinary Support)." *Dongnanya yanjiu (Southeast Asian Studies)*, No. 3, pp. 50–68.

Liu, Hongjun and Sun Bojun (2008). "Cunshi '*Hua-Yi Yiyu*' jiqi yanjiu (The Surviving Manuscript of Chinese-Foreign Translation and Its Research)." *Minzu yanjiu (Ethno-National Studies)*, No. 2, pp. 47–55.

National College of Oriental Languages (ed.) (1946). *Guoli dongfang yuwen zhuanke xuexiao gaikuang (An Overview of the National College of Oriental Languages)*. Nanjing: National College of Oriental Languages.

National College of Oriental Languages (ed.) (1947). *Guoli dongfang yuwen zhuanke xuexiao gaikuang (An Overview of the National College of Oriental Languages)*. Nanjing: National College of Oriental Languages.

Su, Yingying and Han Xiao (2022). "Perkembangan Bahasa Melayu Selama 60 Tahun Memperindah Hubungan Persahabatan China-Malaysia." *Dewan Bahasa*, 27 June. https://dewanbahasa.jendeladbp.my/2022/06/27/4301/.

Syed Hussein Alatas (1974). "The Captive Mind and Creative Development." *International Social Science Journal*, Vol. 26, No. 4, pp. 691–700.

Wu, Jiewei (2021). "An Overview of Less Commonly Taught Languages Education in China: Historical Perspectives and Practical Concerns." *Onomázein: Journal of Linguistics, Philology and Translation*, Special Issue IX, pp. 39–50.

Wu, Zongyu (2011). "Luzai women jiaoxia: wo de wushinian jiaoxue shengya (The Path Beneath Our Feet: My Fifty Years Teaching Career)." In School of Asian and African Studies, Beijing Foreign Studies University (ed.), *Shuren, Zhizhi, Huaiyuan:Beijing waiguoyu daxue Yafei xueyuan changjian 50zhounian jinian wenji (Nurture, Knowledge, Horizon: Commemorative Collection for the 50th Anniversary of the School of Asian and African Studies, Beijing Foreign Studies University)*, pp. 278–287. Beijing: China Intercontinental Press.

Yun, Eunja (2016). "Zhongguo guoli dongfang yuwen zhuanke xuexiao yu Hanguoxue jiaoyu de xianqumen (National College of Oriental Languages and the Pioneers of Korean Studies Education)." *Korean Studies of Modern Chinese History*, No. 70, pp. 121–153.

© 2025 World Scientific Publishing Company
https://doi.org/10.1142/9789819801350_0013

Chapter 13

Xiamen University Malaysia: Origins, Development, and Future Prospects

Yap Hon Lun

Introduction

In 2013, the Malaysian Government issued an official invitation to Xiamen University to set up a branch campus in Malaysia. This was the first time such an invitation was extended to a Chinese university from Malaysia. The project was successfully launched, marking for the first time the overseas establishment of a comprehensive branch campus by a China's top national university. This project is by far the most ambitious and comprehensive among the cases of overseas branch operations by China's universities. The project charted a new chapter both in the history of higher learning in Malaysia and the history of Malaysia–China tertiary education collaboration. In the same year, Malaysia and China entered a new stage of their bilateral relations, as Chinese President Xi Jinping proposed the Belt and Road Initiative (BRI) and the bilateral relationship was elevated to a "Comprehensive Strategic Partnership."

Xiamen University has deep roots in Southeast Asia and Malaysia in particular. The university was founded in 1921 by Tan Kah Kee (1874–1961), the most renowned entrepreneur and philanthropist from the overseas Chinese community in the Nanyang (Southeast Asian) region. Xiamen University was also the first tertiary institution founded by an overseas Chinese in the history of modern education in China. Born in Jimei, Fujian province (now Jimei district in Xiamen city), Tan Kah Kee came to Singapore in his youth and eventually became a very successful entrepreneur and one of the richest persons in the region. Tan was very determined to spend his fortune on education. He went back to China and founded many educational institutions in his hometown of Jimei (including what later became Jimei University and Xiamen University), while in Singapore he also founded several schools. His famous motto was "emptying one's fortune to revive learning" (*huijia xingxue*), and his effort to support education is well known throughout Chinese communities across the world, even inspiring many overseas Chinese to do the same (Yen, 2008).

Today, Xiamen University is an elite university in China, consistently ranked among the top 20 universities in China over the decades and known as the "Strength of the South," an acknowledgment of its status as one of the best in China's southern region. It received recognition from the Chinese government as one of the top-tier universities eligible for Project 211 (a state endeavor in the 1990s to facilitate the development of some 100 higher educational institutions as a national priority for the 21st century) and Project 985 (a national project for building world-class universities, announced in May 1998, with 39 participating universities). In the 21st century, Xiamen University has been granted recognition as one of the 140-plus universities in China with a "double first class" distinction (*shuangyiliu*, meaning distinction in both overall academic standards and in particular academic fields). With a commitment to internationalization strategies, Xiamen University has now "returned" to its roots to set up a branch campus in Malaysia. This has become a celebrated tale in the development of education cooperation between Malaysia and China.

This chapter provides the background on the origins of the establishment of Xiamen University Malaysia (XMUM). It also seeks to offer some observations regarding recent developments in and further prospects of XMUM under the framework of China–ASEAN cooperation and within the context of the BRI.

The Founding of Xiamen University Malaysia

Southeast Asia has emerged as a distinct region in search of its own identity and a sense of community. This is also a region crucial to the future economic development and interests of China (Wang, 2019). China views Malaysia as a forerunner in championing China–ASEAN cooperation.

With Malaysia's open policy in higher education, the branch campus project of XMUM plays an important role in providing positive impact in the fields of education, academic research, culture, and even politics, economy, and diplomacy under the framework of the BRI. From a micro perspective, this cross-border educational cooperation project was made possible by many interwoven ties that are worthy of in-depth exploration.

In September 2003, the then Deputy Prime Minister of Malaysia (who became Prime Minister soon after) Abdullah Ahmad Badawi led an official visit to China, with the then Housing and Local Government Minister Ong Ka Ting being among the members of the delegation. The delegation visited Xiamen and Xiamen University, and Abdullah was impressed by Xiamen University's Research School for Southeast Asian Studies (*Nanyang yanjiuyuan*) and its decades of research devoted to the history, culture, economic development, and politics of Southeast Asia. Upon returning to Malaysia, he proposed the establishment of a research institute on China studies. This proposal led to the establishment of the Institute of China Studies at the University of Malaya (UM). Hou Kok Chung, a scholar at UM and a close associate of Ong Ka Ting, became the first director of the Institute of China Studies at UM. Hou would later join politics and was appointed Deputy Minister of Higher Education in 2008.

The trip had left a lasting impression on Ong Ka Ting. He continued to engage with Xiamen University and was invited to speak at the university many times. He was highly valued by the university and was officially appointed as a visiting professor (Yap, 2018: 142). During a visit to Xiamen University in September 2011, Ong Ka Ting (who was then also the chairman of the Malaysia–China Business Council) and Hou Kok Chung made a proposal to Xiamen University President Zhu Chongshi to consider setting up a branch campus in Malaysia.

Xiamen University followed up by forming of a high-level delegation to conduct several rounds of working visits to Malaysia, beginning first with an official meeting with the Higher Education Ministry in Malaysia. It then carried out on-site inspections and met local tertiary education groups and Chinese associations to exchange views, working out the campus plan from the aspects of both the physical and soft infrastructure. Ong Ka Ting envisioned XMUM as a university that would foster a high degree of cooperation between the two countries and enhance the diversity of Malaysia's higher learning sector. He also enlisted the support of key figures within the ethnic Chinese business community in Malaysia. Most notably, Ter Leong Yap, an entrepreneur who leads the Sunsuria group and was also the then treasurer of the Associated Chinese Chambers of Commerce and Industry of Malaysia (ACCCIM), became a very crucial and determined supporter of the XMUM project. Ter reckoned that his commitment to the XMUM project was inspired by the example of Tan Kah Kee (Francis, 2013). Ong and Ter visited the Xiangan Campus of Xiamen University in April 2012. While this was only a short visit, it became one of the key moments toward setting up XMUM (Yap, 2018: 144). Through this site visit, Ong and Ter were able to gain a better understanding of the concept and physical scope of the Malaysia campus and get a good grasp of Xiamen University's expectations of the Malaysia campus.

XMUM is unlike other commercialized private universities or branch campuses of foreign universities in Malaysia. Since the inception of the branch campus idea, Xiamen University made it clear that it would operate on a not-for-profit model. The university would not fork out a single cent for the establishment of the branch campus, nor take a single cent away. In August 2012, Xiamen University wrote an official letter to the Malaysian Higher Education Ministry to state its intention to set up a branch campus in Malaysia, which said, "The Malaysia Campus of Xiamen University will be a modern University with innovation and global perspective, and it will be internationally recognized for its excellent teaching, research, the quality of community service, and distinctive international character. It is committed to being a leading international institution of higher education in Malaysia, and one of the preferred universities for Malaysian students, researchers, professionals, and business administrators" (Yap, 2018: 145). In early 2013, Xiamen University President Professor Zhu Chongshi received the reply, in which an invitation letter to set up a branch campus was sent from Malaysian Higher Education Minister Khaled Nordin. The XMUM project was officially approved and construction soon began.

On 5 February 2013, Prime Minister Najib Abdul Razak and Chairman of the National Committee of the Chinese People's Political Consultative Conference Jia Qinglin witnessed the signing of a Memorandum of Arrangement between Xiamen University, neither XMU nor XMUM and Sunsuria to establish a Malaysia Campus. Following the signing, Sunsuria created Xiamen University Jiageng Education Development Sdn. Bhd. in

Malaysia on behalf of Xiamen University. In October 2013, President Xi Jinping and Prime Minister Najib witnessed the signing ceremony by China Development Bank to provide investment and financing for the campus. Najib reemphasized the significance of Malaysia being given the privilege of hosting this branch campus project by China: "With its establishment, we can expect to attract more international students from China and the wider region, leveraging our strategic position — not just as a host to several branch campuses of other international and world class universities, but also within ASEAN" (Najib Abdul Razak, 2013).

Other than Ter Leong Yap, another prominent supporter of the XMUM project was Robert Kuok Hock Nien, Malaysia's richest person. On 5 June 2013, Ong Ka Ting arranged for Zhu Chongshi to meet with Kuok in Hong Kong. In the meeting that lasted close to one-and-a-half hours, Zhu presented the campus project and its progress to Kuok, and won over Kuok's approval. A month later, Robert Kuok sent a letter to Zhu Chongshi to express his intention to donate RM100 million. Robert Kuok said in the letter, "As Malaysian Chinese, it is our pleasure and honor to provide a small support to this university" (Yap, 2018: 149). This single largest donation in aid of education in Malaysia triggered a wave of donations for XMUM. Mass media coined the term "one Xiamen University, two richest men" to illustrate the phenomenon of having two legendary tycoons (Tan Kah Kee and Robert Kuok) from different generations contributing huge sums of money to the establishment of Xiamen University and XMUM, respectively. Ong Ka Ting stated that the establishment of this branch campus was the continuation of the legacy of Tan Kah Kee: "The spirit of Mr Tan Kah Kee lives on. Owing to this, both governments have approved the setting up of Xiamen University campus in Malaysia" (Ong, 2013).

2014 was named the Malaysia–China Friendship Year as Malaysia and China celebrated the 40th anniversary of the establishment of bilateral ties. The setting up of Xiamen University's branch campus in Malaysia showcased the increasing educational collaboration between the two sides (Md Nasrudin Md Akhir et al., 2018). XMUM held a groundbreaking ceremony on 3 July, with Prime Minister Najib Abdul Razak as the host. Najib echoed the friendly sentiment, saying, "Xiamen University's decision to open in Malaysia would not have been possible without the very strong ties between Malaysia and China" (Najib Abdul Razak, 2014). The groundbreaking ceremony was symbolic of the friendship between the two nations. At the same time, XMUM also put in an application to the Malaysian Education Ministry for the accreditation of its courses and received a response from a ministry representative providing its agreement to render full support and cooperation. The construction of XMUM began within a short period of time because the governments and leaders of both countries placed immense importance on this project.

XMUM became the first overseas branch in Malaysia with an independent purpose-built campus that is wholly owned by a Chinese university. Spanning 150 acres, the planned building area was about 470,000 sq m to accommodate 10,000 students, with a total investment of RM1.3 billion. The first phase of construction, for a building area of 244,000 sq m, cost about RM800 million. The 13 buildings in the first phase included classrooms, school halls, a student activity center, sports facilities (football field, basketball court, volleyball court, tennis court, etc.), hostels, a bell tower, and two guard posts. Located in Sepang, XMUM is a 15-minute drive from the Kuala Lumpur International Airport and a 25-minute drive from Putrajaya, the administrative center of the government of Malaysia.

On 22 February 2016, XMUM hosted an opening ceremony for the first batch of students to coincide with the Spring Lantern Festival, kick-starting the official operation of the university. Since receiving the invitation from the Malaysian government to establish a branch in 2013, XMUM took only three years to complete the first-phase construction of buildings and get the necessary certifications and approvals from the relevant authorities. The first batch of 187 students enrolled in seven bachelor's degree programs, namely, Chinese Studies, Journalism, Accounting, Finance, International Business, New Energy Science and Engineering, and Traditional Chinese Medicine.

Of course, there were difficulties and challenges in the process with gaps and hurdles relating to the systems and procedures from both sides. As XMUM President Professor Wang Ruifang once said, "There were four main obstacles in the establishment of the branch campus — site selection, preparing the land for construction, language, and policy" (She, 2016). But with full commitment from both sides, XMUM eventually became operational.

To enhance the educational opportunities and cross-cultural exchanges, China's Education Ministry gave XMUM a quota of recruiting 500 students from China via its national exam known as *gaokao*. In its initial years, XMUM recruited many students from China. The first batch of 166 students from China arrived in early 2016, followed by the second batch of 440 students in September (Krishmanoorthy, 2016). The arrival of these students from China, plus the locally enrolled students in the first two batches, meant that within the first year XMUM enrolled about 1,350 students.

Looking back, Tan Kah Kee established the institution in 1921 and Abdullah visited Xiamen University in 2003, which led Ong Ka Ting and Hou Kok Chung to raise the proposal for a branch campus in 2011. In 2013, the approval for the branch campus was given. In 2014, the foundation-laying ceremony was held. In 2015, the main building was completed and admissions were launched. In 2016, classes began officially — Xiamen University finally returned to the place of its founder, Tan Kah Kee. The establishment of XMUM is a story of historical and mutual reciprocation between Malaysia and China.

Observations on the Developments of Xiamen University Malaysia

1. *Strong support from the Malaysian and Chinese Governments*: With the deepening of the diplomatic relations between the two countries, more attention has been paid to bilateral cooperation, and this branch campus project was regarded as a key cooperation project between Malaysia and China under the framework of the BRI.

   In the first five years of implementing this project, leaders of both countries expressed their support for the branch campus during bilateral meetings. The then Malaysian Prime Minister Najib even took it upon himself to call for an acceleration of the process. While Hou Kok Chung coordinated links between the two education ministries, Ong Ka Ting was instrumental in facilitating efforts, through the Prime Minister's Department, that prompted the leaders of Malaysia and China to give their full support to the project, all of which were crucial factors in the project's fruitful conclusion. Various ministries and departments of both countries sped up their processes when handling the branch campus project, which enabled XMUM to complete its initial construction and start classes officially within three years.

   The branch campus has had a great start. Najib reiterated the importance of the establishment of XMUM in a Malaysia–China bilateral cooperation Lunar New Year luncheon in Kuala Lumpur: "It is a testament to our good relations, and will accelerate Malaysia's position as a regional hub for educational excellence" (Najib Abdul Razak, 2018). According to local recruitment agencies, XMUM fits the educational market of Chinese Malaysians, but its future operation will greatly depend on the relationship between the governments (Guo, 2018).

2. *Work culture and reciprocal learning*: The first phase of XMUM's construction was completed within 24 months and classes were able to start on time. The site of the campus was originally an oil palm plantation site, which added to the challenges of construction. The XMUM team had to connect water supply lines to the site and generate electricity using diesel generators. The construction team had people from many different countries, with language being a major barrier. Aside from the time, space, language, and cultural constraints, the team had to navigate many unexpected differences in terms of Malaysia's strict labor system and administrative approval procedures. Nevertheless, Wang Ruifang said that fortunately XMUM had a "trump card" — it had direct access to Ong Ka Ting, who was able to provide major help (She, 2016).

   When XMUM's operations began, the university management had to familiarize itself with Malaysian policies and work culture when applying for course accreditation and implementing the language policy mandated by the government of Malaysia. While courses in Chinese Studies and Traditional Chinese Medicine are taught in Chinese, all other courses are taught in English. In line with Malaysian regulations on higher education, the management has to provide a detailed explanation of its language policy and course content. Both sides had to learn about each other's work culture through regular interactions.

3. *Cutting-edge research cooperation and transnational knowledge transfer*: Apart from teaching, XMUM is committed to producing cutting-edge academic research and initiating close academic collaboration with other colleges and research institutes. For instance, MIMOS Berhad, Malaysia's national R&D center, signed an MOU with Xiamen University and XMUM on 26 April 2024, which was witnessed by Malaysia's Science, Technology and Innovation Minister Chang Lih Kang and China's Minister of Science and Technology Yin

Hejun (XMUM, 2024a). Most recently, XMUM was ranked in the top 1% globally in the disciplines of Clinical Medicine, Neuroscience and Behavior, Engineering, and Social Sciences (General) by to the Essential Science Indicators (ESI) ranking released in May 2024. This was the first time that the Social Sciences (General) discipline of the university had entered the ranking. As of April 2024, a total of 1,573 papers published by XMUM faculty members were listed on the Web of Science platform with a reported 68,359 citations (which translated into 45.88 citations per paper on average), ranking 12th and 1st among the higher education institutes in Malaysia, respectively (XMUM, 2024b). XMUM demonstrates that China is able to provide transnational knowledge transfer at the advanced science and technology level. In many ways, it sets the benchmark of *jingwai banxue* (the "going out" of China's universities) (Ngeow, 2022).

4. *Vibrant campus with broad vision and diverse culture*: The "going out" of Chinese universities is the latest trend of "internationalization" of the Chinese higher education sector. XMUM is the first overseas branch of a Chinese university with an independent campus that is wholly owned by the institution. The 150-acre modern campus of magnificent scale is equipped with advanced facilities, and its overall design has stayed true to Tan Kah Kee's architectural style and is consistent with the three campuses of Xiamen University in China. It can even be said that XMUM is one of the most beautiful campuses in Malaysia. The university also offers scholarships for *Bumiputera* and Malaysian Indian students in order to create a vibrant and diverse campus. Graduates from XMUM are awarded degrees that are recognized by both the Malaysian and Chinese governments, which affords them the opportunities to further their studies or seek employment in both countries. XMUM aspires to become a university with a distinct global outlook, featuring first-class teaching and research, and embracing cultural diversity. It is by far the most ambitious project of all the cases of the "going out" of China's universities, not just in Southeast Asia but in the world (Ngeow, 2022).

As of 2024, XMUM has a student enrollment of more than 7,500 students from 44 countries and regions around the world, which fully reflects the internationalized status of the university. These students gained admission with excellent exam grades. XMUM strives to nurture young talents with strong cross-cultural skills and an appreciation and understanding of each other's culture. These students will become bridges for mutual understanding and pillars for maintaining friendly ties between Malaysia and China. To date, the branch campus has trained 4,813 high-quality graduates. By the end of 2024, the total cumulative number of XMUM graduates is expected to reach 6,300 (Khoo, 2024) — and there will be more to come — making important contributions to the development of talents and human resources for both countries.

5. *Strong continuous support from the Chinese community*: Despite Tan Kah Kee's generosity, universities were too expensive for any one person or any one group of private philanthropists to support continuously (Wang, 2003). Xiamen University was privately funded until 1936 when it could not support itself any longer. For the establishment of XMUM, many businesspeople were initially interested in the potential commercial opportunities that came with collaborating with XMUM and were eager to present their sites to the university. However, they withdrew upon discovering that Xiamen University would not fork out a single cent nor take a single cent away from the project and that any profit would be channeled to academic research and scholarships (She, 2016).

However, in line with its cultural tradition, the Chinese community in Malaysia is generally passionate about supporting education. The Chinese business community, especially those who have often cared about the community's well-being, is often the defender and supporter of Chinese education. Many of these Chinese business elite offered their strong support for the XMUM project. Hence, a critical factor that enabled Xiamen University to set a high bar and achieve its goals was the presence of this large ethnic Chinese community in Malaysia. In examining four Southeast Asian cases of the "going out" of China's universities, Ngeow Chow-Bing argues that the XMUM project was able to tap into the resources of the ethnic Chinese business elite circles in Malaysia, as both Ong Ka Ting and Hou Kok Chong had strong links with the ethnic Chinese business community (Ngeow, 2022). The rapid development of the branch campus can be attributed to the generous donations of Chinese business leaders, as can be seen in the cases of Robert Kuok and Ter Leong Yap discussed earlier, but many other names also deserve mentioning here, such as Lee Shin Cheng, Yeoh Tiong Lay, and Robert Tan Hua Choon.

XMUM can also serve as a bilateral platform for Malaysia to reciprocate and enhance mutual understanding between the two countries. With its branch campus in Malaysia, Xiamen University itself will gain important experiences in operating in a different environment and more exposures internationally. XMUM will reinforce Malaysia's multiculturalism and recapture the traditional intermediary role of the overseas Chinese, as a bridge linking China and Malaysia (Chang, 2022).

Conclusion

In September 2019, XMUM had its inaugural convocation, where 371 students — 242 Malaysian students and 129 students from China — received their bachelor's degrees (Loh, 2019). In September 2023, XMUM held its fifth convocation to celebrate the graduation of 1,455 students from 17 bachelor's degree programs and four master's programs, including 802 local Malaysian students and 653 international students. XMUM currently offers 23 undergraduate degree programs, 11 postgraduate degree programs, six doctoral programs, as well as two foundation programs (Khoo, 2024). Since its establishment, the branch campus has proved to be able to contribute significantly to the development of talent for Malaysia and China. It is also a good example of people-to-people exchange under the BRI framework.

Historically, Xiamen University has roots in Nanyang. As Malaysia and China celebrate their 50th anniversary of diplomatic relations in 2024, XMUM stands as a testament to the robust ties between the two countries and has become an exemplary project of the BRI. As a new force in the higher education sector in Malaysia, it will provide new developments in culture, education, economic, and many other fields. All these developments are exceptionally meaningful, not only because of the institution's historical origin but also its impact on the Malaysia–China relations.

References

Chang, Peter Thiam Chai (2022). "China's Soft Power and the Chinese Overseas: Case Study of Xiamen University and the Confucius Institute in Malaysia." In Leo Suryadinata and Benjamin Loh (eds.), *Rising China and New Chinese Migrants in Southeast Asia*, pp. 91–106. Singapore: ISEAS.

Francis, Isabelle (2013). "Ter: Sunsuria a facilitator in Xiamen Uni project." *The Edge Malaysia*, 14 October.

236   *Yap Hon Lun*

Guo, Jie (2018). "Xiamen University Malaysia: A Chinese Branch Campus." *International Higher Education*, No. 95, pp. 9–11.

Khoo, Linda Hui Li (2024). "Xiamen University Malaysia Campus a Testament to Robust Malaysia-China Ties." *Bernama*, 28 May. https://bernama.com/en/world/news.php?id=2302134.

Krishmanoorthy, M. (2016). "XMUM's Biggest Foreign Intake." *The Star*, 22 September. https://www.thestar.com.my/news/nation/2016/09/22/xmums-biggest-foreign-intake-440-students-from-china-arrive-in-xiamen-varsity-malaysia.

Loh, Foon Fong (2019). "First Batch of Xiamen University Students Conferred Their Degrees." *The Star*, 28 September. https://www.thestar.com.my/news/nation/2019/09/28/first-batch-of-xiamen-university-students-conferred-their-degrees.

Md Nasrudin Md Akhir, Lee Chee Leong, and Hafiz Muhammad Tahir Ashraf (2018). "Malaysia-China Bilateral Relations, 1974–2018." *International Journal of East Asian Studies*, Vol. 7, No. 1, pp. 1–26.

Najib Abdul Razak (2013). "Malaysian Prime Minister Dato' Sri Najib's Keynote Address at the Malaysia-China Economic Summit, 4 October 2013." In *The President of the People's Republic of China, H. E. Xi Jinping's State Visit to Malaysia, October 3–5, 2013* (Program Brochure Booklet).

Najib Abdul Razak (2014). "The Ground Breaking Ceremony of Xiamen University Malaysia Campus Site." 3 July. https://www.pmo.gov.my/ucapan/index.php?m=p&p=najib&id=4255.

Najib Abdul Razak (2018). "Malaysia-China Bilateral Cooperation Lunar New Year Luncheon." 27 February. https://www.pmo.gov.my/ucapan/?m=p&p=najib&id=4400.

Ngeow, Chow-Bing (2022). "China's Universities Go to Southeast Asia: Transnational Knowledge Transfer, Soft Power, Sharp Power." *The China Review*, Vol. 22, No. 1, pp. 221–248.

Ong, Ka Ting (2013). "Speech by Tan Sri Ong Ka Ting, The Prime Minister's Special Envoy to China, at Welcoming Luncheon hosted by Malaysian Chinese in Honour of H. E. Xi Jinping, President of the People's Republic of China." In *The President of the People's Republic of China, H. E. Xi Jinping's State Visit to Malaysia, October 3–5, 2013* (Program Brochure Booklet).

She, Jing (2016). "Xiada huidao xiaozhu fendouguo de difang banxue (XMU Returned to Where Its Founder Sweated and Toiled)." *Xiamen Daily*, 29 March.

Wang, Gungwu (2003). "Who Should Pay for Universities?" In Phua Kok Khoo, Hew Choy Sin, and Ong Choon Nam (eds.), *The Tan Kah Kee Spirit of Today*, pp. 45–73. Singapore: Tan Kah Kee Foundation and Tan Kah Kee International Society.

Wang, Gungwu (2019). *China Reconnects: Joining a Deep-rooted Past to a New World Order*. Singapore: World Scientific.

XMUM (2024a). "MIMOS, Xiamen University China, and Xiamen University Malaysia Forge Pioneering Partnership in Semiconductor Technology." *XMUM News*, 30 April. https://www.xmu.edu.my/2024/0430/c16257a48 6531/page.htm.

XMUM (2024b). "4 Disciplines and 91 XMUM Publications Among ESI Global Top 1%." *XMUM News*, 17 May. https://www.xmu.edu.my/2024/0517/ c16257a487057/page.htm.

Yap, Hon Lun (2018). *Mazhong yuanmeng: Hua Jiading churen shouxiang duihua teshi jishi* (*Fulfilling the Dreams of Malaysia and China: An Account of Ong Ka Ting as the Malaysian Prime Minister's Special Envoy to China*). Kuala Lumpur: Malaysia-China Business Council.

Yen, Ching-hwang (2008). *The Chinese in Southeast Asia and Beyond: Socio-economic and Political Dimensions*. Singapore: World Scientific.

© 2025 World Scientific Publishing Company
https://doi.org/10.1142/9789819801350_0014

Chapter 14

How Satisfied are China's Students Studying in Malaysia's Higher Education Institutions? An Exploratory Survey

Fan Pik Shy and Choo Kim Fong

Introduction

With the advent of globalization, the transnational mobility of tertiary-level students has been a major phenomenon, presenting both great opportunities but sometimes also challenges for the countries and universities receiving large numbers of international students.

Cooperation in the field of higher education between Malaysia and China began in the 1990s after the signing of the Memorandum of Understanding between the Government of the People's Republic of China and the Government of Malaysia on Education Cooperation in 1997. Mutual exchanges and cooperation in the field of education were also gradually carried out. The signing of the Framework Agreement to Facilitate Mutual Recognition in Academic Higher Education Qualifications (the Agreement) on 28 April 2011 by the Governments of the People's Republic of China and Malaysia marked another watershed moment in higher education cooperation between the two countries.

Since the 2010s, and coinciding with the launch of the Belt and Road Initiative from China, which defines "people-to-people exchanges" as one of the five areas of connectivity, there has been a significant increase in the number of international tertiary-level students from China to Malaysia and vice versa. Previously, developed countries such as the United States, the United Kingdom, Australia, Canada, and Japan were the primary destinations for Chinese students studying abroad. In recent years, Southeast Asian countries such as Malaysia and Thailand have grown in popularity among Chinese students. From 2019 to 2022, despite the COVID outbreak in between, Chinese international students were the most common source of international students in Malaysian public and private higher education institutions (HEIs) or universities. As of 2022, there were 39,007 Chinese international students in Malaysia, accounting for 37.3% of the total international student population, more than three times greater than students from Indonesia (9.8%).

Many Malaysian HEIs have embraced the advent of international students and have strived to improve the quality of education and provide better services to international students. International students' educational services encompass a wide range of topics, including the campus environment, instructional equipment and software, housing, transportation, and food. The growing number of Chinese international students studying in Malaysia has created a lot of financial potential for Malaysian HEIs, but it has also unavoidably brought to light certain hitherto hidden weaknesses. Recently, Chinese international students have expressed some of their dissatisfaction and negative views toward some universities or related institutions in Malaysia through social media posts, short videos, newspapers, magazines, and other channels. These criticisms imply that Malaysian HEIs and government agencies are still inadequate in preparing for the arrival of a large number of Chinese international students.

What are the areas of dissatisfaction among Chinese international students? What challenges do they face from the moment they apply for admission until the time they study in Malaysia? How pleased are they with the educational services offered by Malaysian HEIs? What are the deficiencies of universities' hardware and software facilities as well as their management? To remain attractive to Chinese international students, it is critical to have a thorough understanding of their needs and satisfaction.

Using an online survey, this chapter aims to provide a preliminary understanding of how students from China perceive their experiences of studying in Malaysian HEIs and living in Malaysia. Based on the survey results, it seeks to provide some assessment of the level of readiness and

Table 1. International Students in Malaysia (2013–2022).

Ranking	1st			2nd			3rd		
Year	Country	Number of Students	%	Country	Number of Students	%	Country	Number of Students	%
2013	China	4,398	8.4	Nigeria	3,134	6.0			
2014	Bangladesh	25,982	34.6	Nigeria	7,532	10.0	China	7,055	9.4
2015	Bangladesh	30,829	25.6	Nigeria	12,947	10.8	China	10,755	8.9
2016	Bangladesh	34,455	26.4	Nigeria	15,262	11.7	China	11,718	9.0
2017	Bangladesh	30,525	22.8	China	14,854	11.1			
2018	Bangladesh	22,158	17.0	China	16,361	12.6			
2019	China	13,448	14.4	Indonesia	9,340	10.0			
2020	China	16,957	17.7	Indonesia	9,983	10.4			
2021	China	28,593	29.4	Indonesia	10,278	10.6			
2022	China	39,007	37.3	Indonesia	10,234	9.8			

Source: Website of the Ministry of Higher Education, Malaysia (https://www.mohe.gov.my/muat-turun/statistik).

242 *Fan Pik Shy & Choo Kim Fong*

preparedness of Malaysian HEIs in anticipation of an even greater inflow of Chinese international students in the coming years.

Brief Literature Review and Research Framework

Today, HEIs often compete in the world's university rankings, which are determined, at a significant level, by their research output. The satisfaction of students however should continue to be seen as an important indicator of how good or successful an HEI is. There is a large body of academic literature documenting the effect of the quality of services provided by an HEI and the hosting country, including most importantly the educational services but not limited to this domain, on the satisfaction of international students (Arambewela, Hall, and Zuhair, 2005; Aramewela and Hall, 2013; Mai, 2005; Parves and Wong, 2010). The level of satisfaction also influences international students' decision to stay or return to their home countries.

In recent years, a significant amount of research has been conducted on Malaysia's HEIs and international students (Abdul Hakeem Alade Najimdeen, Ismail Hussein Amzat, and Hairuddin Mohd Ali, 2021; Ismail Hussein Amzat *et al.*, 2023; Khan and Haque, 2018; Cynthia and Chong, 2023; Blessing and Ogundare, 2019; Ali *et al.*, 2016; Foo, Russayani Ismail, and Lim, 2016; Jin and Chan, 2023; Mohammed Fadel Arandas, Loh, and Shahrul Nazmi Sannusi, 2021; Ong and Ramasamy, 2022; Saloma Emang *et al.*, 2015; Teah, 2019; Waqas Ali *et al.*, 2020). These studies highlighted various aspects of the services offered by the HEIs, including teaching quality, e-learning, responsiveness, service delivery, campus activities, accommodation and facilities, social experiences, and costs. All these studies underlined how international students' choices and levels of satisfaction were determined by these various factors in different contexts.

In the academic literature, various indexes of international students' satisfaction have been developed to cover more comprehensively the factors affecting the level of satisfaction (Temizer and Turkyilmaz, 2012; Memon *et al.*, 2014). This chapter will utilize a research framework known as the Malaysia International Students' Satisfaction Model (MISS-Model), first conceived of by Malaysian researcher Chong Pui Yee and subsequently developed with her collaborators Tham Siew Yean and Andrew Kam Jia Yi (Chong, 2015; Chong, Tham, and Kam, 2018). The MISS-Model covers five dimensions or aspects in evaluating students'

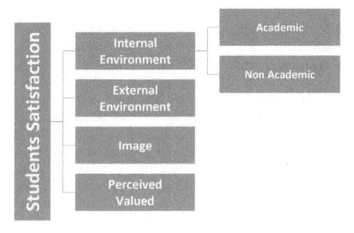

Figure 1. The MISS-Model Assessing International Students' Satisfaction.

satisfaction, namely, internal academic environment, internal non-academic environment, external environment, image, and perceived value (see Figure 1).

Internal academic environment refers basically to academic and educational aspects such as teaching quality, the quality of programs, method of instruction, and facilities and equipment. Internal non-academic factors include accommodation, safety and security, availability of student activities and services, and availability of student-oriented facilities on campus. The external environment takes note of the fact that for international students, experiencing life beyond the university campus forms a vital component of their international study experience. There are both social (societal openness and friendliness toward foreigners, weather, food variety, medical services, etc.) and physical aspects (transportation infrastructure, housing and accommodation, etc.) of the external environment. Image refers to the reputation of both the country and the university — whether they have "branding values" that are seen as positive, reputable, and trustworthy by the international students. Finally, perceived value refers to factors such as tuition fees and the cost of living.

Methodology

An online survey questionnaire was designed consisting of about 32 questions, including demographic questions (gender, place of origin, the university attended, etc.). Questions related to the five dimensions based on the MISS-Model accounted for a majority of the questions. For each question related to the MISS-Model, the respondents were given the option of selecting a score on the 5-point Likert scale, with a score of 1 indicating very dissatisfied and a score of 5 indicating very satisfied. Furthermore, the questionnaire also permitted respondents to further elaborate their responses in some open-ended questions, so that more informative and qualitative data can be captured. The collection of the sample admittedly was not based on a random sampling method, and hence cannot be claimed as scientifically representative of the whole population. However, the methodology of the survey fulfilled the "convenience sampling" rationale, which is also a legitimate sampling method given its practicality and feasibility; the limitations of the sample are well acknowledged and taken note of (Bryman, 2012: 201–202).

The questionnaire was circulated as a Google form among major public and private HEIs in Malaysia, with the link spread primarily through university lecturers and Chinese international students' groups at each of these HEIs, as well as secondary forwarding by responding students. Between January and March 2024, 119 individuals completed the survey. Of the 119 participants, 26 were men and 93 were women. The age distribution was primarily in the 21–30 and 31–40 age categories. 58.82% ($N = 70$), 22.69% ($N = 27$), 12.61% ($N = 15$), and 5.88% ($N = 7$) of the respondents were enrolled in Malaysian HEIs for up to 1–3 semesters, 4–6 semesters, 7–9 semesters, and 10–14 semesters, respectively. 82.35% ($N = 98$) of the respondents were enrolled in public universities, whereas 17.65% ($N = 21$) attended private HEIs. 15.13% ($N = 18$) were enrolled at undergraduate programs, 42.02% ($N = 50$) were attending master's programs, and 42.86% ($N = 51$) were pursuing a doctoral degree.

Data and Findings

Internal Academic Environment

The respondents were first asked to evaluate their satisfaction with the internal academic environment. The result suggests that, so far, Chinese international students had an overall reasonably high level of satisfaction with the academic aspects of Malaysian HEIs, especially regarding the teaching quality of the lecturers. Nonetheless, respondents were less

How Satisfied are China's Students Studying in Malaysia? 245

Table 2. Internal Environment (Academic) by Various Criteria.

Item	Internal Environment (Academic)	Mean	Standard Deviation
1.	Professors have the expertise to answer students' questions	3.81	0.950
2.	The course assessments and evaluations are reasonable and fair	3.72	0.938
3.	The medium of education allows me to completely understand the lectures' substance	3.70	0.979
4.	Lectures are fascinating and energetic	3.61	0.950
5.	The campus is well-equipped with hardware and software resources, including laboratories, computer labs, libraries, and databases	3.61	1.042
6.	The course content is appropriate for the students' skill levels	3.58	0.925
7.	Use of relevant and up-to-date course materials in the area of specialization	3.55	0.870
8.	The course content is current and relevant to the needs of the work market	3.48	0.919
9.	Classrooms are equipped with innovative and comfortable hardware (desks, chairs, upholstery, air conditioning, whiteboards, projectors, etc.) and software (computer software, maintenance services, etc.)	3.39	1.067

satisfied with the equipment and the use of software technology in the classroom and course content.

Despite the relatively satisfactory scores shown in Table 2, in the open-ended questions, numerous respondents revealed that there were problems and weaknesses in the program management and administration in their HEIs. Many HEIs were ill prepared, whether in terms of hardware facilities or software (management), following the rapid increase in enrollment. Even the University of Malaya, the top-ranked university in Malaysia, struggled to cope with the increase and has not been able to provide a better service to these students. Respondents complained that the course selection system was too rigid and failed to provide adequate instructions and information. Three respondents described the situation.

The education system could be better, and the increase in the number of international students has not been supported by a comparable faculty [hence the course offerings are limited], making it difficult, if not impossible, for students to select courses. Furthermore, the university failed to handle the situation correctly by instructing individual students to log on to the system at a specific time to select courses. It was unfair and non-transparent.

(Respondent R97)

I am a new student enrolled in the spring of 2024, and in the second semester of this academic year I didn't choose a course that is required for graduation, which means that I can't graduate within the time as indicated in the offer letter, and therefore my study will have to be extended by half a year to a year, and the cost of living and accommodation during this period is a considerable amount of money.

(Respondent R98)

As the university approaches its 120th anniversary, it should have increased its efficiency in administration, course design, teaching personnel, and communications, given that the number of overseas students is increasing. It is futile to use the QS ranking as a shield if the university keeps raising money without taking any action.

(Respondent R119)

Unfortunately, as reported in the survey, these are not isolated occurrences. Respondents studying in other HEIs (both public and private) have reported similar issues and grievances to varying degrees.

Internal Non-Academic Environment

Table 3 shows that the overall satisfaction level for non-academic services within the HEIs is on the lower side of the scale, with six of the items having mean scores between 3.13 to 3.44 and five items receiving unsatisfactory mean scores of less than three.

As shown in Table 3, respondents were generally unsatisfied with the accommodation facilities on campus and transport. When asked about the accommodation arrangements in Malaysian HEIs, respondents mentioned obsolete facilities and insufficient provision of on-campus accommodation; this resulted in a majority of the respondents living off campus, with

Table 3. Internal Environment (Non-Academic) by Various Criteria.

Item	Internal Environment (Non-Academic)	Mean	Standard Deviation
10.	Campus security provides me with peace of mind	3.44	1.047
11.	The International Student Office and other administrative entities are able to offer accurate information	3.39	1.201
12.	The university campus is conveniently located	3.31	1.177
13.	Orientation week offers useful information	3.30	1.225
14.	Good medical services (including for mental issues) are accessible on campus	3.20	1.062
15.	Adequate and punctual on-campus mobility and feeder transport to and from campus	3.13	1.127
16.	Good and acceptable on-campus housing and facilities	2.97	1.175
17.	The food in campus canteens and restaurants is reasonably priced, clean, and tasty	2.96	1.108
18.	The International Student Office and other administrative departments on campus can fix difficulties quickly	2.91	1.328
19.	Cultural differences sometimes cause misunderstandings or confrontations with professors and administrative staff on campus	2.56	1.337

only a few staying in university-provided dormitories. The students could sometimes be subject to high rental costs in the private rental market. Another concern for students living off campus is the availability of school feeder transport. Respondents generally viewed the school shuttle bus and public bus system as not very reliable timewise and insufficient in number, affecting their arrival and attendance in class.

On-campus food options in Malaysian HEIs were also generally seen as lacking in variety. As a respondent commented, *Food in the campus should not be solely Malay meals, which is highly uncomfortable, it should be more diverse* (Respondent R8). This is especially the case in public universities, where dining alternatives are generally limited.

Inefficiency was also a commonly stated issue among the respondents. Many students were less than satisfied with the speed and problem-solving abilities of the international student offices or other administrative departments of their HEIs. International students place a high value on the speed, accuracy, and accessibility of information in overseas education

248　*Fan Pik Shy & Choo Kim Fong*

services, and an inefficient administrative department or inadequate information surely affects their level of satisfaction. Many respondents reported poor encounters with HEI departments, stating that they were not only unable to handle the difficulties they had enquired about but also frequently could not be reached. For example, Respondent R15 stated, *I don't know who to contact when I have problems, the email processing speed is slow, they don't solve the problems seriously, they just forward the emails, there is no progress, and there is no channel for complaints.* Respondent R91 felt that *the school administration needs to improve administrative efficiency, actively solve students' problems, and reduce the occurrence of the phenomenon of 'kicking the can down the road'.*

Finally, when asked about daily communication and social perceptions, many respondents reported experiencing miscommunication, conflict, or even discrimination when communicating with lecturers or administrative staff on campus due to cultural differences.

External Environment

Respondents, a majority of whom resided off campus, appeared to have no difficulty adjusting to their new surroundings off campus. Table 4 shows

Table 4.　External Environment.

Item	External Environment	Mean	Standard Deviation
20.	I have the freedom to cook in my rental property	4.14	0.847
21.	The community I live in is safe and my neighbors are friendly	3.96	0.995
22.	I feel safe studying in Malaysia because of the good bilateral relations between China and Malaysia	3.77	1.004
23.	I live in a neighborhood where food is easily accessible, hygienic, and selective	3.61	1.082
24.	I can communicate in both Mandarin and English in my daily life without any barriers to understanding	3.56	1.005
25.	I have easy access to public transport to reach my campus	3.24	1.295
26.	Public and private healthcare services in Malaysia are affordable and available off campus	3.14	1.044
27.	I am satisfied with the application process, documents required, time taken, and fees charged to renew my international student visa	2.71	1.224

that the respondents were generally very satisfied with all of the external environment issues assessed, with the three highest scores being for the safety of the environment in the place of residence, interpersonal relationships, and freedom of activities, with mean scores of 3.77, 3.96, and 4.14, respectively. However, visa issues appeared to generate a lot more dissatisfaction.

The primary issue with the current international student services in Malaysia appears to be the ineffectiveness of the visa application and processing procedure. From applying for a student visa before enrolling to requesting a visa renewal after enrolling, most respondents found Malaysia's visa procedure to be time-consuming and inefficient. This topic was mentioned 43 times by the survey respondents as a priority area for improving services.

The prevalence of visa difficulties is the result of a systemic issue. Malaysia's international student visas are subject to an annual renewal system, and international students must submit a renewal application at least 60 days before the visa expires, which typically takes about a month to process. It can take up to half a year from document preparation to application submission, plus time spent waiting for the examiner's feedback. Furthermore, due to the annual renewal process, the application process must be repeated a few months after receiving the new visa. International students believe they are in a constant process of compiling documents, submitting applications, and waiting for results. In contrast, China's international student visa service typically issues a new visa 8 to 13 working days after the application paperwork is completed.

The problem has grown, especially in the last two years as the number of applications has increased dramatically. According to Education Malaysia Global Service (EMGS, 2024), there were 12,174 applications from new Chinese international students in 2019, 8,876 in 2020, 19,202 in 2021, 21,975 in 2022, and 26,627 in 2023. The high volume of applications stretched the processing capacity of the relevant departments, resulting in a huge number of visa applications that could not be processed on time, resulting in many cases in which prospective students had to postpone their planned study in Malaysia. As the number of students from China is anticipated to continue to increase in the coming years, the lack of manpower and efficiency of the relevant agencies deserves more attention.

Perceived Value

The cost of studying in Malaysia is a major factor for the Chinese international student community. Whether or not the actual costs of studying in Malaysia match the expected costs directly impacts their willingness to continue their education in the country as well as their willingness to recommend Malaysia as a study destination to others in their home country. Table 5 reveals that respondents are highly satisfied with the cost of living, with a score of 3.61. In terms of tuition fees, while the score of 3.37 is satisfactory, many of the respondents stated that the recent increase in tuition fees in some HEIs caused hardship for them. For instance, Respondent R14 suggested that *tuition fees should not be increased any further.* Respondent R81 indicated that *fees for international student should be improved.* Respondent R85 also indicated that *international student should be charged a reasonable fee and should not be charged more than twice as much as domestic students.*

Perceived value is not only about paying for and receiving services but also, at the conceptual level, about the extra value derived from studying abroad. Studying abroad implies leaving a familiar environment in one's home country and society, learning to overcome challenges, and adapting to new situations. This kind of experience can have a significant impact on one's worldview, values, and outlook on life. Most respondents strongly agreed that living in a diverse environment in Malaysia enhanced their personal experiences and perceptions.

Table 5. Perceived Value.

Item	Perceived Value (Cost)	Mean	Standard Deviation
28.	My personal experience and knowledge have been enhanced by living in a multi-lingual, multi-cultural, and multi-religious environment in Malaysia	3.97	0.901
29.	The cost of living in Malaysia is affordable and payment options are varied and convenient	3.61	1.019
30.	I feel that the tuition fees charged by the universities are reasonable and commensurate with the quality of education received	3.37	1.213

Image

Image assesses the extent to which the degrees and qualifications awarded by the attended HEIs are recognized in the home country and internationally. In the improved MISS-Model framework created by Chong and co-authors (Chong, Tham, and Kam, 2018), respondents' views have been further expanded to include HEIs' efforts to improve their world rankings as an assessment item. There are various reasons why Chinese international students are interested in studying in Malaysia, and a particularly prominent reason is value for money. The factor behind the high value for money is the performance of Malaysian public and private HEIs in the world's major university rankings. For example, in the QS World University Rankings 2024, 28 public and private HEIs in Malaysia were ranked among the top 1,498 universities in the world. Of these, the University of Malaya was ranked in the top 100. Four other Malaysian universities were ranked in the top 200, 14 in the top 1,000, and 9 outside the top 1,000. Compared to other Southeast Asian countries, Malaysia appears to offer the most cost-effective choice for Chinese international students who value the reputation of the degrees they receive.[1]

The phenomenon of value for money is fueled by the highly competitive environment in China today. There is a common saying at job fairs in China: *bosuo duoduo yishan, benke dengdeng zaikan, dazhuan kandoubukan* (PhDs and Masters are always welcomed, undergrduate degree holders are only considered, junior college degree holders are not considered at all). A number of respondents confirmed the accuracy of this assertion. They all agreed that this type of highly competitive environment (often called "involution" or *juan*) still exists in China. From their point of view, the goal of participating in postgraduate courses and degrees is to improve their employment chances and social competitiveness once they return to China. Respondents R44 and R45, both university lecturers, decided to

---

[1] The QS World University Rankings for other major economies in Southeast Asia in 2024 are as follows: A total of four universities in Singapore were selected, with the highest ranking of 8th; a total of thirteen universities in Thailand were selected, with the highest ranking of 211th; a total of twenty-four universities in Indonesia were selected, with the highest ranking of 237th; a total of five universities in the Philippines were selected, with the highest ranking of 404th; and a total of five colleges and universities in Vietnam were selected, with the highest ranking of 514th.

252 Fan Pik Shy & Choo Kim Fong

Table 6. Image.

Item	Image	Mean	Standard Deviation
31.	I am proud to be enrolled at my university	3.76	1.071
32.	My university has a good international profile and reputation and is ranked highly in the world	3.69	1.056

study in Malaysia after weighing the financial and time implications in order to prepare for future job promotions. They stated that a Ph.D. degree is now considered a baseline academic requirement for Chinese domestic universities, even for those universities that are not part of the 985 and 211 projects.[2] Table 6 demonstrates that the respondents were highly satisfied with the image and reputation of the HEIs they were attending.

Conclusion

In conclusion, the mixed satisfaction of the respondents regarding the assessment indicators signifies that, on the one hand, they were generally satisfied with Malaysia's education and academic offerings but, on the other hand, there were many weaknesses that required further improvement. The Chinese international student population is large, and it is also a rapidly growing market for many Malaysian HEIs; hence, reforming education services and management will help Malaysia retain its attractiveness as a study destination for future Chinese international students.

The Malaysian government, the Ministry of Higher Education (MOHE), and HEIs must create a comprehensive and effective strategy in terms of the development of international education. This should include

---

[2] In 1995, the Chinese government carried out a major reform of higher education to implement the strategy of "revitalizing the country through science and education" by focusing on the construction of about 100 higher education institutions and a number of key disciplines for the 21st century, referred to as the "211" project. Later, in order to achieve modernization, the "211" project supported some higher education institutions, such as Peking University and Tsinghua University, to build world-class universities and high-level universities, referred to as the "985" project. After more than 30 years of implementation, the two projects have now been integrated into the "Double First Class" construction program.

a clear understanding of the educational needs of the international students, with sufficient investment and input to upgrade the readiness of the higher education sector. The strategy should also include steps to simplify the application and enrollment process, optimize teaching and learning services and administration, and improve support services. Furthermore, it should contain a quality assurance, assessment, and monitoring structure to ensure that international students receive high-quality services. In the meantime, the strategy should avoid blanket admission just for the sake of increased intake and ensure a diligent process of admitting international students who are qualified to undertake rigorous studies in Malaysian HEIs. The goal of this study is to equip Malaysia to welcome and retain good-quality international students from China and other countries, while also increasing the competitiveness of the Malaysian higher education sector. Ultimately, the goal is to enhance Malaysia as an international educational hub.

References

Abdul Hakeem Alade Najimdeen, Ismail Hussein Amzat, and Hairuddin Mohd Ali (2021). "The Impact of Service Quality Dimensions on Students' Satisfaction: A Study of International Students in Malaysian Public Universities." *IIUM Journal of Educational Studies*, Vol. 9, No. 2, pp. 89–108.

Ali, Faizan, Yuan Zhou, Kashif Hussain, Pradeep Kumar Nair, and Neethiahnanthan Ari Ragavan (2016). "Does Higher Education Service Quality Effect Student Satisfaction, Image and Loyalty? A Study of International Students in Malaysian Public Universities." *Quality Assurance in Education*, Vol. 24, No. 1, pp. 70–94.

Arambewela, Rodney, John Hall, and Segu Zuhair (2005). "Postgraduate International Students from Asia: Factors Influencing Satisfaction." *Journal of Marketing for Higher Education*, Vol. 15, No. 2, pp. 105–127.

Arambewela, Rodney and John Hall (2013). "The International Effects of the Internal and External University Environment, and the Influence of Personal Values, on Satisfaction among International Postgraduate Students." *Studies in Higher Education*, Vol. 38, No. 7, pp. 972–988.

Blessing, David and Emmanuel Ogundare (2019). "Factors Influencing International Students' Satisfaction towards Higher Education Providers (HEPS) in Malaysia." *International Journal of Education, Learning and Training*, Vol. 4, No. 2, pp. 1–20.

Bryman, Alan (2012). *Social Research Methods*. 4th Edition. New York, NY: Oxford University Press.

Chong, Pui Yee (2015). "Internationalisation of Higher Education: Proposed Framework on International Students' Satisfaction." *Pertanika Journal of Social Sciences and Humanities*, Vol. 23(S), pp. 73–90.

Chong, Pui Yee, Tham Siew Yean, and Andrew Kam Jia Yi (2018). "Verifying International Students' Satisfaction Framework for the Development of MISS-Model in Malaysia." *Pertanika Journal of Social Sciences and Humanities*, Vol. 26(S), pp. 1–18.

Cynthia, Robert and Chong Pui Yee (2023). "Factors Influencing International Students' Choice to Study at Malaysian Private Higher Education Institutions." *Malaysian Journal of Social Sciences and Humanities*, Vol. 8, No. 5, pp. 1–13.

Foo, Chuan Chew, Russayani binti Ismail, and Lim Hock Eam (2016). "Retaining International Students for Advanced Degree in Malaysia: Quality Matters." *Journal Ekonomi Malaysia*, Vol. 50, No. 1, pp. 133–144.

Ismail Hussein Amzat, Abdul Hakeem Alade Najimdeen, Lynne M. Walters, Byabazaire Yusuf, and Nena Padilla-Valdez (2023). "Determining Service Quality Indicators to Recruit and Retain International Students in Malaysia Higher Education Institutions: Global Issues and Local Challenges." *Sustainability*, Vol. 15, No. 8, pp. 1–25.

Khan, Ashraful Azam Khan, and Ahasanul Haque (2018). "Factors Affecting International Students' Level of Satisfaction Towards Selected Public Higher Learning Institutions in Malaysia." *International Journal of Education and Knowledge Management*, Vol. 1, No. 3, pp. 1–19.

Jin, Yufang, and Benjamin Chan Yin Fah (2023). "Perceived Determinants of Studying in Malaysia among the International Students." *International Journal of Management, Accounting, Governance and Education*, Vol. 3, No. 1, pp. 49–58.

Mai, Li-Wei (2005). "A Comparative Study between UK and US: The Student Satisfaction in Higher Education and its Influential Factors." *Journal of Marketing Management*, Vol. 21, Nos. 7–8, pp. 859–878.

Memon, M. A., Rohani Salleh, Mohamed Noor Rosli Baharom, and Haryaani Harun (2014). "Factors Influencing the Satisfaction of International Postgraduate Students in the Malaysian Context: A Literature Review and A Proposed Model." *International Education Studies*, Vol. 7, No. 11, pp. 76–83.

Mohammed Fadel Arandas, Loh Yoke Ling, and Shahrul Nazmi Sannusi (2021). "Exploring the Needs and Expectations of International Students towards The National University of Malaysia (UKM)." *Journal Personalia Pelajar*, Vol. 22, No. 2, pp. 137–144.

Ong, Chris Siew Har, and Ravindran Ramasamy (2022). "Service Quality and Corporate Image Leads to Student Loyalty Mediated by Student Satisfaction in the Malaysia Context." *International Journal of Social Science Research*, Vol. 4, No. 1, pp. 146–156.

Parves, Sultan and Wong Ho Yin (2010). "Service Quality in Higher Education: A Review and Research Agenda." *International Journal of Quality and Service Sciences*, Vol. 2, No. 2, pp. 259–272.

Saloma Emang, Amran Rasli, Xu Ke, and Nadhirah Norhalim (2015). "Antecedents of Satisfaction among University Students from People's Republic of China in Malaysia." *Sains Humanika*, Vol. 5, No. 2, pp. 1–8.

Teah, Chloe Woo Seam (2019). *Investigating Key Factors Influencing International Students' Choice of Private Higher Education Institutions (HEIs) in Malaysia.* Unpublished Doctoral Dissertation, Victoria University.

Temizer, Leyla and Ali Turkyilmaz (2012). "Implementation of Student Satisfaction Index Model in Higher Education Institutions." *Procedia-Social and Behavioral Sciences*, Vol. 46, pp. 3802–3806.

Waqas Ali, Saeed Muhammad, Muhammad Masood Khan, and Nasir Ali Khan (2020). "Financial Satisfaction of International Students in Malaysia." *Sarhad Journal of Management Sciences*, Vol. 6, No. 1, pp. 49–67.

© 2025 World Scientific Publishing Company
https://doi.org/10.1142/9789819801350_0015

Chapter 15

Malay Public Opinion on China-Related Issues in TikTok: A Case Study of Four TikTokers

Ling Tek Soon and Karl Lee Chee Leong

Introduction

TikTok has undoubtedly become an integral part of the daily lives of many Malaysians, especially Malay netizens. Since the imposition of Movement Control Order (MCO) in Malaysia from 2020 to 2021 (during the COVID-19 pandemic), TikTok has become a new platform on which Malay netizens connect and engage with each other as well as provide assistance to those who are in need, especially during the pandemic years. In the post-pandemic period, the use of TikTok in Malaysia has become even more widespread, and it has become one of the most important social media platforms for shaping views and opinions.

As the second most-used mobile app by the number of downloads in Malaysia (Digital Business Lab, 2022), the rise of TikTok among Malaysian netizens is staggering. With more than 50% usage among Malaysians aged 16 to 64 who use social media platforms each month, TikTok has become the sixth most popular social media platform in Malaysia five years after its global release in 2017 (*ibid.*). Unlike other major social media platforms such as WhatsApp, Facebook, Instagram, and Twitter, TikTok originates from China's "Douyin" (literally, "shaking sound") app, and the social media platform is wholly owned by the

Chinese tech company Bytedance. In Malaysia, TikTok is the only China-originated social media platform that has garnered a wide following in such a short span of time — an achievement that the other Chinese app, WeChat, has been unable to replicate despite being released globally six years before TikTok.

Currently, in Malaysia, TikTok has taken a wide range of functions. While showing solidarity and providing assistance were the main functions of TikTok during the pandemic, it has now become a platform for creative content dissemination, e-commerce activities, and even electoral campaigning (Hakem Hassan, 2020; Juliana Kristini Khalid, Wardatul Hayat Adnan, and Shazleen Mohamed, 2023; Hadi Azmi, 2023; Mohd Faizal Musa, 2022). In particular, the ethnic Malay community is the most engaged in using these expansive functions of TikTok compared to other ethnic communities in Malaysia.

As far as creative content expressions are concerned, TikTok is also the main platform for Malay artists, comedians, and wider content creators to showcase their skills and gain recognition from the wider public. With a user-friendly interface and function tools, TikTok is both attractive and enjoyable for users who seek entertainment, information, and knowledge in a refreshing manner that is not available on other social media apps. Influential Malay TikTokers with extensive followings have emerged — with the likes of Puteri Sari (@puteriisarii), Rozyana Roslan (@rozyanaroslan2), and Neng BabyShima (@babyshimaofficial) making up the top 3 Malay TikTok influencers with 6.4 million, 5.6 million, and 4.9 million followers, respectively (Promoty, n.d.). As creative content creators with their own niches to garner a wide following, their content often reflects the experiences and perspectives unique to the Malay community itself. In other words, the presence of such diverse representation in TikTok contributes to the variations of Malay narratives on a myriad of issues, including their public opinion on issues related to China.

Unlike Chinese Malaysians who are able to access information in the Chinese language, Malay netizens do not have such an advantage to start with. Despite that, there is a high level of interest in China-related issues since the COVID-19 pandemic, as evident from the frequency and intensity of discussions on social media platforms. Even after the end of the pandemic, the high level of interest continued among Malay TikTok users who were seeking to understand China through posts, comments, and shared content. It is through such lenses that this chapter seeks to address the following overarching research question: How do Malay TikTok users perceive China through the videos posted by the TikTok influencers (or TikTokers)? In what Mohd. Faisal Musa (2022) claims to be the new "constituency" to describe a new political space with no physical boundaries, it is both timely and crucial to comprehend the diversity of Malay public opinion toward China-related issues in such digital space as represented by TikTok.

Malaysian Perceptions toward China

There are growing studies that seek to examine Malaysians' public opinions toward China and China-related issues in Malaysia. Among them, three previous studies are particularly important as they provide the contextualization of this chapter that delves into Malay public opinion on China-related issues in TikTok. Be it on-field surveys or sentiment analysis within Twitter, these three studies sought to understand Malaysians' public opinion toward China-related issues in three different domains of Sino-Malaysian people-to-people interactions.

At the nationwide level, the polling company Merdeka Centre provided the most comprehensive public opinion survey on China-related issues among Malaysians of different communities in the country. Conducted from 17 March to 26 March 2022, a total of 1,204 respondents from each parliamentary constituency had been selected for the survey. Overall, most Malaysians were neutral toward China (45%) while those who were favorable and unfavorable to China made up the remaining 39% and 12%, respectively (Merdeka Centre for Opinion Research, 2022: 5). In terms of ethnic groups, most of the Malay respondents were neutral toward China (50%), with 28% favorable and 17% unfavorable (*ibid.*). By contrast, the ethnic Chinese respondents reported the highest favorability to China (67%), with 29% neutral and a mere 3% being unfavorable to the rising power (*ibid.*).

If compared to a similar survey conducted by Merdeka Center in 2016, there is, however, a noticeable decrease in the favorability toward China among the Malay respondents. As reported by Merdeka Centre (2022: 6), there was a 5% drop in favorability toward China among the Malays in 2022 as compared to the percentage in 2016 (33%). At the same time, the favorability toward China among the Malaysian Chinese respondents in 2022 had jumped as much as 26% from the percentage in 2016 (41%) (*ibid.*). Thus, two entirely different trends are noticeable for the

Malay and Malaysian Chinese respondents when comes to their favorability toward China before and after the COVID-19 pandemic.

Apart from the favorability indicator of Malaysian public opinion toward China, the respondents were also measured on their impression of China from the year 2020 to 2022. Such a survey design is critical in understanding if any shift of opinion or relatively static view toward China has been affected by the country's developments during the pandemic period. Overall, the impression of China among Malaysians has been unchanged (38%) while those who have better and worse impressions amount to 34% and 21%, respectively (Merdeka Centre for Opinion Research, 2022: 7). Based on ethnic groups, most Malays (38%) had an unchanged view on China, with better and worse impressions of China more or less equal at 27% and 26%, respectively. As for the Malaysian Chinese, an increasingly positive trend was also present in which 55% of respondents reported having a better impression of China whereas 32% remained unchanged and 8% had a worse impression. Interestingly, the Malaysian Indians recorded the largest percentage of those with a worse impression of China (56%) as opposed to those who had a better (22%) or unchanged (19%) impression of China. In all, it is clear that the developments in China during the COVID-19 pandemic period had a bearing on the Malaysian Chinese community's impression of China but not on the Malays in Malaysia.

On the other hand, also in 2022, Merdeka Centre, Rongzhi Corporate Social Responsibility Institute, Asia Foundation, and Carnegie Corporation collaborated on a project that assessed the local level of community perception of China's Belt and Road Initiative (BRI) projects in two different localities, namely, Kuantan and Batu Gajah. With the two localities being the locations of China Railway Rolling Stock Corp's Rolling Stock Center (CRRC) and the Malaysia–China Kuantan Industrial Park (MCKIP), a perception survey was purposely deliberated to gauge the perceptions of the local communities toward China's BRI as well as the overall Chinese investments in their localities. Unlike the Merdeka Centre's public opinion survey earlier, this particular survey examined the perceptions of the local communities collectively without taking an additional ethnic lens like the former.

Based on the responses from 400 respondents in each of the localities, it was found that a majority of the locals were not aware of Malaysia's involvement in China's BRI in their localities. This percentage was 62% for the local respondents in the CRRC locality of Batu Gajah (state of

Perak) while it went up to as high as 74% for the MCKIP area (state of Pahang) (Merdeka Centre for Opinion Research *et al.*, 2022: 17). These high percentages show that there was a severe lack of communication and engagement by the central and state governments, politicians, and corporations that operate in these two localities with the local communities. Conversely, when asked about their perception of Chinese investments in Malaysia, a majority of locals in both localities were positive about them — with 39% in the CRRC area and 37% in the MCKIP locality (Merdeka Centre for Opinion Research *et al.*, 2022: 20). Only 13% and 17% of those polled had bad and very bad perceptions, respectively, of the Chinese investments in the two localities (*ibid.*). The presence of such a mismatch demonstrates that the local communities were largely welcoming of Chinese investments but there was a need for a lot more effort to communicate and engage with the local communities to ensure they are consulted on matters that affect their lives in the future.

Another study, also released in 2022, delved into the social media world by analyzing the overall sentiment of Malaysians on China's BRI based on the 860 English Tweets selected from 1 January 2018 to 1 January 2020. Using the lexicon-based analysis tool, VADER, the study's authors found that a majority of the Malaysian tweets were positive toward China's BRI (around 50%) while those having neutral and negative views were at 37% and 13%, respectively (Chong *et al.*, 2022: 77). The following were the top ten trending BRI keywords with the highest counts on Twitter (presently known as X): "link", "bri", "city", "forest", "China", "ecrl", "Malaysia", "project", "Johor", and "hotel" (Chong *et al.*, 2022: 77). In other words, "China's BRI," "Forest City, Johor", and "Malaysia ECRL Project" were the top trending phrases collected from the Tweets. As pointed out by the authors (Chong *et al.*, 2022: 79), the absence of cultural phrases in the Tweets showed that there was much work left to be done in integrating Chinese culture and values into the BRI — an effort which the authors believed will optimize the benefits of the BRI in Malaysia.

All three studies have provided a great amount of information about Malaysia's public opinion on China-related issues for the past five years. Among them, only Merdeka Centre's public opinion surveys ventured into ethnic community-based perceptions toward China and China-related issues. There is a clear need for more research to be done to understand the views on China-related issues among the Malay community in different domains, including new social media platforms. As a fast-rising social media platform that has been extensively used within the Malay community today, TikTok is therefore the focus of this chapter.

Research Methodology

"Melayu cakap China" (Malay/Malay speaking/commenting on China) was used as the key phrase to identify suitable TikTok accounts for this study. Upon conducting such a search, four Malay accounts were chosen with the highest number of followers between 1 January 2023 and 31 December 2023. In order to achieve a focused analysis of the contents of their posts, five videos from each of these four TikTok accounts were selected based on three criteria: uploaded within the above-mentioned dates; content that is related to China; and garnering the highest number of views among followers.

It is important to note that the number of views for the first video of each TikTok account is the highest based on the keyword search of "Melayu cakap China." However, in order to ensure that there is a better understanding of the thoughts and expressions of these TikTokers, four additional videos were also selected with the highest number of views for each TikToker based on the three criteria as mentioned above. After watching and thoroughly analyzing a total of twenty short videos from these four TikTok accounts, the research findings are as reported as follows.

Research Findings

Case 1: @husnaliangliang

The first case is the TikTok account @husnaliangliang. This TikTok account has the video with the highest number of views among all the four TikTok accounts in this study. Entitled *Siapakah orang China ini yang pandai cakap Bahasa Melayu? Mahu memperkenalkan diri kepada anda semua!* (Who is this Chinese who can speak fluent Malay? I will introduce myself to you in this short video), the video had garnered 2.7 million views at the time of writing (@husnaliangliang, 9 October 2023 in Appendix 1). The TikToker is actually Liang Liang, a Chinese reporter for *International Online*, a key central news website sponsored by China

Central Radio and Television. Known by her Malay name, Husna Liang, she opened a Facebook account for the first time during the pandemic and communicated with the Malaysian audience in fluent Malay, which then attracted a large number of followers.

Similarly, she is followed by a large number of users on TikTok. In the above-mentioned TikTok video, the Malaysian media discovered that she could accept interviews fluently in Malay when they covered the Hangzhou Asian Games. After being widely reported in varied media formats and languages, her TikTok account gained a wide following among Malay netizens, with hundreds of thousands to millions of viewers for some of her short videos. Even a simple video of her old Malay language textbooks that she used during her studies in China garnered a total of 96,300 viewers in a day (@husnaliangliang, 12 October 2023). In fluent Malay, she tells Chinese stories with a positive influence on the Malay audience.

Malaysian political leaders were also featured in her TikTok posts. Two separate videos of her interviewing two Malaysian Deputy Prime Ministers, namely, Ahmad Zahid Hamidi and Fadhillah Yusof, in Malay, attracted 395,000 viewers and 173,500 viewers, respectively (@husnaliangliang, 1 June 2024; @husnaliangliang, 11 November 2023). In her videos, she asked for words of encouragement from the Malaysian Deputy Prime Ministers for the younger generation of Malaysians and Chinese to engage with one another through new study exchanges and so forth. Another interesting video was when Liang Liang and the Chinese Music Society in China performed the Malay folk song *Rasa Sayang* with Chinese music (@husnaliangliang, 30 September 2023). This showcased an astute blend of elegant Chinese culture (the performer also wore a full set of traditional *hanfu*) and Malay culture through a musical performance of the most representative folk song within the Malay community. Similar to the previous videos with the Deputy Prime Ministers of Malaysia, this video garnered 102,500 views as of the time of writing.

Case 2: *@laoshi_mandarin*

The second case is the TikTok account @laoshi_mandarin (Mandarin teacher). Unlike Liang Liang, this TikToker, Azim, is a young Malay who had studied in China earlier, which explains his high proficiency in the Chinese language in all his videos. Through his TikTok account, most of his short videos are about the introduction, explanation, or teaching of Chinese or Chinese culture in the Malay language. The most viewed video on his account is one in which he imitates another English short video to demonstrate how to use chopsticks to pick up food. With two pencils serving as "chopsticks," he picked up the rubber eraser representing the food (@laoshi_mandarin, 23 July 2023). This video was meant to teach Malays, who use their right hand to eat, to use chopsticks correctly when there is a need for them to do so. At the same time, Malays can also learn to experience Chinese culture and integrate it into their daily lives. This video recorded 1.5 million views.

His second video, which received 677,000 views as of the date of writing, pertains to the Chinese New Year celebration. While playing the Chinese New Year song *Gongxi Gongxi*, he used a pencil to point to the relevant Malay translations of the song, letting the audience know the meaning of this song, which was aired in public spaces and in the media in Malaysia (@laoshi_mandarin, 20 January 2023). In the comment section of this video, many commenters stated that after listening to this song for so many years, they finally understood the meaning of the lyrics through the video. Malay netizens thought *Gongxi* meant "Happy New Year" but it was not. Instead, he corrected that as to mean "wishing you" and which often pairs up with "prosperity" (fa cai) for Chinese New Year's greeting. This has helped Malay viewers clear their misunderstandings about popular Chinese characters, thereby fostering a better understanding of Chinese culture as well.

Other videos by @laoshi_mandarin also explained the meaning of certain Chinese characters, which attracted tens to hundreds of thousands of viewers (@laoshi_mandarin, 15 January 2023; @laoshi_mandarin, 17 April 2024; @laoshi_mandarin, 6 June 2023). In the comment section of each video, there were two notable observations. First, the interest from some Malay viewers to learn Chinese was quite clear, as they took the opportunity to ask Azim about the diverse methods of learning the Chinese language. Second, the TikToker provided the Malay perspective on certain issues despite his China-positive stance throughout his videos. For instance, he dresses like a Muslim, recites Koranic verses from time to time, teaches Malays how to express support for Palestine in Chinese sentences (the number of views for this video is not high). It is precisely due to such a Malay perspective that the TikTokers China-positive stance did not attract criticism from his ethnic group.

Case 3: *@faizmywau*

The third case is the Tik Tok account @faizmywau. Like Azim, Mohd. Faiz is another Malay TikToker who is very enthusiastic about sharing information on contemporary China. However, unlike Azim, Mohd. Faiz focuses more on sharing his business experiences in buying wholesale goods in China. Judging from the content of the videos, it is clear that he owns a business and is not necessarily proficient in the Chinese language. When he went to wholesale markets in Guangzhou and Yiwu, he communicated with local vendors in English and recognized that the Chinese partners were reliable and capable of long-term cooperation. More importantly, he shares tips on wholesale goods from China to help Malay netizens who are interested in conducting such wholesale business.

One video with the title *Nampaknya ramai still tak tahu flow beli barang dari China, kalua nak tahu jom tengok video ni sampai habis* (Looks like many still do not know the flow of goods purchased from China, if you want to know let's watch this video till the end) showed how he planned to ship goods to Malaysia through his own app platform after batching goods in China. Although he provides such services for a fee, it can help solve problems for e-commerce companies that are just starting to transport Chinese goods overseas. This video accumulated 436,800 views as of the time of writing (@faizmywau, 2 March 2023). The TikToker also stated that he set up different groups at different periods to teach Malays to buy wholesale goods in China for a fee. At present, he uses the MyWau group to share wholesale knowledge for a fee and has successfully helped 30,000 merchants buy wholesale goods in China. The latest group was been renamed *The Great Wall Borong China* ("borong" is the Malay word for wholesale) (@faizmywau, 13 September 2023).

In addition, the TikToker also announced in another video (*Jom daftar sebelum penuh*😄, with 180,500 views) that he would provide free training for East Coast Malay e-commerce entrepreneurs on three aspects: how to buy wholesale goods from China; how to sell goods on TikTok; and how to establish a business network for a wholesaler (@faizmywau, 14 September 2023). This particular video shows that TikTok has become a virtual platform for Malay people to learn how to do business with their Chinese counterparts. The impact of such educational content is far-reaching. According to conservative estimates, the commercial benefits of TikTok are exceedingly high, with people from different backgrounds tapping into the social media platform to conduct their business. By sharing his experiences, Mohd. Faiz is in a way encouraging those with a small capital to venture into businesses through the use of TikTok and the Chinese supply chain. More importantly, one does not need to have a Chinese language background to purchase goods in China. By distinguishing Yiwu and Guangzhou as different batching sources, Mohd. Faiz made things easy for business novices who now know which location is more cost-effective for them to start batching goods since they have their own capital limitations (@faizmywau, 23 October 2023, with 119,400 views). Due to his rich experience in dealing with wholesale goods in China, he knows where to buy electronic products for a rate cheaper than in stores in Malaysia. In this fifth video, he stated that the price of the Play Station 5 game console purchased in Dashatou Town, Guangzhou, was much cheaper than one in Malaysia (@faizmywau, 21 June 2023, with 124,900 views).

Case 4: @zierazain

The fourth case is the TikTok account @zierazain. Similar to Mohd. Faiz, Ziera Zain, the owner of this account, also focuses on sharing her experiences of shipping Chinese goods to Malaysia. In two of her videos (with 79,800 and 31,700 views, respectively), she tried out an electric scooter and a mobile suitcase in China. After acknowledging the good price/performance ratio of these goods, she decided to bring a batch of them for sale in Malaysia (@zierazain, 8 June 2023; @zierazain, 3 November 2023). Judging from these two videos, it seems that she notified her retailers of these new products so that they could buy the goods from her. In the third video with 19,000 views, she shared how, as a Muslim, she ensure that the food she buys is halal. She demonstrated that she went to a supermarket in China and scanned the barcode of food packaging through a specific app on her mobile phone. The barcode would show whether the food contained unauthorized ingredients, especially pork meat (@zierazain, 20 June 2023).

Her fourth and fifth videos (with 12,000 and 11,400 views, respectively) were about her experiences of traveling to China. In one of them, she returned to the tourist streets in Guangzhou to buy seasonal fruits and taste them following the end of travel restrictions in China (@zierazain, 24 May 2023). The other video was in response to a netizen's question on whether the public environment in China was dirty and unhygienic. With relevant examples, she shared her own personal experiences that most of the Chinese streets she visited were very clean. As for public toilets in China, her only complaint was that the doors of these toilets were not necessarily higher than the height of an average person (@zierazain, 29 June 2023). This is, of course, very different from Malaysian public toilets.

Conclusion

These four cases of TikTok accounts represent the positive Malay perceptions toward China or China-related issues, as can be seen in their short videos. The four TikTokers have become major content creators in helping Malay netizens obtain more information or knowledge with regard to China. With bilateral relations expected to deepen and broaden in the coming years, and as people from both sides travel for business, tourism, and studies, there could be increasing positive attitudes among Malay netizens on China-related issues as evidenced from the four TikTok accounts.

In the near future, non-governmental organizations (NGOs) that promote exchanges between Malaysia and China, such as the Malaysia–China Friendship Association, the Malaysia–China Chamber of Commerce, and various BRI associations, will find TikTok to be a new social media platform to disseminate relevant information for the enhancement of business-to-business ties and people-to-people exchanges. These organizations should open TikTok accounts in order to more effectively reach Malay netizens and enhance their understanding of China. Videos on travel, cuisine, education, culture, and art, in both countries, are especially important as these experience-sharing videos are very interesting and appealing to many TikTok viewers.

Moreover, we also recommend a two-way dissemination of popular culture through the introduction of related products on TikTok. In the entertainment aspect, both Malaysia and China can utilize TikTok to introduce movies, TV series, variety shows, paintings, and pop songs of the two countries that have the potential to gain a following in both countries. The language barrier can be overcome while mutual understanding and appreciation can be fostered. As for the halal food aspect, TikTok can become a new social media platform to promote halal food from both countries. Again, systematic sharing of informative videos on Malaysian and Chinese halal food (nasi lemak, mee tarik, roti canai, and so forth) on TikTok will be a comprehensive approach to facilitate two-way exchanges between the netizens of the two countries.

Appendix 1. Videos of the Four TikTokers

Azim (@laoshi_mandarin) (2023). "*Asal Tahun Baru Cina Je Kita Biasa Dengar Lagu Ni Kan? Haa Jom Tengok Lirik Dia* (*In Every Chinese New Year, We Used to Hearing This Song, Right? Let's See His Lyrics*)." 20 January.

Azim (@laoshi_mandarin) (2023). "*Nah Tutorial Gunakan Chopstick Cara Laoshi* (*So, This is the Tutorial of Laoshi's Chopstick Use Version*)." 2 July.

Azim (@laoshi_mandarin) (2023). "*Saya Suka Bakai Baju Merah! Awak Suka Bakai Baju Warna Apa?* (*I Like to Wear Red Shirt! What Color of Clothes Do You Like to Wear?*)" TikTok, 17 April.

Azim (@laoshi_mandarin) (2023). "*Sedih Kadang Ajar FREE Dkt Tiktok Pun Tak Ramai Support* (*It's Sad that Sometimes There Isn't Much Support for FREE Teaching On TikTok*)." TikTok, 6 June.

Azim (@laoshi_mandarin) (2023). "回复 @*Nurul Wani I Saw Where This is Going Sis...* (*Reply @Nurul Wani I Saw Where This is Going Sis...*)." 15 June.

Liang, Liang Husna (@husnaliangliang) (2023). "*Artis China Memainkan Lagu Rasa Sayang Dengan Menggunakan Alat Muzik Tradisional China!* (*Chinese Artists Play Rasa Sayang Songs Using Traditional Chinese Musical Instruments*)." 30 September.

Liang, Liang Husna (@husnaliangliang) (2023). "Buku Teks Bahasa Melayu Universiti China! Walaupun Buku Ini Dah Usang, Tapi Semuanya Kenangan Kampus Saya Yang Manis! ♡ (*My Malay Textbooks During Studies at China University! Although This Book is Outdated, It's All My Sweet Campus Memories!*)." 12 October.

Liang, Liang Husna (@husnaliangliang) (2024). "*Chinese Reporter Interview the Hon. Deputy Prime Minister #AhmadZahidHamidi in Malay Language. Wawancara Kali Ini Dilakukan Sempena Sambutan Ulang Tahun ke-50 Hubungan Diplomatik China-Malaysia, Amat Bermakna Bagi Saya. Terima kasih banya!* (*Chinese Reporter Interview the Hon. Deputy Prime Minister #AhmadZahidHamidi in Malay Language. This Interview in Conducted in Conjunction of the 50th Anniversary of China-Malaysia Diplomatic Relations*)." 1 June.

Liang, Liang Husna (@husnaliangliang) (2023). "*Chinese Reporter Interviews the Deputy Prime Minister #fadillahyusof in Malay Language.* ☆ *Terima kasih Dato'Sri, Saya Akan Terus Berusaha.* 😊 (*Chinese Reporter Interviews the Deputy Prime Minister #fadillahyusof in Malay Language. Thank you Dato' Sri, I Will Keep It Up).*" 23 November.

Liang, Liang Husna (@husnaliangliang) (2023). "*Siapakah Orang China Ini Yang Pandai Cakap Bahasa Melayu? Mahu Memperkenalkan Diri Kepada Anda Semua!* (*Who is the Chinese in Malay Who Speak Fluent Malay? I Will Introduce Myself to You in This Short Video).*" 9 October.

Mohd. Faiz (@faizmywau) (2023). "*Amacam Geng Padu Tak Padu? (How Are You Bro? Is Anything Wrong?)*" 21 June.

Mohd. Faiz (@faizmywau) (2023). "*Anda Nak Mula Memborong di Guangzhou atau Yiwu? Cuba Komen (Do You Want to Start Wholesale in Guangzhou or Yiwu? Please Comment).*" 23 October.

Mohd. Faiz (@faizmywau) (2023). "*Jom Daftar Sebelum Penuh*😄 (*Let's Register Before It's Full).*" TikTok, 14 September.

Mohd. Faiz (@faizmywau) (2023). "*Nampaknya Ramai Still Tak Tahu Flow Beli Barang Dari China, Kalau Nak Tahu Jom Tengok Video Ni Sampai Habis* (*Looks Like Many Still Do Not Know the Flow of Goods' Purchase from China, If You Want to Know Let's Watch This Video till the End).*" 2 March.

Mohd. Faiz (@faizmywau) (2023). "*Sampai Bila Nak Biar Business Anda Tak Berkembang?Ramai Yang Dah Join dan Tak Menyesal Sebab Business Semakin Improve Lepas Join Class Ni*😄*Confirm Puas Hati Sebab Kami Akan Ajar Step By Step Sampai Anda Berjaya Memborong Dari China* 🤝 (*How Long Do You Want to Leave Your Business Not Growing? Many Have Joined and Have No Regrets Because Their Businesses Are Improving After Joining This Class*😄 *Confirm Your Satisfaction Because We Will Teach You Step By Step Until You Successfully Wholesale from China).*" 13 September.

Ziera Zain (@zierazain) (2023). "*Awal2 Dulu Masa Pergi China, Kawan2 Ziera Semua Cakap Jangan Masuk Convenient Store Diorang Sebab Katanya Semua TAK HALAL. Tapi Betul Ke? Fuhh… (When I First Went to China, My Friends All Told Me Not to Go to Convenience Stores Because They Said Everything Was NOT HALAL. But Is It true?)*" 20 June.

Ziera Zain (@zierazain). (2023). "*Jalan-jalan Dekat Guangzhou Setelah 3 Tahun xmasuk China (Walk around Guangzhou after 3 years of Not entering China).*" 24 May.

Ziera Zain (@zierazain) (2023). "*Personal Opinion Tentang Airwheel Luggage: Tak Boleh Corner Tajam dan Buat Speed Laju2, Tak Balance Nanti Tersembam. Kalau Berbont*t Besar Fikir 2x Nak Beli, Risau Tak Muat. Nak Bawak Naik Flight Boleh, Tupi Ada Trick Dia, Sbb Airwheel Ni Berat 9kg Tau. Apa-apa Pun, Mudah La Ada Luggage Berjalan. Oh Lupa Dia Boleh Jalan 5km. Ok Sekoan Review Saya (Personal Opinion About Airwheel Luggage: Can't Make Sharp Corners and for Fast Speeds, It Won't Balance and It Will Fall. If You Have a Big Butt, Think Twice about Buying It, worried It Won't Fit. You Can Take It On a Flight, But There's a Trick to It, Because*

This Airwheel Weighs 9 kg. Anything, It's Easy With a Walking Luggage. Oh, I Forgot, It Can Walk for 5 km. Okay, That's My Review)." 3 November.

Ziera Zain (@zierazain) (2023). "*Replying to @Huzaifie Azman Ahmad Basikal Je Banyak Sewa, Scooter dan Motor Selalunya Kami Beli Je* (*Replying to @ Huzaifie Azman Ahmad, There are a Lot of Bicycles for Rent, We Usually Buy Scooters and Motorbikes*)." 8 June.

Ziera Zain (@zierazain) (2023). "*Replying to @tyrajichan Haha Jangan Percaya Rumours! Jahat Tau Depa ni* (*Replying to @tyrajichan Haha Don't Believe in Rumours! This is Bad*)." 29 June.

References

Choong, Heng Hui, Salwani Abdullah, Goh Hong Lip, and Lee Pei May (2022). "Sentiment Analysis of China's 'One Belt One Road' Initiative and Its Effects on China's Soft Power." Paper presented at *International Conference on Regional Cooperation for Sustainable Economic Development*, Kajang, Malaysia, 21 April, pp. 66–81.

Digital Business Lab (2022). "Social Penetration in Malaysia (Research)." 26 July. https://digital-business-lab.com/2022/07/%e2%91%a1-social-media-penetration-in-malaysia-research/.

Hadi Azmi (2023). "Malaysia State Polls: Could TikTok Domination Give Perikatan Nasional the Edge?" *South China Morning Post*, 10 August. https://www.scmp.com/week-asia/politics/article/3230623/malaysia-state-polls-could-tiktok-domination-give-perikatan-nasional-edge.

Hakem Hassan (2020). "TikTok Gaining Popularity among Malaysians." *The Sun*, 30 September. https://thesun.my/local-news/tiktok-gaining-popularity-among-malaysians-XH4339330.

Juliana Kristini Khalid, Wardatul Hayat Adnan, and Shazleen Mohamed (2023). "The Use of TikTok Social Media in Influencing Generation Z Online Purchasing Behaviour in Malaysia." *Management Research Journal*, Vol. 12, No. 2, pp. 40–52.

Merdeka Centre for Opinion Research (2022). *Public Opinion Survey: Perception towards China among Malaysian Public*. 19 May. https://merdeka.org/9813-2/.

Merdeka Centre for Opinion Research, Rongzhi Corporate Social Responsibility Institute, The Asia Foundation and Carnegie Corporation (2022). *Social Impact and Community Perception of Belt and Road Initiative Projects in Malaysia*. 14 April. https://asiafoundation.org/publication/social-impact-and-community-perception-of-belt-and-road-initiative-projects-in-malaysia/.

Mohd Faisal Musa (2022). "'P225' TikTok: Malaysia's New Constituency?" *Fulcrum*, 15 November. https://fulcrum.sg/p225-tiktok-malaysias-new-constituency/.

Promoty (n.d.). "Influencers in Malaysia — TOP 20 on Instagram and TikTok." https://promoty.io/influencers-in-malaysia/.

© 2025 World Scientific Publishing Company
https://doi.org/10.1142/9789819801350_bmatter

Index

A

Abdul Razak, 1, 2, 4, 6, 9, 11, 62, 77, 132
Abdullah Badawi, 6, 18–19, 208, 227
Academy of Malay Studies, Universiti Malaya, 208–209, 214
Ahmad Zahid Hamidi, 263
Amboyna Cay, 72, 77–78
Angkatan Belia Islam Malaysia (ABIM), 181–182
anti-corruption, 20
Anwar Ibrahim, 2, 8, 11, 23, 27–28, 36, 44, 47, 49, 105, 162, 180–181, 194
artificial intelligence, 9, 102, 151, 153, 169, 221
ASEAN–China Environment Cooperation Center, 164, 172
ASEAN–China Free Trade Area (ACFTA), 9, 17, 21, 94, 105, 133
ASEAN–China Green Envoys Program, 165
ASEAN–China Strategy on Environment Protection Cooperation, 165
ASEAN Plus Three, 5, 17, 105, 165

ASEAN Treaty of Amity and Cooperation (TAC), 17
Awang Sariyan, 208–209

B

Beijing Foreign Studies University (BFSU), 194–195, 203–209, 211, 213–214, 216, 222
Belt and Road Summit, 6
Beting Patinggi Ali, *see* Luconia Shoals

C

China–ASEAN Free Trade Area (CAFTA), *see* ASEAN–China Free Trade Area (ACFTA)
China–Malaysia Qinzhou Industrial Park (CMQIP), 20, 98–99
"China Plus One," 49
"China Threat" theory, 4, 15, 17
China–US strategic competition or rivalry, 8, 10, 38, 41–42, 49, 60, 69, 79
Chinese international students (in Malaysia), 240, 244–252
clash of civilization, 179–180, 184, 188

274 *Index*

climate change, 25, 161–162, 164, 171
Clinton, Hillary, 59
Code of Conduct in the South China Sea (COC), 57–58
Communist Party of Malaya, 3–4, 14, 47
community of shared future/community with a shared future, 8, 14, 20, 24–28, 62, 162, 172, 194
Confucian–Muslim (*huiru*) scholars, 185–186
COVID-19 pandemic, 23, 112, 119, 123–124, 146, 157, 240, 257, 260

D
Declaration on Conduct of the Parties in the South China Sea (DOC), 57
Defence White Paper, 37
Deng Xiaoping, 2–3, 13, 63
digital development cooperation, 145–146, 150, 157
Digital Free Trade Zone (DFTZ), 132, 136–139, 141–142
Digital Silk Road (DSR), 150–157
digital transformation, 132, 136, 140–141, 147, 150–151, 154, 158
"dual-track approach," 58

E
East Coast Rail Link (ECRL), 7, 22–23, 102, 112, 136, 141, 261
electric vehicles (EVs), 161, 167–168, 170, 172

F
Five Powers Defence Arrangement (FPDA), 44
Forest City, 136, 261

G
Ghazalie Shafie, 27
Global Civilization Initiative, 8, 10, 24, 25–27, 222

Global Development Initiative, 10, 24–25, 222
Global Security Initiative, 10, 24–25, 222
Global South, 26, 163, 222
Good neighbor policy, 11, 16–17, 196
Green Belt and Road Initiative (Green BRI), 163, 169–170

H
hedging, 35–50, 69–70
Hu Jintao, 15–17
Huawei, 152–153
Hussein Onn, 2, 72

I
Institute of China Studies, Universiti Malaya, 227
intermediate goods, 91, 93
international oil crisis, 71
intra-industry trade (Malaysia and China), 122–125, 128
Ismail Sabri Yaakob, 7, 23

J
Jiang Zemin, 5, 57
Joint Communique between China and Malaysia (1974), 6, 9, 62
Joint Communique between China and Malaysia (2004), 19
Joint Communique between China and Malaysia (2014), 20
joint development (in the South China Sea), 63–64

K
Kasawari oil field, 46
Kuantan Port, 7, 102–103, 115
Kuok Hock Nien (Robert Kuok), 229

L
Li Keqiang, 5
Li Qiang, 28, 47

Index   275

Liang, Husna, 263
Luconia Shoals, 46, 78

M

Madani Malaysia, 8, 28, 194
Mahathir Mohammad, 2, 3–6, 11, 14,
  17–18, 22–23, 48, 63, 72–73,
  111–112, 140, 205
Malay Studies in China, 193, 195,
  197–198, 206, 208–210, 213–214,
  218–221
Malaysia Digital Economy Blueprint,
  140, 149
Malaysia International Students'
  Satisfaction Model (MISS-Model),
  242–244, 251
Malaysia Studies in China, 212, 219,
  222
Malaysia's digital infrastructure, 145,
  147, 150, 154, 157
Malaysian Investment Development
  Authority (MIDA), 101,
  115
Malaysia–China comprehensive
  strategic partnership, 20, 110,
  164, 225
Malaysia–China Friendship
  Association, 1, 267
Malaysia–China Kuantan Industrial
  Park (MCKIP), 7, 20, 98, 103–104,
  114–115, 136, 261
Malaysia–United States relations,
  44
Marcos, Bongbong Jr., 43
Mao Zedong, 2
Merdeka Centre, 259–261
Mischief Reef, 57, 59
Muhyddin Yassin, 7, 23, 213

N

Najib Abdul Razak, 2, 5, 6–7, 11,
  18–22, 44, 71, 111, 136, 207–208,
  228–229, 231–232

National College of Oriental
  Languages, 197–202
Nishan Forum, 184, 188

O

One China policy, 47
Ong Ka Ting, 227, 229, 231–232,
  234
Osman Bakar, 180–182, 186–187

P

Pakatan Harapan, 22
"Peaceful Rise" of China, 15–19

Q

QS World University Ranking, 251

R

Raja Nushirwan Zainal Abidin, 28
Regional Comprehensive Economic
  Partnership (RCEP), 12, 21, 94–95,
  102, 105, 110
Regional Islamic Dahwah Council of
  Southeast Asia and the Pacific, 3
regional production network, 93, 95
renewable energy, 9, 163–164,
  166–167, 169, 172
Research School for Southeast Asian
  Studies, Xiamen University, 227
Royal Malaysian Air Force, 45, 68
rules-based order, 26, 28, 40

S

San Francisco Peace Treaty, 74–76,
  79
Seyyed Hossein Nasr, 180, 186, 188
solar investment, 115–116
South-South cooperation, 26–27, 162
steel investment, 113–114
strategic embedment, 28
Sultan Nazrin Muizzuddin Shah, 27
supply chain, 9, 84, 91–95, 103–104,
  122, 124, 127, 166, 266

276 *Index*

Swallow Reef, 68, 72, 77–78
Syed Hamid Albar, 19, 27
Syed Hussein Alatas, 222

T
Taipei Treaty, 74–76, 79
Taiwan, 42, 75–76, 115–116
Tan Kah Kee, 225, 228–229, 231, 233–234
technology innovation, 103, 164
technology transfer, 103–104, 132, 197, 141, 170
terra nullius, 74–76
Tiktok influencers, 258–259, 262–267
Tu Wei-Ming, 180–181, 183–188
Tun Abdul Razak Chair, Ohio University, 194
Tunku Abdul Rahman, 3

U
United Nations Convention on the Law of the Sea (UNCLOS), 60, 73–74

United Nations Sustainable Development Goals (SDGs), 25, 27

W
Wang Yi, 61
Wen Jiabao, 20, 57
West Capella incident, 43
World Trade Organization (WTO), 15, 85, 90, 94, 113
Wu Zongyu, 204–205, 207–209, 216–217

X
Xi Jinping, 7–8, 24–25, 27, 150, 162, 184, 194, 209, 225, 229
Xiamen University Malaysia (XMUM), 6, 21, 226–235
Xinjiang, 47–48

Y
Yao Nan, 198–199, 201

Z
Zheng Bijian, 15–16
Zhou Enlai, 1, 75, 203

www.ingramcontent.com/pod-product-compliance
Lightning Source LLC
LaVergne TN
LVHW011503020525
809945LV00002B/34